The politics of Englishness

Manchester University Press

The politics of Englishness

Arthur Aughey

Manchester University Press
Manchester and New York

distributed exclusively in the USA by Palgrave

Published by Manchester University Press
Oxford Road, Manchester M13 9NR, UK
and Room 400, 175 Fifth Avenue, New York, NY 10010, USA
www.manchesteruniversitypress.co.uk

Distributed exclusively in the USA by
Palgrave, 175 Fifth Avenue, New York,
NY 10010, USA

Distributed exclusively in Canada by
UBC Press, University of British Columbia, 2029 West Mall,
Vancouver, BC, Canada V6T 1Z2

British Library Cataloguing-in-Publication Data
A catalogue record for this book is available from the British Library

Library of Congress Cataloging-in-Publication Data applied for

ISBN   978 0 7190 6872 0 *hardback*
ISBN   978 0 7190 6873 7 *paperback*

First published 2007

16 15 14 13 12 11 10 09 08 07   10 9 8 7 6 5 4 3 2 1

Typeset
by Action Publishing Technology Ltd, Gloucester
Printed in Great Britain
by Biddles Ltd, King's Lynn

Contents

Preface and acknowledgements

The idea for this book began during England's football World Cup campaign in 2002 and so perhaps it is fitting that its completion should coincide with England's exit from the World Cup competition of 2006. The question of support for the English team became a political issue in 2006, an (erroneous) touchstone of Britishness for those who either ought to know better or who were intent on making mischief. If the tone of a book is to be measured by sporting affiliation then this writer did support the English team both for the positive reason of wishing it well and for the negative reason of taking pleasure in the discomfort of those who take pleasure in the discomfort of England. *Schadenfreude* is a satisfaction best doubled and when pleasure is replaced by sorrow, it is a sorrow halved. That may be a view peculiar to this side of the Irish Sea but perhaps it is a view sufficiently sympathetic to the subject of study yet sufficiently distant from it to provide a useful perspective on Englishness. One justification for this book is that it does.

Its writing was assisted by the positive attitude to research of the University of Ulster which provided support along the way and at all levels from the Vice-Chancellor, Professor Richard Barnett, and Pro Vice-Chancellor Research, Professor Bernie Hannigan, to the Dean of Social Sciences, Professor Anne Moran, the Director of the Social and Policy Research Institute, Professor Bob Osborne and the Head of School of Economics and Politics, Carmel Roulston, and to my colleagues in the School, especially Professor Henry Patterson and Dr Fidelma Ashe. Graduate students in the Faculty – Carol-Ann Barnes, Lyndsey Harris and Sean Swan – were prepared to relieve me of some of the burden of undergraduate teaching for which I am very grateful. All members of the secretarial staff were unfailingly helpful and particular mention should be made of Hazel Henderson who devoted a considerable amount of time and energy to make the manuscript (as the jargon now has it) 'fit for purpose'. Dr Karyn Stapleton assisted me in some of the initial research and was absolutely essential in rectifying my incompetence in keeping proper track of references. I owe her a large debt. My understanding of Englishness was significantly enhanced by collaboration with the Constitution Unit at University College London, a collaboration which enabled me to benefit directly from the wisdom of all those scholars involved in the edited book *The English Question* (2006), scholars whose knowledge is far greater than my own. My special thanks goes to Professor Robert Hazell who was kind enough to include me in that project and who has been exceptionally generous in his support ever since. Dr Christine Berberich of the University of Derby helped me think through some of the literary aspects of the subject and her comments on my ideas were always insightful and stimulating. My greatest intellectual debt is owed to Dr Julia Stapleton of the University of Durham who gave so much of her precious time to read and comment on the manuscript in the course of its writing. Where there was doubt she provided belief and where there was confusion she provided clarity. I am forever grateful to her and hope that this book does some justice to the suggestions she made. And thanks are due to Tony Mason at Manchester University Press for his encouragement and support. Of course, all the errors and failings are mine alone.

Finally, I would like to thank my daughter Sky for being such a bright star and I dedicate this book to her.

1

Put out more flags

According to Philip Larkin, sexual intercourse in England began in the
annus mirabilis of 1963, some time between the ending of the ban on
Lady Chatterley and the Beatles' first LP. What had formerly been a
rather shameful thing had now become an unlosable game in which
everyone felt the same – though it had come too late for Larkin (2003:
146). According to many accounts something similar appears to have
happened to English national identity in the *annus mirabilis* of 1996,
some time between New Year and football's Euro96. What had also
been formerly a rather shameful thing had now become an unlosable
game in which everyone could share. It also seemed to have had a
comparably erotic impact. The English had come out of the national
closet and declared a patriotic love that could now speak its name. It
was better late than never. How often was one to read or to hear
subsequently the couplet from G. K. Chesterton's *The Secret People*,
'Smile at us, pay us, pass us; but do not quite forget. For we are the
people of England, that never have spoken yet.'
  The people were secret no longer and were prepared to speak openly
about what England meant to them with all the fervour of a new affair.
As la Rochefoucauld observed, lovers enjoy each other's company
because they are always talking about themselves. The heralds of this
new 'soccer fan Republic of St George', as one critic called it, had
certainly fallen in love with England and they could not stop telling
themselves about it (Pocock 2000). 1963 helped to dispel the myth of
the English preferring the comfort of a hot water bottle and a cup of
cocoa at night to the delights of sexual pleasure. 1996 helped to dispel
the myth of the English being reserved and reluctant to engage in
collective celebration. One observer, who was later to write a large
book that attempted to make historical sense of the *annus mirabilis* of
1996, argued that something 'has changed in the English national
landscape'. What had changed, he proposed, was that the supposedly
undemonstrative (Sir Ernest Barker once called them the 'never reflec-

tive') English, were now insistent on coming out and flaunting their nationalism: 'The flag of St George, for centuries confined largely to the spires of rural parish churches, flew from cars, pubs and shops' (Weight 1999: 25). If the particular occasion was support for the national football team, the political significance was the extraction of the English cross from the Union flag. Popular flag waving meant that the English were 'gaining a deeper awareness of their own nationhood' and England was in the process of becoming a nation once again. What the old Union flag represented 'is becoming a foreign country' to most English people (1999: 25). Here was the condition for a new Podsnap who, if not so bombastic as Dickens's character, would know again what England *is* (see Heathorn 1996 for a summary of the texts). For all the hyperbole of the moment, in *recent* historical terms at least, the change was quite striking and was also remarked upon by those who did not share unequivocally such enthusiasm for either football or for English patriotism. The historian Hugh Kearney, for example, noted how interest in England and Englishness had now become commonplace while all but a few decades earlier it would have seemed bizarre (2003: 251). And it is interesting to note just *how* bizarre the flag waving would have appeared.

Consider, for example, one of the standard texts on the politics of nationalism in the United Kingdom, A. H. Birch's *Political Integration and Disintegration in the British Isles* (1977). Writing at a time when the Labour Government had introduced proposals for devolution to Scotland and Wales, when the 'Troubles' in Northern Ireland were at their height and concern about the 'break-up of Britain' was the topic of the moment, Birch wrote of England: 'It should also be noted that the English pay little attention to national symbols apart from those which relate to the United Kingdom.' They did not celebrate St George's Day and left that sort of thing to the Scots, the Welsh and the Irish. Significantly, they 'rarely fly the English flag and it is not certain that most Englishmen would even recognise it' (Birch 1977: 142). To emphasise his point about English inattentiveness to national symbolism, Birch used not football, as the post-96ers were to do, but boxing. He reminded his readers that when 'that super-patriotic boxer John H. Stracey defended his world championship in 1976, he entered the ring carrying a Union Jack and celebrated his victory by leading the audience in a rousing chorus of the only nationalistic song that could come easily to their lips, namely *Maybe It's Because I'm a Londoner*'. It is a measure of how times have changed that Birch's comments read now like a report from another country about another people.

For some patriotic Scottish intellectuals, this lack of explicitly

English national celebration was a frustrating state of affairs. Hugh Seton-Watson complained that the English, or at least those English officials with whom he spoke, 'seem to have lost a national consciousness, they seem to have ceased to think of themselves as English'. One of the difficulties in contemporary British politics, he thought, was that 'whereas the Scots have very strong and indeed developed national consciousness increased by economical and other frustrations of the last thirty years, the English do not seem to have any national consciousness' at all. The English political class 'think in bureaucratic categories, use bureaucratic language and are on a different wavelength' from the Scots, Welsh and Northern Irish (Seton-Watson 1979: 45). The cultural consequence was that being insensitive to one's own nationality meant that the English were also insensitive to the nationality of others. The political consequence was that most English politicians were incapable of thinking seriously about constitutional reform, something that was remarked upon at the same time by Nevil Johnson in his subtle study *In Search of the Constitution* (1977). Seton-Watson's invitation – and a similar one can be found in Tom Nairn's *The Break-up of Britain* (1977) – was that the English should put out more flags.

Writing a decade later, the historian J. H. Grainger observed that in the English tradition 'flying the Cross of St George was a protest or a foible, usually Socialist or Anglican' (1986: 53–5). It was definitely not the symbol of popular patriotism and its cultural associations were indeed rather bizarre, an interpretation in line with Orwell's judgement in *The Lion and the Unicorn* that 'the patriotism of the common people is not vocal or even conscious' (1941: 16). From that perspective, wrapping oneself up in the Cross of St George would have been a decidedly un-English thing to do (and it should not be forgotten that there are many who continue to think so). Even in his multi-volume *Patriotism: The Making and Unmaking of British National Identity* which did much to prompt discussion of such issues, Raphael Samuel did not predict this new moment of flag-waving Englishness. In his introductory essay to the first volume, although he felt it was now rather 'exciting to be English', Samuel also thought that there had been a retreat from traditional patriotism. On the left there was militant particularism and on the right there was privatisation. Neither of them, according to Samuel, left much space for the idea of the nation: 'A new pluralism has put corporate loyalties of all kinds into question, not only flag-waving patriotism but also those other forms of collective belonging which underpinned, or reproduced, the national idea: religious affiliation, class loyalty, the public-service ethic.' The meaning of identity in politics was likely to be found not in the similarities of nationality but in the differences of gender or ethnicity (1989: xx).

To provide one further illustration of how things have changed Bernard Crick – perhaps influenced by his time with Scottish intellectuals in Edinburgh – was arguing as late as 1991 that the promotion of English identity had become an important political objective. A self-conscious and political Englishness needed to be popularised – or, perhaps to put that more precisely, Crick believed that the right *kind* of English identity was not popularly expressed. 'We English', he wrote, 'must come to terms with ourselves' and it was time to stop infusing 'everything that is English into the common property of Britishness' (Crick 1991: 104). By 1995 he was still of the view that the answer was not 'less English nationalism' but more. Like the Scots, the Welsh and the Irish, the English needed to develop 'a self-confident and explicit national feeling' (1995: 180). If Samuel had traced the outlines of the contemporary condition and Crick had defined what the English were missing, their imagination was obviously insufficient to grasp the historical cunning of St George in 1996. At the beginning of the new millennium an editorial in the *New Statesman* examined the *Zeitgeist* and observed that 'as so many sources of identity and community wither away, the people fall back on the only identities left to them: colour of skin, ethnicity, nation' (2000). The implication was that the one thing remaining for English patriots by 1996 was to fly the flag of St George.

In 1996, then, the flying of the English flag (at least in such large numbers) was a startlingly new form of behaviour. By 1998, it had become commonplace. In the course of the football World Cup of 2002, the *Sun* (with its accustomed exaggeration) wrote that the patriotism displayed by all classes and creeds during the English team's campaign meant that 'England is a different country today from the one which entered the World Cup three wonderful weeks ago' (cited in Garland 2004: 89). During Euro 2004 the flag was everywhere. Not only was the flag everywhere but the symbol of English identity had become a more or less permanent feature of the national landscape. It had entered the popular cultural mainstream. As Boris Johnson wrote in the midst of English football fever: 'Never in history has the flag of St George been so popular. Never has it been so prevalent in the décor of our streets' (2004a). Even the hesitant *Observer* noted as the World Cup finals of 2006 approached that something culturally significant was going on though it was, justifiably, not too clear about what that something was (Campbell and Asthana 2006).

How very distant all this seemed from the condition that was conveyed in the title of Clive Aslett's book (1997) *Anyone for England?*, a book completed before, though published after, the *annus mirabilis* of 1996. Aslett's point, like Samuel's, was that patriotism now seemed unfashionable and unattractive to the English. After 1996, the impression appeared to be that now *everyone* was, or could be, for England and not just the usual suspects like football hooligans. Still, the question of what it means to be 'for England' remains an open one. Is it waving (blissful dawn, the heaven of a youthful, vibrant Englishness) or drowning (the last refuge of a decadent nationalism)? Or is it both waving (rediscovering England) and drowning (discovered only when it is too late)? Rodney Barker has argued that national identity in England (rather than in the rest of the United Kingdom), 'like religious allegiance, had been a virtually dormant theme in political argument during the whole of the short twentieth century'. When one came to look at these matters afresh, he thought, the student of politics would have little to draw on (Barker 1996: 15–17). Perhaps the truth lies elsewhere. There is indeed much to draw on but it will not necessarily be found in traditional academic commentary. As Melvyn Bragg once discovered in his evocation of lives in his home town of Wigton: 'Obvious things are always easy to overlook, and always important' (1976: 447). When younger academics, unburdened by older fashions, have looked elsewhere, patriotic sentiment becomes rather more visible (see, for example, the excellent work of Julia Stapleton in intellectual history and Susan Condor in social psychology). As Barker suggested, there is scope for reconsidering the assumptions about national identity in England since the conclusions drawn from them appear to be unsatisfactory. Dissatisfaction here is perhaps best understood in the sense in which Raphael Ingelbien identified the 'misreading' of England in recent literary criticism. He too was dissatisfied with some of the key terms in which the debate about Englishness and modern poetry was being conducted. *Misreading England* was a study about both the subject and the object of this misreading, England itself. These misreadings provided Ingelbien with 'productive distortions' and provocative reactions to other texts (2002: 3–4). To be productively provoked into making a critical response is sufficient acknowledgement that much has been learned in the process of such an engagement. What this book takes to be political misreadings are also ones from which much has been learnt and to which intellectual debts are owed. Furthermore, to accept that misreadings are examples of neither ignorance nor irrelevance is also to accept the possibility that the reading found in this book may be a misreading as well.

One thing is not attempted at the outset and that is a straightfor-

ward definition of Englishness. Such a definition is not required for the
tasks this study has set for itself nor is it the precondition for saying
something intelligible about contemporary England. This is not to
argue that such definition may not be attempted or even accomplished,
only that it may be either inexpressible or succumb to banality.
According to Paul Laity, whenever Englishness or any other '-ness' is
the subject of reflection 'you can be sure the cliches will come jogging
along close behind' (2001). This is often attributable to a very
common misreading which solidifies brief moments *in* the English past
as *the* English past (see Grainger 1969: 280). It has become the
convention to argue that such solidifying of values and characteristics
is exclusively a habit of the conservative or traditionalist. However,
radicals too have often been in unacknowledged thrall to particular
'solidifications of Englishness', especially when the subject has been
the working class. There are, of course, 'perils of the *non*-definition of
Englishness – the assumptions, prejudices and exclusions which can go
unacknowledged when Englishness is simply accepted for what it says
it is' (Maslen 2004: 46). This is a peril which this book hopes to negotiate. On the one hand, to define Englishness comprehensively would
entail the discussion of absolutely everything. But as Voltaire wrote,
the secret of being boring is to omit nothing and even then without
guarantee of success. On the other hand, to define it concisely has its
own dangers. Borges tells the story of the Irish poet charged by the
High King to write a compendious ode, a tale of the island's history.
At each attempt the ode becomes more mysterious, more beautiful and
more exact until the poem consists of a single line, so ineffable that it
can never be repeated. The poet loses his life and the king loses his
mind. Borges gave this story the title *The Mirror and the Mask* and it
is tempting to think that the final poem is the mirror, permitting us to
see ourselves clearly, a 'gift forbidden to men', only to provoke self-
destruction (Borges 1978: 79). It is perhaps wiser to accept that such
transparency will always be impossible, always fabulous and that
behind each mask will be always another. While he was capable of
drawing up a list of what England 'stands for' – from Women's
Institutes to branch-line trains – John Betjeman thought he was less
than capable of explaining England 'at once so kind and so complicated' (1943: 296). Even Billy Bragg, a modern bard who has been
quite expansive in his thoughts on contemporary English identity, told
an academic conference in Warwick that if 'you try to write songs
about Englishness it is nigh on impossible' (1999: 25). It was a view
shared also by Crick who thought that the 'identity of the English is
almost as difficult to specify as the name of the state' (Crick 1991: 91).

This may very well be in the nature of the subject matter rather than in the peculiarities of the English. One writer confessed that 'the very nature of Identity Studies' means that rarely is a definite, clear finding ever arrived at (Garton Ash 2001: 12). For example, in his comprehensive survey of the identity of France, Fernand Braudel was equally compelled to admit that 'we are faced with a hundred, a thousand different Frances of long ago, yesterday or today' (cited in Stringer 1994: 10). Yet that discovery does not detract from the reality of France. Another scholar noted that the unitary term 'national identity' had only recently become ubiquitous in cultural history and had unfortunately become a catch-all for different forms of national consciousness which would be better kept separate or distinct – patriotism, nationality, national character and nationalism (Mandler 2004: 110). To identify these difficulties does not mean that the contours of the mask are not worth studying or that the journey of discovery is not worth making. To accept the complexity of national identity and to accept that national identity alone is not everything should not mean subscription to the proposition that everything is fragmented, fractured, 'de-centred' and in a constant process of transformation (for a criticism of this view see Schlaeger 2004). Because we cannot give a precise account of the nation does not mean that we cannot know of it, much less experience it. The negatives are judiciously positive. They should be sufficiently positive to prevent the inescapable mystery of nationhood becoming a cult or even occult affair.

Coming to define Englishness is not so much a preface as a postscript, as Michael Oakeshott might have put it, and the result cannot avoid being incomplete. One can only attempt to make it less so. Because this is the case, the approach of this book is inspired by Oakeshott's view of political education – in this case knowledge of England – as participation in a conversation, an imaginative rather than a functional engagement with Englishness. For Oakeshott, conversation involves an exploration of the 'intimations' of a tradition of behaviour and Englishness is such a 'tradition' with many intimations. And as he observed, 'a tradition of behaviour is a tricky thing to get to know' and (perhaps like the fable of Borges) it may be 'essentially unintelligible' (Oakeshott 1991: 61).

> It is neither fixed nor finished; it has no changeless centre to which understanding can anchor itself; there is no sovereign purpose to be perceived or invariable direction to be detected; there is no model to be copied, idea to be realized, or rule to be followed. Some parts of it may change more slowly than others, but none is immune from change. Everything is temporary.

However 'flimsy and elusive' such a tradition may be, it is not without an identity. Everything is temporary, yes, but Oakeshott adds the crucial qualification that 'nothing is arbitrary'. Moreover, nothing that ever belonged to that tradition of behaviour is completely lost. There is always a 'swerving back to recover and make something topical out of even its remotest moments; and nothing for long remains unmodified'. This is not a 'fixed and inflexible manner of doing things'. It is, rather, 'a flow of sympathy' (1991: 59). And though it is customary to call Oakeshott a conservative, such an understanding of Englishness is not necessarily conservative at all, as Robert Colls's appreciative remarks about Oakeshott would indicate (Colls 2002: 374–9). Indeed, it reveals its own remarkable 'flow of sympathy' with Orwell's observation in *The Lion and the Unicorn* that 'England will still be England, an everlasting animal, stretching into the future and the past and like all living things having the power to change out of all recognition and yet remain the same'. Even a self-conscious opponent of 'tradition' is often the unconscious proponent of another, drawing upon imaginative and rhetorical resources distinctive to English political culture. Tradition in this sense suggests that two views of national identity are inherently implausible. The first would indeed propose a changeless centre to which the present generation of English people can anchor itself or some authenticity to which they can return. The second would indeed propose that everything about national identity is not only temporary but also arbitrary, a transparent set of 'invented traditions'. The first intimates homogeneity, the second infinite adaptability. Both can make reasonable claims on our attention because they have some intelligibility but neither appears fully adequate to understanding the identity of modern England.

Moreover, tradition should not be confused with essence or teleology. Tradition, according to Oakeshott, is not blind but only 'blind as a bat'. In a brilliant philosophical examination of these matters in language that anticipated Oakeshott's own mature reflections in *On Human Conduct* (1975), M. B. Foster argued that a political society 'possesses the characteristic of all created things, that its essence is not distinguishable'. The philosopher cannot distinguish its 'essence' and the critic cannot condemn it by 'reference to a timeless standard'. This does not mean that a political identity is above criticism. What it means is 'that it is susceptible only of an historical understanding and liable only to an historical judgement'. In other words, a political tradition 'so far as it is the product of a creative activity in man, may be understood as a development, without being interpreted as a teleological process' (Foster 1935: 188, 203). The consequences of this view have been summed up politically by Bikhu Parekh: 'S national identity is a product of history, it can also be remad ... history unless one naively assumes that history somehow came to an end at a particular point in time.' However, this does not imply that identity is a *tabula rasa*. 'To say that each generation is free to redefine its national identity in the light of its needs is to ignore the basic fact that its very definition of the needs and of what it considers acceptable ways of satisfying them are shaped by the inherited way of life' (Parekh 1994: 504). In short, a national identity is 'neither fixed and unalterable nor wholly fluid and amenable to unlimited construction'. It 'is both given and constantly reconstituted' (Parekh 2000: 5–6; see also Miller 1995a). The challenge is to be able to understand how such 'processes of ideological construction cohabit with a depth of commitment and passion' (Reicher, Hopkins and Condor 1997: 84). It is often thought that this is a distinctly modern view of things; that in the past contemporaries were one-eyed (sameness) and could not see things bifocally (sameness and change). This is an obvious misreading. What could be more contemporary, for instance, than Sir Ernest Barker's conclusion to *The Character of England* where the claims of change and continuity are both noted and given their due? Barker thought that it was possible to be too historically minded. 'But this long slow movement of the character of England,' he asked, 'has it not something enduring?' The answer was in the question (Barker 1947: 575).

These philosophical musings find support amongst the historians. According to J. G. A. Pocock, national history (and so identity) can be read as both contingent and relative. It is contingent in that 'it has been shaped by factors exterior to itself,' and it is relative in that traditions are invented in relation to others (or to the Other). However, Pocock thought it the merest cant to suggest that acknowledging contingency meant accepting that national identity is some sort of illusion or mistake; or to suggest that acknowledging the relativity of identity meant accepting that it was 'false' or should be 'righteously demolished' (1995: 298–301). And while he used the term 'patriotism' rather than identity, J. C. D. Clark argued similarly that it meant 'that "we" are related to "our" history by something more than contingency' and that 'we are part of our past, inhabitants not tourists'. The key point, as Clark also observed, is that although these assumptions can be shared by left and right, 'different conclusions are drawn' (1990a: 41). Does not the Oakeshottian view assume, however, some internally coherent tradition that is unfriendly to cultural diversity? Is it necessarily exclusive in its understanding of who constitutes the English people? Does such a reading (or misreading) not inscribe too many 'exclusion clauses' in its notion of national identity (see Lunn 1996: 85)? That may be one interpretation of Oakeshott's view of political activity 'as a concrete whole' which has the 'source of its movement within itself' (1991: 46). However, the political activity of which Oakeshott wrote is learned behaviour and not esoteric practice (though much of it may appear esoteric to those without sympathy for it). To be part of a tradition does not mean that one is *determined* by that tradition. An agent 'has a history but no "nature"' (Oakeshott 1989: 64). If so, Englishness is indeed a construct, though not a product of the moment, and its political arrangements are not permanent fixtures, but ones that are modifiable by circumstance and by will. If tradition 'writes' the individual, the individual also writes the tradition. The individual and tradition cannot be separated in any simple way and neither is the essence nor the effect (of power, of invention or of inertia, even if they all play a role). Famously, Oakeshott defined politics to be 'the activity of attending to the general arrangements of a set of people whom chance or choice have brought together' (1991: 44). Neither the word 'chance' nor the word 'choice' implies a particular foundation – indeed any foundation at all – to Englishness. If the first suggests fate (or perhaps birth) and the second an act of will (or perhaps immigration) both are bound up in the political association that has been brought together. The 'conversation' of which Oakeshott writes suggests a general participation in conceiving the constitution of Englishness. As the novelist Andrea Levy legitimately put it: 'If Englishness does not define me, then redefine Englishness' (cited in Nunning 2004: 150). That is true up to a point, the point being that those claiming that England should redefine itself are also required to undergo redefinition in terms of the England in which they find themselves (and one of the failures of multiculturalist rhetoric was often the failure to acknowledge that reciprocal requirement). Every contribution to the conversation makes a claim of that sort and nations survive, as Slavoj Žižek reminds us, because they are capable of transforming themselves (1996: 128). The only illusion, as Oakeshott observed, is to think that there is a harbour for shelter or a floor for anchorage, a starting-place or an appointed destination – in other words, the illusion that the conversation will end, that the definition will be final, that there is an origin that specifies authenticity, or that there is some grand objective outside tradition itself. Oakeshott's conclusion was that a tradition of behaviour, like nationhood, 'is not a groove within which we are destined to grind out our helpless and unsatisfying lives'. In short, if 'the doctrine deprives us of a model laid up in heaven to which we should approximate our behaviour, at least it does not lead us into a morass where every choice is equally good or equally to be deplored' (1991: 60). The model nation laid up in heaven and the morass of cultural relativism may be political illusions but they are powerful ones; it is sometimes difficult for the imagination to avoid succumbing to them, and they are both revealed in the politics of Englishness. Even so, illusions can be part of the 'flow of sympathy' which is also distinctively English. Every society, Oakeshott argued, by the underlinings it makes in the book of its history, 'constructs a legend of its own fortunes which it keeps up to date and in which is hidden its own understanding of its politics; and the historical investigation of this legend – not to expose its errors but understand its prejudices – must be a pre-eminent part of political education' (1991: 63). These underlinings, or what this book calls 'legends', resemble what Joan Scott intriguingly called 'fantasy echoes'.

Scott encountered the phrase 'fantasy echo' in a student essay. Only by following up the outline of the lecture schedule did she come to the conclusion that 'fantasy echo' was a misunderstanding of the French expression *fin de siècle*. However, Scott was struck by something imaginative and creative in the Anglicised – and so, transformed – phrase. The words seemed to offer 'a way of thinking not only about the significance of arbitrary temporal designations (decades, centuries, millennia) but also about how we appeal to and write history'. All sorts of historical references, she thought, appear to echo assessments of the past in terms of predictions about the future and the process itself was also rather fantastic. It involved both the repetition of something imagined and an imagined repetition. This, Scott argued, was the key to identity formation since retrospective identifications 'are imagined repetitions and repetitions of imagined resemblances'. When a person or a community claimed an historical identity, the 'echo is a fantasy, the fantasy an echo; the two are inextricably intertwined' (Scott 2001: 285–7). On the one hand, 'fantasy is the means by which real relations of identity between past and present are discovered and/or forged'. It is that act of historical imagination, which imposes order on events and thereby 'contributes to the articulation of political identity'. On the other hand, echo connects past to present and present to past yet the 'return of partial phrases alters the original sense and comments on it as well'. While we can acknowledge the differences between historical experience and contemporary conditions, those differences are also familiar since they are an echo of *our* history. Historical identification, according to Scott, operates as a fantasy echo, 'replaying in time and over generations the process that forms individuals as social and political actors' (287–92). The value of this term is that it avoids both the essentialism of that sort of historical understanding which supposes an unchanging or timeless identity (echo) and also that sort of historical understanding which supposes that all identities are mere inventions or constructions (fantasy).

Structure of the book

'Never', according to David McCrone, 'has there been such interest in the English question as there is today' (2006: 267) and this book is a modest example of that interest. It is divided into three parts and each part consists of three related chapters. The first part, Legends of Englishness, looks at traditional narratives of the English polity. It considers them as legends – or fantasy echoes – of political Englishness and identifies the various underlinings and the range of prejudices that are to be found there. Unlike Oakeshott's rationalist, the purpose of this study is not to bring the social, political, legal and institutional inheritance of England before the tribunal of intellect and to act as a grand inquisitor (1991: 5–7). The intention is not to put England on trial but, as far as possible, to provide a portrait of 'great diversity and likeness' and though Englishness is abstracted for reasons of academic focus it should be said that most of what goes for England also goes for Britain (Colls 2002: 7). Chapter 2 considers a legend of integration, a narrative that may be said to constitute the English answer to problems of stable governance. As Dyson argued, modern English political theorists tended to come from a receptive elite that was historically accessible to ideas of reform. 'Consequently, there was a remarkable continuity of assumptions among intellectuals, a relative indifference to theoretical disputes elsewhere and a tolerance for theoretical and ethical muddle' (1980: 195). It was a tradition that generally preferred, as Disraeli once said, government by Parliament rather than by logic; one, like Macauley, that thought little of symmetry and much of convenience, and one that could see no point in removing an anomaly simply because it *was* an anomaly. It was a tradition in which, as A. J. P. Taylor once quipped, Whig plus Tory equalled eternal truth (1976: 35). Where Whig and Tory met in the English case was at the intersection of the notion of being different from others (especially continental Europeans) and of the notion of being prototypical, 'blazing trails which others followed' (Collini 1985: 41; Clark 2003: 210). This English legend is the legend of the exemplary exception.

Chapter 3 takes its bearings from E. P. Thompson's essay 'The Peculiarities of the English' and its purpose is not to defend the English tradition, neither to minimise its limitations nor to pronounce on the inevitability of its demise. It is to provide 'a more collected and informed analysis', one which tries to take account of the historic strengths and weaknesses of what is called, following Thompson, the 'English idiom', (Thompson 1978: 57). In this idiom it has been traditionally bad form to confuse formal logic with politics or to substitute a rational vision for what is convenient, an idiom that may be otherwise described as pragmatic or even empiricist. It has contributed to the tone of England's political culture and Karl Mannheim thought it revealed 'a peculiar genius for working out in practice the correlation of principles which seem to be logically opposed to one another' (cited in Kent 1998). Chapter 4 considers an equally influential, if more recent, legend of disintegration which charts England's loss of supposed self-possession. This narrative of disintegration has proved attractive because it appeared to synthesise two apparently contradictory developments: nationalism and a new, post-imperial, global framework for politics. It traced England's loss of both uniqueness and universal significance. In this view, as the Anglo-centric narrative of Britishness waned then England, formerly first among nations, was now to be pitied as the laggard of historical destiny. That was *Schadenfreude* indeed, a transition from a Celtic fringe to an Anglian fringe. The invitation now was to pity poor old England rather than to emulate her. The wide appeal of this legend can be attributed to the fact that it provided a compelling explanation of British circumstances in the late twentieth century. It explained the new significance of nationalism after 1989, it related that new nationalism to the process of European integration and it also seemed to make sense of larger global trends. The one writer who integrated all parts of the narrative of disintegration was the Scottish intellectual Tom Nairn and his polemical synthesis of the return to the particular (nationalism) and the loss of the universal (English institutional decay) influenced a generation of radical criticism.

Part II considers the Anxieties of Englishness and this is shorthand for the recent debate about English political identity. Chapter 5 considers the imaginative effect of the post-war experience. In 1950 the historian George Kitson Clark reminded his readers that if the ancient constitution faltered, the English had been English before they were British and that English identity could be found behind or beyond the institutions of the United Kingdom. One interpretation of recent British history suggests that the diminishing authority of the old institutions has indeed provoked the present re-assessment of Englishness. As one literary critic suggested, some of the drive towards re-assessment has come from authors attempting to find and to reclaim Kitson Clark's 'Englishness before Britishness'; that the very act of naming England has been an attempt to bring it back to a virile existence (Cowley 1999: 29). There may be some exhilaration in the pursuit of authentic England since the pursuit of the authentic is a sort of romanticism in politics. The urgency of cultural Englishness has also been attributed to the widespread impatience with either a sense of the country's 'disconnectedness' or with a sense that England is somehow 'forbidden' (Easthope 1999; Scruton 2000). This is the condition of anxiety upon which the politics of identity thrives and it provides intellectual space for all sorts of historical and cultural revisions. Whereas in the past these English anxiety attacks could be attributed to high political concerns about external security, the current one, this chapter argues, is mainly concerned with inner self-confidence (or the lack of it). In short, the question of English identity today is bound up with the new complexity of British governance and with the new uncertainty of how England fits into it. Chapters 6 and 7 explore the ambiguous and ambivalent outworking of these anxieties in contemporary engagements with the 'particular' of Englishness. The first is a left/liberal version of the English 'particular' that celebrates a civic, liberal, multi-ethnic idea of Englishness, an idea that it struggles to reconcile with native populism. The second is a conservative version of the English 'particular' that celebrates – if not unreservedly – a more populist idea of England, an idea that it struggles to reconcile with civic, liberal and multi-ethnic values.

Part III revisits these legends and anxieties by examining them in terms of the actual and metaphorical 'locations' of Englishness that cut across the usual patterns of political partisanship. Chapter 8 considers the regions of England not only as territories of administrative convenience but also as potential 'identity resources', as Bond and McCrone have termed them, for the fashioning of a new sense of local patriotism following the pattern of devolution elsewhere in the United Kingdom (2004). English local allegiance is deeply ingrained but it has rarely meant identification with a region – however it may be defined. Mobilising support *of* the English for the prospect of regionalism *in* England has been a conundrum and has not been without either controversy or ambiguity. Chapter 9 looks at the 'necessary context' of Europe in which many of the arguments about English identity are now discussed. Those who welcome integration into a dynamic European Union believe that the process is not only historically inevitable but also politically desirable. Those hostile to that process believe it to be both misconceived and politically undesirable. Both dramatise through the medium of Europe issues of English identity: sovereignty, self-government and legitimacy. Which pole one tends towards is not determined by any simple question of patriotism. In their very different ways both sides are serious about patriotism but draw different conclusions from their patriotism. Chapter 10 reconsiders the Britishness of England and returns the study to its beginnings, albeit in the very different conditions of the present. The claim is not, in some mystical sense, to understand England for the first time. It is to understand it as voyagers might do at the end of a long journey, when consulting the journal of their encounters, to reflect on what the evidence obliges them to believe. Since the United Kingdom is still the political location for the continuing legends and anxieties of Englishness it seems appropriate to draw things together under that heading. A brief conclusion restates the major themes of the study.

One final and personal comment is worth making. Larkin wrote in 'The Importance of Elsewhere' that as an Englishman living in Belfast 'strangeness made sense'. Living in England, no 'elsewhere' underwrote his existence but bound him up in 'customs and establishments'. Perhaps the importance of elsewhere, in this case viewing England from Belfast albeit without Larkin's poetic force, is a useful tactic. The elsewhere of Northern Ireland is, of course, not English but it is (I would argue) 'half-English', a place where Larkin's English customs and establishments are familiar but also strange. It is the strangeness of a familiar England and the familiarity of a strange England which requires one's attention. As one critic has argued 'being English means not being *just* English' since 'self-obsession becomes the same thing as self-deception' (Gervais 2001: 167). The intimate connection of the strange and the familiar appears – to anyone who looks attentively – to be close to the truth. Being not just English but rather a British *half-English* (an explanation must wait until the final chapter) may provide some protection against such self-deception. Perhaps, rather in the manner of Samuel Johnson's acquaintance Oliver Edwards, having tried to identify Englishness my Irishness will always be breaking in. On the other hand, this may go some way to addressing more satisfactorily the problem identified by Krishnan Kumar. In his justly influential book, he argued that 'initially at least' it was necessary to 'lay aside the traditional approaches to English national identity'. Their limitation, he argued, is that they tended to consider Englishness 'from inside the national culture'. Their drawback is that they 'take for granted the very thing that needs investigation'. Consequently, Kumar argued that 'English national identity cannot be found from within the consciousness of the English themselves. We have to work from the outside in' (Kumar 2003a: 17; for a criticism of this view, see Colls 2005: 581–3). However, as Kumar's own footnote to this point reveals, this is neither fully the case nor exactly what he means. Not only is the 'inside' insufficient; so too is the 'outside' ambiguous. To be both inside – to share in the solidarity, or 'flow of sympathy', to be British in other words – and yet to be outside – not to be English by nationality – may provide some new insight on what Englishness has been and what it has become. That is one more justification for writing this book.

Part I
Legends of Englishness

2

An absorptive patria

It is rather striking that much of the literature on Englishness in the last few decades has assumed a peculiar lack, and what is thought to be lacking is a politically significant national identity. At the centre of Englishness there seems to be a void and only when national sentiment becomes visible in public displays of the Cross of St George – and these certainly have become more frequent since the 1990s – is it thought that the void is being filled. There is something deeply unsatisfactory, indeed rather superficial, about that assumption. In short, it suggests a misreading. This misreading has informed the most subtle and intelligent interpretation of Englishness, Krishnan Kumar's *The Making of English National Identity* (2003a). To make this claim is not to question the significance of Kumar's book since it provides a wealth of insight into the history of Englishness. Moreover, the book's intellectual merit is sustained irrespective of any particular misreading since that particular misreading is generally at odds with Kumar's display of the historical evidence. The subject would not be so alive today if it were not for this kind of misreading since it helps to keep the conversation going (on this see Žižek 2000).

Kumar introduces *The Making of English National Identity* with the statement that 'there are virtually no expressions of English nationalism' and 'no native tradition of reflection on English national identity' (despite the subsequent 273 pages which trace both the strengths and the limitations of that very tradition). However, the *nationalism* which finds virtually no expression and the identity upon which there is no native tradition of reflection in England turn out to have, on Kumar's reckoning, a rather specific character. It is what he calls 'classic nationalism' and it is an ideal type which the English version fails to match. This, unfortunately, establishes a conceptual framework within which English peculiarity and distinctiveness can indeed be acknowledged but only on the basis of their historical deviance. 'The enigma of English nationalism', thought Kumar, lies in the fact that though the

English must have *a* sort of nationalism, they puzzle everyone by thinking that they do not have a *real* nationalism (2003a: 34). It is only at the end of the twentieth century that 'the English have been forced to ask themselves the kinds of questions that other nations have engaged in for a long time'. Unfortunately for them, just when they need it most, they now realise what they lack and the consequences have been 'glaringly revealed' in the incoherence of the English response to changing political circumstances in the contemporary world. The conclusion of Kumar's thesis (though it is not necessarily the conclusion to which his scholarly evidence tends) is stark: 'The English, having for so long resolutely refused to consider themselves as a nation or to define their sense of nationhood, find themselves having to begin from scratch' (2003a: 269). *The Making of English National Identity* finishes with the announcement of English Identity: Year Zero.

The spectre haunting this framework is one specific idea of nationalism and Kumar's definition, as one critic observed, means that the sociology unfortunately undermines most of the history. For Robert Colls, Kumar's concern to hold on to the attributes of 'classic nationalism' as an exclusively modern phenomenon means that he 'is obliged to reject the idea that any previous expressions of national identity can be as authentic as the modern variety'. It is the modern variety which has become the test against which Englishness should be measured but this, Colls thinks, is all very implausible. The thesis required its readers to accept that 'up to a very late stage English identities were built on the winning of empires and not on the authentic expressions of the English people' and only when empire was no longer an option did the English feel compelled to 'come out as full-on nationalists'. The English, then, have been made to wait a thousand years for the 'authentic' formation of a national identity but 'such has been the clamour of new identities, and the fading of old ones, the English now find themselves living through an identity crisis' and it is a crisis from which they may or may not recover. For Colls, this argument suffered from the fault of substituting logical seriousness, or definitional exactitude, for the messiness of historical experience. Indeed, he noted that while Kumar requires rigorous subscription by others to a modern or 'classic' definition of nationalism, he himself can resort to a wide range of terminological devices to explain Englishness on the one hand and to keep pure his definition of nationalism on the other (2005: 581–3). Such intellectual virtuosity may choreograph a theoretical dance around the historical elephant. Even if English people did, or still do, find it difficult to understand the nationalism of other people they surely had some sense of their own national belonging (see Chadwick 1945: 3). Mr Podsnap's knowledge of what England *is* may have been complacent but it was not at all unusual and as Idries Shah noted, the exceptional thing about the English is that they are obsessed with themselves while contriving to remain unaware of it (Shah 2000). To argue thus is not to trivialise the distinction that Kumar is making – that one should not confuse national sentiment with the political programme for autonomy called nationalism – but to re-think it (Smith 2003: 26; see also Mandler 2004). Hard cases make bad law, it is said, but in politics perhaps hard cases are the law because there are no easy cases. The English past, according to Bernard Crick, 'can only be misread if read in terms of modern nationalism' and, in this sense, the reading one finds in Kumar is actually ambiguous (1995: 175). On the one hand, it confirms Crick's statement since it claims that past *cannot* be read in terms of modern nationalism but on the other hand it challenges it since it assumes that past can *only* be read in terms of (the lack of) modern nationalism.

The key question is the one once asked by Wittgenstein – what is being judged by what? Surely there is some problem with a definition of the subject if Kumar's superb survey of historical interpretation must operate under such a self-denying ordinance. To use a literary example, if one tried to define tragedy by excluding *King Lear*, then 'you would not reject the instance but the definition, since any account of tragedy that does not include that instance must be wrong' (Watson 2000: 90). Perhaps, as Germaine Greer has suggested (and this is something that will be encountered frequently in the course of the book), the lack in this case may not be national identity or even a form of nationalism but exactly that 'chronic lack of seriousness' in English culture which frequently baffles outsiders and disorders neat defini- tion (Greer 2005). And it is often the case that outsiders, especially the Scots, Welsh and Irish, encounter this lack of seriousness as itself a nationalistic move. Some English commentators acknowledge this as well. Probe English sensitivities too seriously and, on the one hand, 'they get you for earnestness' or, on the other, 'put you down with their toleration' (Walden 2004). In sum, one element of English nationalism is its tendency to make other nationalisms appear vulgar. Yet Greer is capable of seeing this positively as a kind of patience that accepts 'inconsistency and contradiction, an awareness of the contingency of all things'. For Greer this is 'the soul of irony' and 'it is also what makes Englishness both so enduring and so difficult to grasp' (2005). One can add that insofar as this awareness of contingency is itself a form of non-contingent self-understanding it is one of those paradoxes that have been defined as peculiarly English (see Chapter 3).

It may be difficult to grasp, yet those who have tried – like genera-tions of writers, liberal, socialist and conservative – had no doubt about its existence even if some modern academics are only belatedly beginning to discover it again (see Canovan 1996). The lack of an overtly defined nationalism did not and does not mean the absence of a profound sense of nationality or even a certain idea of England. The truth has been quite the opposite. It is the 'self-conceptualisation' of England, Julia Stapleton believed, 'that constitutes the most striking general feature of political thought from the British perspective between the mid-nineteenth and the mid-twentieth century' (1998: 860). This self-conceptualisation has certainly undergone changes but it remains a conversational part of public life. Here is a long and diverse tradition of reflection on matters of national identity and, in a convincing re-consideration of the history of England, Jonathan Clark thought that certain ways of conceptualising 'group identity' had become 'so well developed in England, and occupied the intellectual terrain so thoroughly, that there was insufficient conceptual space for nineteenth-century ideas of nationalism to flourish'. However, the absence of nineteenth-century ideas of nationalism did not mean that English identity was lacking because Clark also observed that 'England, Britain and the United Kingdom comprised a society that was highly self-aware, but one which normally took as symbols of identity a shared libertarian culture, and institutions that promoted the advance of civilization, law and history' (Clark 2003: 88). This was the basis of a civic patriotism and the important point is that it was both civic *and* patriotic, another theme that will recur in the course of this book. Even today English people feel that any distinc-tion between the nation as a set of civic rights and the nation as a patriotic affection eludes common sense (Condor 2001: 180). This conceptualisation and awareness, if it was not exactly *classic* nation-alism as Kumar understands it, did constitute the dominant public doctrine which, it was widely thought, should (and often did) inspire both admiration and emulation.

According to Watson, this 'English idea of government', or what he called the 'English ideology', was 'the idea of liberty expressed through parliamentary institutions' (1973: 1). It proposed an English narrative of integration, a narrative that reconciled different visions of English exceptionalism *and* its exemplary quality. This narrative was integrative in two respects. It served to legitimise and celebrate English institutionalism but it also helped to integrate the other nations of the United Kingdom into that culture of English institutionalism. Though the persuasiveness of this narrative has been severely diminished, it managed to survive remarkably well throughout the twentieth century and even today it can still claim adherents, and not just amongst Orangemen in Northern Ireland. Kohn, in his seminal study of the genesis of English nationalism in the seventeenth century, argued that England, *pace* Kumar, was actually the first country with a popularly based national consciousness and that it had become so deeply ingrained in the English mind that it appeared self-evident. English philosophers may not have thought it necessary to meditate upon nationalism but absence did not mean that national belonging was neglected (Kohn 1940: 92–3; see also Greenfeld 1992: 86–7). Lord Rosebery believed this to be a case of England's 'notable self-possession' and he implied that England's constitutionalism (or Watson's English 'ideology') had accommodated within it the other nations of Britain and, without undue pressure, had absorbed them into its own consciousness (Grainger 1986: 52–3). The dominance of England within the United Kingdom had elements of both design and imposition but its dominance was mainly a consequence of its being so powerfully present. Within, the identity of England extended its exceptional and exemplary qualities to the multi-national polity, even if these qualities – especially in Ireland – were not always gratefully received. Without, the identity of England represented itself in the Empire where the spirit of its rule was also thought to be both exceptional and exemplary. It has become somewhat of a cliché to remark upon England's exceptionalism and to dismiss the notion now that England has become merely one amongst many medium powers in a globalised world. Nonetheless, it is worth considering in some depth what that term once meant because it is an idea that lingers still.

The English exception

In any country of notable self-possession, the claim of exceptionalism would not be unusual. However, as with arguments about the 'lack' of English nationalism, it has been suggested that the English have not been overly conscious of their difference but confuse their difference with the norm. If the Americans have American exceptionalism, the French *l'exception francaise* and the Germans *der deutsche Sonderweg*, the English do not have an equivalent expression: 'it seems they take their exceptionality so much for granted that they don't even bother putting a name to it' (Bell 2000). Perhaps, but the absence of a distinctive word does not deny the experience or the exceptionality. The American sense of manifest destiny, for instance, remains simultaneously exceptional and universal, 'unique in the good fortune of its institutions and endowments, and exemplary in the power of its radiation and attraction' (Anderson 2002: 23). Like Kumar's notion of English 'missionary' nationalism, Anderson also argues that in the American case the national interest is the ground both of the particular (exception) and of the general (example), sometimes mixing force with the cultural neutralisation of competing power centres. To adapt the expression of Daniel Bell, exceptionalism does not mean uniqueness, a term which applies to all nations. It means being somehow fated to achieve greatness, being exempt or immune from the decadence of other countries, and being the beacon of modernity or, more conservatively, stability. The idea of exceptionalism is a distinct theme which, in its exemplary virtue, tends to recur in the history of the favoured nation (Bell 1991: 50–1).

Exceptionalism as a mode of historical self-understanding established a particular debate about the character of England and the high moral idiom in which politics was discussed engaged contesting notions of the exception. Either in praising the country for its high ideals and standards or in condemning the country for its very betrayal of those ideals and standards, participants to the debate shared in the notion of England being the bearer of universal values. As Amy Kaplan noted, this style of debate often reduced the complexity of things to a Manichean conflict between good and bad versions of both history and policy (2004: 156–7). In such circumstances it becomes difficult to get a proper perspective in a contest between two cults: a cult of historic self-esteem and its opposite, a cult of self-loathing, and by blinding people to the complexity of historical circumstances, these cults could easily lead to self-delusion (Kearney 2003: 254). Thus, for every argument which claimed that England's history revealed an exceptional virtue there was also an argument which claimed that it revealed an exceptional vice. Hence the question of whether the British Empire was, in Seeley's terms, all 'wonder and ecstasy' or whether it was an 'excrescence' that exposed England to war and corruption (Watson 1973: 216); whether, as Elton put it, 'English history most convincingly demonstrated how man should order his existence on earth' (what he called the Froude complex) or whether it served 'to demonstrate the opposite with equal coherence and conviction' (what he called the *New Statesman* complex). Whatever the public rhetoric and whatever side was taken in these arguments, Elton continued, the nature of the debate testified to the belief 'that England and her history enjoyed the special privilege of providing an example to mankind' (1991: 110–11). The conversation of English public culture would not have become what it is without these distinctive complexes

There is a strong element of the 'chosen people' about this self-understanding that in England's case may be traced back to the Protestant Reformation in the sixteenth century and which resurfaces at times of great crises (Hastings 1999: 393). However, one must be careful about attributing too much in this regard to English Protestantism as some writers have done. To consider oneself to be part of *an* elect nation is not the same thing as being *the* Elect Nation even though the two notions were sometimes confused. Protestantism and English patriotism, by the beginning of the seventeenth century, were largely regarded as one and the same and the Church of England, for most of its history at least, 'rarely hesitated to claim that it embodied the Englishness of English Religion' (Robbins 1982: 468; see also Loades 1982; Collinson 1986). However, Kohn was in little doubt about the 'peculiar character' of English nationalism and thought that it was 'imbued with the spirit of liberty asserted in a struggle against ecclesiastical and civil authority' and as such it 'never made the complete integration of the individual within the nation the aim of nationalism'. He also argued that the peculiarity of English socialism similarly could be traced to that single cultural root with the result that 'English socialism carried the deep impress of the Independentism of the seventeenth century, religious, liberal and humanitarian, but so also did English imperialism'. For all the brutalities in the course of English history, there was never lost 'the demand for and the promise of political and intellectual liberty and equal justice under the law' (Kohn 1940: 92–4).

This was a distinctive political inter-relationship that Colls brilliantly explored sixty years later. 'The bonding of the English with their common law could make conservatives into radicals and radicals into conservatives.' When, in the course of the nineteenth century, national identity became bound up with notions of the 'British Constitution' and 'Empire', the same bonding applied for this too 'was said to be a people's story'. Radicals usually stood 'for a constitution that took them for *Englishmen*' in all their exceptional good fortune and a substantial element of that good fortune lay in England's religion (Colls 2002: 28). This was a common understanding, popularly held, that lasted well into the twentieth century. The importance of Protestantism to this self-understanding of English good fortune was remarked upon by George Santayana: 'What could England have been,' he asked, 'but for the triumph of Protestantism there?' His answer was: 'Only a coarser France, or a cockney Ireland.' Protestantism had stiffened the English national character and this proved 'essential to raise England to its external dignity and greatness' (Santayana 1922: 82). As it remains proclaimed on the banners of Orange lodges, displaying the mid-nineteenth century painting by Thomas Jones Barker, the secret of England's greatness was not just its exceptional prosperity but also its reformed faith, and the two were intimately linked. This *English* Protestant ideology was part of a larger national identity which the majority of British people shared (MacColl 2004: 608). This was the foundation of a civilisation that preserved both civil and religious liberty, in which, it used to be said, Labour politics owed more to Methodism than to Marxism and the Church of England was the Conservative Party at prayer. It is only relatively recently in English/British history that national 'values', with the exception of 'tolerance', can be discussed without some reference to religious faith and within a purely secular frame.

This recent secularism has encouraged a widespread indifference to the public profession of the Anglican faith (or any Christian faith) ironically, perhaps, because the passion of the clerical/anti-clerical divisions so common in Europe was never significant (a lack of religious controversy which has worked to the advantage of the monarchy). This has led some to argue that one of the key props that sustained England's, and the United Kingdom's, distinctiveness has now gone. The Protestantism implicit in how the English used to understand themselves no longer resonates because Protestantism, with its cult of individual conscience, has paved the way for its own undoing in the triumph of liberal secularism. However, the extent of English secularism is peculiar both in European and even British experience and this may be an enduring aspect of England's claim to exceptionalism. It certainly contributed to the attitude that English people had with the Troubles in Northern Ireland which was an embarrassing echo, especially to liberal opinion, of England's own past. Civilisation had its discontents and also its history of conflict but this is something that the English have chosen, conveniently, to forget. The 'strange death of Anglican England' has been probably *the* 'most striking cultural transformation in modern English history', all the more remarkable and exceptional for the amnesia of the English (Johnson 2001)

That this civilisational perspective emphasised institutions and law rather than race and nation did not mean that the perspective was neither self-consciously English nor self-consciously patriotic since this was not thought to be at odds with the Britishness of the Union and the Empire. The exception of English political institutions and their civilising role did appear exemplary to many Scots, Welsh and to some

Irish and in the nineteenth century even *The Edinburgh Review* was prepared to declare that 'the nearer we [the Scots] can propose to make ourselves to England the better' (cited in Massie 2002: 13). England, while remaining England, especially for poets, in a real sense also *did* become Britain, as its industrial transformation drew in the Irish, Scots and Welsh. England became not a tract of land but 'an ideal, a dynamic vision with which many Irishmen, Welshmen and Scotsmen have identified themselves' and their national distinctiveness could be absorbed into the English consciousness (Read 1933: x). And vice versa, the English consciousness could fully embrace the Britishness of its larger territorial context. This was not a loss but a mutual gain, not an absence but a very powerful presence and an 'absorptive *patria*' of this sort had no need to base Englishness on blood, soil, flag or even classic nationalism (see Grainger 1986: 53–5). Sharing law, Parliament, government, and liberties was sufficient and this ruling perspective was capable of resisting, or transforming, more essentialist definitions of belonging. In turn, the virtues of this social and political integration were thought to rely in large measure upon the relatively stable national identity that England gave to both Union and Empire (Stapleton 1999a: 130). Historically, the hegemony of England promoted two anxieties amongst the other nations: the anxiety of provincialism, in which acknowledgement by England was thought necessary to validate local cultural achievement; and the corresponding anxiety of influence, in which such validation became an expropriation of the local into the English cultural mainstream. In short, there was, and for some there continues to be, the feeling that matters non-English were insufficiently recognised. Only recently has that reciprocal bond become an issue for some English commentators as well and they too have responded by parading their own particular anxieties (see Chapter 4).

The continuity of political institutions, which was thought to display the peculiar genius of the English, also informed the English attitude to their European neighbours (for a criticism of such supposed continuity see Davies 1999). 'English observers of the nineteenth century,' according to Kumar, 'watched with concern but also some complacency the failure of parliamentary institutions to take firm root in countries such as France, Italy and Germany' (Kumar 2003b: 16). The tendency of Europeans either to revolutionary or to despotic excess was at odds with assumed English moderation and this unfortunate tendency was thought to lie in the uncivil character of European politics. In short, the failing was the inability to achieve the exceptional English integrity of the civic and the patriotic. Nor was this an exclusively insular view. The 'English nation', according to Voltaire, had discovered the secret of the balanced constitution where monarchical power was limited, where aristocratic influence was moderated and where the people could share in government without confusion (Salmon 1999: 87). English difference continued to be remarked upon by outsiders throughout the nineteenth and twentieth centuries and some of them did indeed find it exemplary. Their 'Anglophilia' derived from admiration for England's exceptional combination of civility, freedom and order, albeit with some wonder at these paradoxical circumstances (Buruma 1999).

The link between the history of a people and its political institutions was a key feature of English reflection on the modern state. For Ernest Barker, law and institutions were ultimately ideas 'and ideas do not grow – they are made by human minds'. Though it was difficult to trace the origins of such ideas it was not, he thought, a mystical process. Rather, it involved a complicated process of the historical interaction of many minds and circumstances. It was differences in the action and the history of the state which fundamentally explained the differences between the institutional inheritance of, for example, France and England. In the sphere of what he called 'social organisation' Barker thought that the influence of the common law had possibly a greater effect on the behaviour and temper of the nation than even Parliament: 'When all are thus bound by law, the nation acquires a fundamental unity, which is a unity of the common framework of law.' If this did not entail equality of status or social position it did secure 'a formally equal legal standing of all its members' (Barker 1927 Chapter VI; see also Colls 2002). Moreover, English respect for the common law represented 'a habit of mind more vital to social well-being than most of the articles of any progressive programme'. The great danger of 'progressive legislation' was that, by failing to command general assent, it would undermine that distinctive English habit of mind and in this case, progressive legislation could be harmful to progress itself, that other vital identity of modern England (Barker 1927: 157). The *Englishness* that appealed to liberties and right derived from the past here embraces the *Britishness* of industry, empire and moral improvement (see Evans 1994: 160). In her study of the contrasting concepts of the state in France and England, Cecile Laborde emphasised that Barker's views, albeit liberal and celebratory, were widely held. Liberty was associated with the continuity of institutions and law and the continuity of institutions and law were associated with liberty. Here were the features 'of a much-cherished heritage, one which even the most radical Utilitarians, Idealists, and

socialists rarely repudiated explicitly' and one which found renewed
life in the assumptions of post-1945 academic political science. For
most of recent history, argued Laborde, 'British theorists could afford
a more relaxed, sometimes even sanguine, approach towards the state
– an approach which never set the state in a wholly pro-active or
conflictual relation to society' (2000: 553). On this point she
confirmed Dyson's long-standing thesis that what distinguished
English intellectual life was 'a relative indifference to theoretical
disputes elsewhere and a tolerance for theoretical and ethical muddle'
(1980: 195). But this distinctively English logical muddle was only
workable because the practical integration of the civic and the patriotic was what mattered.

If national character, as Barker understood it, was intimately related
to history and institutions then the civic decency of public life was
bound up with the concrete patriotic reference that was England itself.
By contrast, European intellectuals were too often thought to be
tempted by the lures of 'abstract' values and this only led to bad politics. Here again the civil bias of Englishness could be contrasted with
the state-centredness or regime bias of traditions like the French or the
German (Stapleton 2001: 114). This nineteenth century 'national faith
in the evolution of England' may not necessarily have been the best
grounding for the brutal challenges of the twentieth since the 'belief in
history as evidence of national rectitude was in many ways a surrogate
religion' where God was a reasonable Englishman or at least ought to
be. Thus was the study of English history as a 'bridge between secular
and rational convictions' and its study helped to develop character and
to reveal the secret of institutional success (Soffer 1994: 9). If pure
theory was irrelevant then experience was instructive and perhaps the
attractiveness of this approach also helps to explain the secularism of
modern English society where history textbooks, according to David
Cannadine, became the new prayer books. This is an exaggeration of
course, but his survey of the standard histories did show that 'they
were all conceived, written and marketed as histories of *England*' and
that 'these books were almost without exception in praise of England'.
These texts 'took English exceptionalism for granted: it existed, it was
good, and it was the historian's task to explain it and to applaud it'.
Moreover, these popular as well as scholarly works 'generally
supposed that this history was a success story: as the authors of *1066
and All That* argued, when England ceased to be top nation, history
came to a full stop' (Cannadine 1995: 16–17). *1066 and All That* was
first published in 1930 but *Histories of England* continued to appear
as late as the 1970s and 1980s by which time they were no longer

either so confident or so convincing. It was the Second World War that had given a new lease of life, understandably so, to the virtues of English constitutionalism and the rule of law in contrast with barbarity in Europe.

Nor did that particular understanding of English exceptionalism have to be either pious, pompous or the stock-in-trade of the propagandist (though England's PR has been rather good). There were those who, while drawing sympathetically on a wide philosophical inheritance, remained in no doubt about the value of England's political tradition especially when it had been tested so severely by the armed doctrines of continental Europe. Michael Oakeshott, for one, stated the case concisely: 'Reputable political behaviour,' he argued, 'is not dependent on sound philosophy.' Rather 'constitutional tradition is a good substitute' and in this respect English politics was remarkably rich. He concluded that the form of parliamentary democracy which England had made 'British' was not an abstract idea but 'a way of living and a manner of politics which first began to emerge in the Middle Ages'. In that era was fashioned a unique way of life and manner of politics, 'an outline which has since been enlarged by experience and invention and defended against attack from without and treason from within'. This way of life, according to Oakeshott, was 'not the gift of nature but the product of our own experience and inventiveness'. Left at that, this estimate of the English/British political tradition would have been unexceptional. But it was not left at that since the freedoms bequeathed by England to the United Kingdom, guaranteed by law, represented an exceptional method of social integration, 'the most civilized and the most effective method ever invented by mankind' (Oakeshott 1948: 476, 489–90). Others were less impressed. In 1953, for example, Eric Voegelin commented that Oxford political philosophers assumed that 'the principles of right political order have become historical flesh more perfectly in England than elsewhere at any time'. Happy the political philosopher, then, who finds that universal principles are 'identical with those of his own civilisation' (cited in O'Sullivan 2004). Voegelin and other exiles from fascism and communism (like Elias Canetti) were rather contemptuous of this English parochialism and the continuity of its assumptions though they were happy enough to benefit from its security and its sanctuary. English intellectual complacency could be attributed to luck, to contingent events or to geography but the fact remained that the stability of Britain/England was not *just* because of these things. It *did* have much to do with national political values, the exceptional nature of which British politicians were still keen to celebrate at the

end of the twentieth century with the 'whiggish fanfare' of Cool
Britannia (Kidd 2001). At the beginning of the twenty-first century the
exceptional values of Britishness were proclaimed anew as politicians
and public intellectuals tried to rebalance the civic and the patriotic
that the second half of the twentieth century appeared to unbalance
(see Brown 2004: 10).

This was not always how things had been, especially in the inter-war
years when the integration of the civic and the patriotic seemed most
under threat. Edward Shils certainly noticed the intellectual transformation that the war had had on English intellectual attitudes, reinvig-
orating beliefs that had been formerly challenged. Whereas in the
1920s and 1930s it was the decadence of institutions and practices
that most intellectuals thought repugnant, by the 1950s Shils discovered that the intellectual class found English society and culture very
much to its satisfaction. This was not just the conceit of conservatives
because in 1953 Shils 'heard an eminent man of the left say, in utter
seriousness, at a university dinner, that the British constitution was "as
nearly perfect as any human institution could be" and no one even
thought it amusing'. Shils observed that those 'who had ridiculed and
abhorred patriotism began to find themselves patriots' and he attributed this to the divesting of what many on the left saw as 'its immoral
imperial appurtenances'. Furthermore, that patriotism was also
informed by the contrast with a troubled Europe and also by a strain
of 'anti-Americanism' (Shils 1972: 137–42). From these remarks, one
is conscious that history does have a habit perhaps not of repeating
itself but of providing analogies with the present. However, Shils was
not only aware that there was more continuity than discontinuity in
these attitudes but also convinced that they were not an unmixed
blessing. On the one hand, English intellectuals were exceptional in
European terms because they promoted a national identity that tended
towards social harmony rather than conflict. If this was morally and
politically an advantage it was also intellectually a disadvantage: 'It
made them less good as intellectuals, among whose tasks – there are
many others – is the truthful interpretation of their national society
and its culture to their own countrymen and the world' (Shils 1972:
149). In short, intellectuals had a habit of believing rather than challenging England's own PR. Shils was certain that this sensibility would
encourage a reaction as the ranks of the intellectual class expanded.
He was right, and one of the consequences of this reaction will be
examined in Chapter 3. Although the traditional understanding of
English and by extension, British, exceptionalism has been questioned
by recent research, *an* understanding of it remains influential and this

is something that is considered again at the end of the chapter. Historians, as one seminal study concluded, 'who have stressed the peculiarity of the English or British experience have been right to do so. There *was* a British *Sonderweg*' even if it was not so distinct as the public doctrine imagined it to be (Eastwood, Brockliss and John 1997: 207). What, though, constituted the exemplary in the English exception?

The English exemplary

In Anderson's view, a state that by definition is exceptional 'will possess features that *cannot* be shared by others, since it is precisely those that lift it above the ruck of its rivals'. At the same time, however, 'its role requires it to be as close to a generalizable – that is, reproducible – model as practicable'. The irony is this. Though the particular and the universal 'are condemned to each other' they 'can only be realized by division' (2002: 21). In this sense the exemplary (as universal) sits uneasily with the particular (as exceptional) and one's voice in the conversation of Englishness often depended on whether one emphasised the civic (exemplary) or the patriotic (particular). Historically, if public institutions rooted in national experience represented the form of English exceptionalism then the code of civility represented its spirit and it was this spirit of the English, as A. L. Rowse called it, that was considered exemplary. In turn, that code of civility found expression in the 'genteel tradition' of English political thought, one of the most articulate exponents of which was again Ernest Barker (see also Aughey 2001: 32–7, 165–7).

In *National Character and the Factors in its Formation*, for example, Barker argued that nationhood was a function of nurture not nature. It was made, and because it was made it was also modifiable (Barker 1927: 7). A nation was not the physical fact of one blood but was an effort of the imagination which had created a common tradition. And it was out of such a common tradition that one could speak of both the English *and* the British nation. This lightness of touch explained Barker's pre-disposition towards 'neighbourliness' as the appropriate relationship in political matters rather than an integral or 'classical' form of nationalism. For him, true nationality was to be found in 'the sweet ties of neighbourliness' which were strengthened by common traditions, a perfect conception of political Englishness, conjuring up as it does the privet hedge of civility and the village green of patriotism. Even after the slaughter of the First World War, Barker could still feel confident enough in the tradition of civility to argue that neighbourliness 'is a quiet virtue – quiet but deep and permeating. It is a virtue that pays' (1919: 144). The conception was also historically functional in that it identified the proper conditions for the management of England's connection with the other nations of the United Kingdom and its association with the Empire. For Barker, Englishness was revealed politically by its pragmatic adjustment to changing circumstances, the code of which was one of 'changing and moving with the times, and actively helping the times to change and move' (1945: 19). This was the compromise between precedent and progress which he thought characteristic of the history of England. The distinctive political *modus operandi* of the English, then, was 'that tentative method of gradual experimentation which is rooted and grounded in its national temper' (1947: 558). This sort of benign, Burkean adaptability would not only define the course of English politics but also regulate political relationships within the United Kingdom and between the United Kingdom and the rest of the world (1927: 157). The English might not be very good at theory like the French but they were generally good in practical matters (that this might be a legend of their own PR see Watson 2000).

Their vice (though one feels that Barker does not really think it to be a vice) was the vice of piecemeal solutions and their temper was what could be called 'wait and see' (1950: 7). There was, Barker believed, self-confidence in the wisdom of that approach which tended to make the English rather self-righteous even if, in the course of the twentieth century, much of that self-righteousness had been knocked out of them. Of course, the genteel tradition that Barker espoused was not without its critics and there were those who thought that its persistence revealed an incorrigible disposition towards appeasement both before and after the Second World War. There were others who thought that its lack of imagination was crippling, that it was platitudinous, vague and politically unsound displaying only smugness, complacency and lack of vigour. Moreover, it ignored not only the sufferings the English had visited upon their colonial subjects but also the self-interestedness of the 'values' it so piously proclaimed. Here was not evidence of a civilising mission but a self-understanding which could be summed up in an evocative single word: humbug. Yet what this tradition implied (for it was too genteel to make a claim) was a worldly wisdom which, like Hobbesian logic, always sought internal stability and external peace. Barker's principle of sweet neighbourliness, that quiet virtue which sought to restrain the popular passions and to make of them a 'nation of the spirit', helped to inform the self-image of British policy-making (1919: 144–5). It understood gover-

nance to require calm and self-conscious moderation, level-headed-
ness, even *sang froid* (some might say, *insouciance* and others bloody-
mindedness). Not only did outsiders take this to be quintessentially
British and thus very English, for they too commonly (and correctly)
confused the two but also the British (and not just the English) thought
that this was how things were done or ought to be done and that it
represented the best of British. And for all its undoubted elements of
humbug, this code of civility did help to convey something of value in
the political culture – a habit of civic tolerance and decency – which
acted as a countervailing power to those more atavistic and chauvin-
istic instincts in English (and British) patriotism. It may have fostered
a rather cool individualism that lacked *bonhomie* but it did help to
cultivate an official *bonne nature* (see Barnard 2001: 101). The
English 'bobby' came to embody this exemplary civil achievement, the
perfectly decent protector of liberty and order but someone implaca-
ble in a sense of duty (McLaughlin 2005: 12). This was a remarkable
modern transformation since the music hall meaning of 'If you want
to know the time ask a policeman' implied that those who were
charged with upholding the law were those most likely to steal your
watch. As the gentlemanly cult of Englishness died so too did the belief
in institutional *bonne nature* diminish and this has affected the reputation of the police as well as all other aspects of public life. The older
view, however, implied a common set of public values which promoted
a sense of commonality in the multinational United Kingdom, at the
centre of which stood England itself.

It was this code of civility that Barker thought to be England's exemplary 'national mission' and its liberality contrasted with the exclusive
nationalism he associated with expansionist European powers like
Germany. For all the sins of England's mission, argued Barker, 'exclusive nationalism' was not one of them since there has never been an
attempt within its own imperial reach by example 'to proselytize all its
peoples into acceptance of a single culture' (Stapleton 1994: 95–9). If
this represented a good measure of the liberal view and its subscription to the universal virtue of English civility, it was a view also generally shared as a patriotic marker of British society. Though English
public doctrine was arrayed here in its Sunday best its sense of
'mission' did help to explain the world historical significance of
Britain's role with which Churchill justified resistance to Hitler. The
'English-speaking peoples' had authored a style of politics sympathetic
to the growth of freedom and law, constitutional government and the
subordination of the state to civil society and at times of crisis they
must not only be the trustees of this style of politics but there was a

time in which they had to 'become the armed champions' of that world view (cited in Roberts 2002: 54). Churchill's visionary sense of responsibility confirms Kumar's view that 'the English could not see themselves as just another nation in a world of nations' but it does not necessarily confirm his related point that the English did not so much celebrate themselves as identify with their mission or the related point that English national identity shifted 'the emphasis from the creators to their creations' (Kumar 2003a: x). In one mode of the exemplary, it did indeed do this and that is why a judiciously intelligent writer like Barker could contemplate serenely the idea that the 'free expansion of English society overseas could create new nations of no less quality than the old' (1947: 558). 'Indirect rule' could be the British *modus operandi* because the code of civility, once learnt by colonial subjects, was a self-evidently exemplary mode of civic governance. Barker thought that even with the weakening of the ties of Empire into Commonwealth, the civil community fostered by this free expansion would continue to survive. On the other hand, as it was reported of the historian A. J. P. Taylor, Englishness may have preferred admiration to emulation, that is they preferred to be exceptional rather than exemplary (Cannadine 1998: 286).

What, though, if the exemplary did not fit so neatly with the exception? What if there was a contradiction between the exceptional, rooted in the distinct historical, patriotic experience of a political community, and the exemplary, the civic codification of a way of life abstracted from its original cultural sources? In other words, what if there was a contradiction between the particular and its own universal, between the creators and their universal creations? Might the English feel that without their own privileged influence and control the 'creation' was probably unsustainable or not even worth sustaining? Would these feelings translate into a rather different self-understanding as England's sense of exception and example diminished? These concerns can be found in Oakeshott where he observed that English experience had become 'the model for peoples whose powers of social and political invention were unequal to their needs'. Unfortunately, if the rights and duties were exported 'the genius that made them remained at home'. Because the code of civility was not the fruit of their own experience, those who had benefited from the gift had forgotten that it derived from the experience of a particular culture. What 'went abroad as the concrete rights of an Englishman have returned home as the abstract Rights of Man, and they have returned to confound our politics and to corrupt our minds'. Furthermore, Oakeshott feared English principles 'returning to us, disguised in a foreign dress, the outline blurred by false theory and the detail fixed with an uncharacteristic precision' (1948: 490). This (exemplary) corruption he later called rationalism in politics and for Oakeshott, and others who thought like him, it appeared to pose a challenge to the (exceptional) English tradition of civility because the civic and the patriotic could not be separated. The civic exemplary alone distorted history and for it to make complete sense it also required the rootedness of English experience. To argue in this fashion does not make Oakeshott a classical nationalist but it does highlight the permanent tension between the civic and the patriotic, the creation and the creators. It also highlights the very specific historical condition in which the exception and the exemplary appeared so harmoniously linked. Indeed, one can argue that what distinguished the English/British 'mission' of civility appeared to be the interchangeable relation between the person and the principle. And what characterised the mission in its supreme self-confidence was its expression of the values of the particular selves that composed it (even if it was a limited proportion of society). If the principle was civility then the person was the gentleman. Achieving the code of civility meant others adopting, or at least adapting, the code of the gentleman.

Writing in 1958, the Dutchman J. H. Huizinga thought he had discovered the reason for the politeness, civility and charm of official-dom in England and it was 'due to the fact that the British system of government was not representative government or popular govern-ment but something very different, Government by the Right People, Government by Gentlemen'. The world's 'model democracy', he found, was an exceptional one. It did not define itself in the abstract terms of liberty, equality and fraternity or popular sovereignty but in the particular terms of the historical triumph of Parliament. In this perspective, freedom was something that had been achieved in the past, was enshrined in the present (that 'shrine' was Westminster) and not something to be worked for in the future. Like Oakeshott, Huinzinga was impressed by the capacity of that mode of governance for political stability even if he was, unlike Oakeshott, unimpressed by the conservatism of its institutions. Even when it appeared that in egal-itarian times the day of the gentleman was coming to an end, he reflected that it was not improbable that 'in spite of all bloodless revo-lutions the system of government by gentlemen might maintain itself' (Huizinga 1958: 96–108). Moreover, the ideal of the English gentle-man, it has been argued, 'once embodied a national ideal as idiomatic and irreplaceable as the American Dream' and was what made 'the English English'. Culturally it entailed a preference for 'character' rather than 'brains' (Collins 2002: 91–3). Whether the gentlemanly ideal was a cause or a consequence of the civil tradition in England; whether it was attached to Britain's expansive civil 'mission'; or whether it was a domestic response to that mission's retreat are questions that remain open (see Mandler 2000). Even non-conservatives could acknowledge its worth since the defence of 'good form' meant a defence of 'conventions' rather than 'principles' and that this empirical attitude helped to defuse the potential for political extremism (Crick 1989: 33). After 1945, the class-based characteristics of the gentleman appeared to be transformed into the universally available 'temperament of decency' upon which the new welfare society was to be founded (Green 1976: 416). Even the affectionate parody of the English gentleman as John Steed in the 1960s TV series *The Avengers* (wonderfully played by an Irish actor) acknowledged its debt to 'traditional' English qualities. By then, however, it had become a style and not a culture and was soon to be commercialised into a fashion 'statement'. In the populist, classless commercial world of contemporary England the style for which it was once celebrated is more likely to be affectation rather than culture and some may see that as a democratic achievement. Nevertheless, the doubts raised by Oakeshott about the *politically* exemplary value of the English-derived code of civility without the patriotic, gentlemanly, character of the people from whom the example was derived are central to questions about England's notable self-possession and the country's self-regard.

This was also the question asked of Ian Buruma's study of Anglomania by David Fromkin. Can Englishness be taught – is it exemplary? – rather than admired – does it remain an exception? Buruma's answer appeared to be that it could be exemplary but 'for that to work, Englishness must be exportable'. That is the question 'upon which all else depends' (Fromkin 1999). That it could be exportable was a central element in the faith of those who celebrated the post-war British Commonwealth as the basis of, as R. A. Butler once argued, 'the scaffolding for a system of world order' or, as *The National and English Review* claimed, 'a sublimation or magnification of our better self' (cited in Huizinga 1958: 197). That represented an updating of Seeley's imperial 'wonder and ecstasy' and appealed as much to those on the left – a possibility to redeem a former 'excrescence' – as to those on the right – the continued extension of British power overseas. Perhaps, as Huizinga concluded, the Commonwealth was regarded as a 'second miracle' that would preserve the country from the fate of the ordinary, the un-exemplary and un-exceptional, precisely the fate that had befallen all previous empires (1958: 202).

On the other hand, if it were indeed true that the virtues of the English constitution were the same virtues which the middle-class English found in their own persons then what happened to 'abroad' when those same people returned, physically or metaphorically, from their imperial excursion (Baucom 1999: 40; see Colls 2002: 176–9)? By the same measure, what happened to England? It was the prospect of this very return to the particular from the grand universe of Empire that helped to prompt the re-definition of Englishness and the re-imagining of its national identity, sometimes as if the imperial, British nation had been never existed or had never been a nation at all. When export turned to import, when large scale immigration began in the 1950s, this re-definition and re-imagining began to take on an urgent intensity. Because England remained England, that too was couched in the language of exception and example.

The exemplary exception

If one can trace any trajectory in recent English history it would be, in Bell's terminology, from England as *the* exceptional nation to England as only one nation among many; from *the* exemplar of modernity to merely *one* exemplar of modernity. Something of this powerful myth lingers as romance but English/British difference no longer seems so different nor does its example appear so exemplary. This has had a significant impact on the expectations long held by liberal thinkers like Ernest Barker who believed in the (exemplary) 'ecumenical possibilities of English civility' and the beneficent potential for the 'globalisation of English culture'. If both of these things now have been abandoned as active political projects, then the reasons were not only the diminished world influence of the United Kingdom which, as Huizinga noted, had been masked by the ideal of the Commonwealth, but also the diminished appeal of Englishness which must exist beneath the shadow of global America. The trajectory detected by one scholar over the last 50 years has been a sort of 'group closure which has been practised by the English nation itself' (Stapleton 2001: 218–19). As the political need for – perhaps political persuasiveness of – an exceptional reading of English history has waned, so also has historical research challenged exemplary conceptions of the past. The 'new' British history has even shifted England from its notable self-possession, orchestrating the fate of Ireland, Scotland and Wales, to one element in a mosaic of political influences in the 'Atlantic Archipelago'. Indeed, as Clark has claimed in a number of essays on the subject, historians have substantially re-thought the notion of

English exceptionalism and all estimates of its exemplary character have been severely qualified. 'British history,' he argued, 'has been more fundamentally reconstructed since c. 1980 than at any time in the last one hundred and fifty years.' As such, the general map of the English past has altered significantly, at least for professional historians (Clark 2003: 211). However, the popular attraction of the older national story remains strong and, for all the changes in the way in which historians now understand the past, the idea of England as the exemplary exception continues to exert its influence. The integration of the civic and the patriotic – England as the exemplary exception – is finding new forms of expression. Sometimes the new England continues to bear strong traces of the old England.

Stefan Collini observed that those academic historians and literary critics who had laboured to uncover the ways in which 'our less self-conscious ancestors derived *their* identities from *their* less complicated relation to *their* chosen past' were often less than self-critical about themselves. This style of criticism sometimes helped to perpetuate absorption 'in the alleged distinctiveness of the English past which it ostensibly desires to criticize'. It was obvious enough to him, moreover, that the myths of the exemplary exception which had been supposedly unmasked were likely to survive for quite a while yet because politicians found them both useful and popular (Collini 1993: 372–3). Although Collini was writing about the Conservative Government of John Major, it was a style that was common enough in the public pronouncements of Labour Governments since 1997. As one academic supporter of the New Labour 'project' put it, there still remained a tendency for Prime Ministerial statements to propose that the United Kingdom was either 'a beacon to the world or its moral leader'. He concluded that 'to imagine that we have some special talents in this area and that the rest of the world looks to us for moral guidance is to invite disappointment and the charge of hubris' (Parekh 2000: 13). What he was challenging was a deeply rooted tradition of notable self-regard that appeared oblivious to what the historical and political evidence obliged us to believe. The number of occasions in which the expressions 'leading player' and 'taking the lead' appeared in the early pronouncements of the Blair administration confirmed a tradition of rhetorical self-understanding of the exemplary exception (see Barder 2001: 369). This suggests that the discourse serves not only a political function but also that it satisfies a deeper national longing. In other words, the persuasiveness of a particular policy in some way depends upon its fit with that older narrative, however historically challenged it has become. That is why the politically sensitive and intellectually gifted editors of *The Political Quarterly* (1998: 1–3) felt obliged, when recommending a regional answer to England's place within a devolved United Kingdom, to present their case within a familiar frame. 'In reinventing itself,' they proposed, 'England may yet help to reinvent much else.' In particular, it would provide the appropriate example to constitution-building in the European Union. The respected political journalist Andrew Marr provided an even more interesting example. Scottish education had been 'fiercely Anglocentric, lantern-jawed, vivid and self-confident' but he thought himself to be sufficiently emancipated from that past to 'stuff ... the Whig view of history' and all the old complacent arrogance of English/British mythology. But if Marr had abandoned one side of the myth (the exceptional) it was only to embrace more tightly the other (the exemplary). 'Britain,' he believed, 'as a multi-national, multi-ethnic, democratic political club is a potential model that Europeans will eventually enjoy' (1998: 27).

The narrative continues to surface in unlikely places as well as in the likely ones. To take an example of the former, Michael Ignatieff's examination of nationalism in both its televised and written versions was criticised for using the United Kingdom (or English experience) as an exemplar of the ideal civic nation-state (see Fine 1994: 433). To take an example of the latter, David Starkey speculated that the new England he thought was in the making would become 'a nation unlike any other the world has seen', one of the first of a new species of 'post-national' states, though one that would essentially 'still be England'. The country would remain exceptional, a trail-blazer, and exemplary, showing others the way to go (1999). If both interpretations are considered either esoteric or provocative, this does not apply to Paxman's *The English* (1998), a generational best-seller. He concluded (in what can now be understood as a very English way of thinking about these matters) by acknowledging that although national identity was a good thing, in England's case its future would *not* be one of flags and anthems. English nationalism would be, apparently, 'modest, individualistic, ironic, solipsistic' and it could well be the 'nationalism of the future' (1998: 265–6). In other words, Englishness would *not* be a serious nationalism at all (it would be exceptional) and, unsurprisingly, it would become *the* model for others to copy (it would be exemplary). That is a discovery that may tell us a lot about the English and their sense of themselves. There can be self-possession even in coping with the loss of former self-possession. Moreover, and perhaps most surprisingly of all, this position is also to be found in the closing passages of Kumar's book. He argued strongly that 'the English should not allow themselves to forget what have been the strengths of their tradition'. Kumar concluded his book by arguing that if England had lost its exceptional status – 'England too at last needs to see itself as a nation among other nations' – it could 'by example' show the world a new sort of nationalism: 'English nationalism, that enigmatic and elusive thing, so long conspicuous by its absence, might newborn show what a truly civic nationalism can look like' (2003a: 273). Even in revising their past, it seemed the English were destined to confirm it and Kumar's was ultimately a generously positive reading of that sort of destiny.

David Gervais once wrote that the thought of England was often a cue for self-indulgence (1993: 172). Not always, of course, but English success did encourage a style of political reflection that was often indulgent of its own self-understanding or its assiduously propagated national PR. Reflection on Englishness has been generally conducted in an idiom that was remarkably enduring and still informs political discussion. That idiom is the subject of the next chapter.

3

The English idiom

In *The English Inheritance* George Kitson Clark presented a very different assessment of the institutions of the country than one of unchanging constancy. Here 'the constitution which our forefathers so earnestly believed in, toasted after so many dinners, celebrated with such pompous oratory and called the palladium of their liberties, has been reformed out of all knowledge'. In the course of the nineteenth and twentieth centuries it had been replaced by democracy and in practice this meant 'the concentration of power' (1950: 40). Despite the Christian seriousness of Kitson Clark's study, there were also traces of that playful humour we find in Dickens's own treatment of Mr Podsnap. If Mr Podsnap was one of those pompous orators of the palladium of liberties it should be remembered that he is challenged by one of his listeners who believed that 'dying of destitution and neglect' must, for many, be the main consequence of English liberty. National sentiment and social conscience may have their separate say, but the complex truth of English experience in the nineteenth – as much as in the twenty-first – century lies in their interpenetration. Kitson Clark's reflection on the English past is not a nostalgic one for he admits that much of the old constitution was bad, full of technical absurdities and sometimes irrational. The fate of the poor and destitute under it was indeed often a cruel one. Yet for all that, he believed (like Churchill), 'English law with all its defects performed a function for human freedom which no other power in the world could have performed'. The English inheritance, then, is one of ruins and survivals and some-times it is difficult to know which is the more valuable, the ruin or the survival. Whether one cares to agree with that judgement or not, it is the tone that is significant. It is a tone that strives to be balanced and one that seeks to be measured. It is a tone that Ernest Barker thought was distinctive of the English literary imagination and, by extension, of English culture in general. 'The note is elegiac,' he wrote, 'but it is not a note of self-pity: there is little sentimentality, and if there is a feeling for the still sad music of humanity, there is no indulgence in *Weltschmerz*' (1947: 558). Or, as one historian argued: 'Cultural pessimism in England rarely gave way to full-blown chauvinism or racism' (Trentmann 1994: 599). It tended to be confined to a sort of Tory longing for a world of community and wholeness sometimes found in the work of a public intellectual and popular author like Sir Arthur Bryant (see the excellent study by Stapleton 2005a). Even when a conservative nationalism did develop at the end of the nineteenth century, it borrowed many of its central notions from the liberal tradition of civil politics fashioned in the age of Queen Victoria (Mandler 2000: 244). The conservatism of the liberal nation and the liberalism of the conservative nation constrained the limits of political rhetoric within civic patriotism and helped to fashion the idiom of English politics. Melancholy there might be in English moods but it was unlikely to be either all-consuming or serious-minded and this lack of sentimentality and soulful longing has been attributed by some critics to English empiricism (see Easthope 1999). Barker, on the other hand, thought it had to do with the spirit of adaptability, a virtue he also associated with the vice of hypocrisy. The English, for all their practicality, had 'a tendency to live in a make-believe world' and the continuity of constitutional development, 'preserving antiquities which have become formalities', encouraged that tendency. Barker's conclusion was that when 'you preserve so much of the past in the present you are apt to get mixed between shadow and substance' (1947: 564). The legend of civic patriotism perhaps indulged too much the imaginative shadow and perhaps too little the practical substance, acknowledging mainly virtue rather than vice. Nonetheless, it forged a distinctive tone which has been characteristic of political Englishness for most of the twentieth century.

This tone, as Barker claims, may be attributed in part to the institutional continuity that provided the stability for such a disposition to flourish. If *Weltschmerz* is associated with the tragic transience of all things, and politically with the desperate anticipation of the transience of all things, then the English sense of continuity (however 'make-believe' or 'invented' it may be) was not conducive to it. The English may not be spiritually insensitive but they are, thought Robert Grant, often spiritually indolent (1998: 31). It can enrage those, like Unionists in Northern Ireland, who believe with good reason that the English are insufficiently concerned about principle and concerned only with their own convenience. Barker certainly believed that the essence of English politics was the willingness, albeit based on a mass of subterranean cultural understandings, to 'make do'. That sort of pragmatism, it can be suggested, is uncomfortable with romanticism and enthusiasm, especially if they demand absolute commitment or absolute choices. To institutionalise, Barker argued, was to domesticate and this English habit had given to public life the familiarity of an old coat 'which frees you from worry' (1947: 503). This was a celebration of the civic achievement *as* a form of patriotism but a celebration, of course, that tended towards political complacency. Others attributed this tone to the 'character' of the people, the cultural practices of whom found expression in political behaviour and from which institutional stability was derived in the first place. Here was the boast of the patriot who would list these characteristics as good humour, the sporting spirit, tolerance and so on (for an entertaining examination see Langford 2000). The Conservative Walter Elliot, for example, thought that his own nation of Scotland 'can never be by instinct as tolerant as the English, as fair as the English, as forbearing as the English' (cited in Ward 2005: 25). These explanations, the institutional and the cultural, abstract from historical experience and their weakness can be judged by how easily they turn into their opposites. Thus institutional stability may have been possible only because of a culture favourable to the exercise of the rule of law (Kitson Clark 1950: 26). But celebration of English character may confuse a public phenomenon with a private set of values not shared universally and their positive quality could be a product of public stability rather than vice versa and the negative qualities conveniently forgotten (Miller 1995b: 161). The truth, and perhaps this is a very *English* truth, is likely to involve a blend of both institutions and character. For Kitson Clark, 'why there are such things as nations' is a consequence of the varying mixtures and components in the historical experience of different countries. The English could pride themselves on their legal system but that was only possible 'because England was a country whose soil was impregnated with law' (1950: 26–7). This is a theme that still resonates and one of the best histories of English identity by a contemporary historian has argued that ideas about the law and the people 'had the force and standing of a popular nationalist ideology, an ideology that was absorbed into the mainstream identity of modern England' (Colls 2002: 13). To be 'freeborn', as the English thought, rather than 'true-born', as others might feel, conveyed a very different conception of nationhood from that of ethnic particularity and expressed it in a very different tone.

Yet others have added the element of historical contingency. As C. F. G. Masterman argued in 1910, 'no living observer has ever seen England in adversity: beaten to the knees, to the ground'. All those virtues that the

English attribute to themselves – 'kindly' or 'good-natured' – might rapidly transform into vices when adversity did strike. 'And no one can foresee what a nation will do in adversity which has never seen itself compelled to face the end of its customary world' (Masterman 1910: 12–13). To speak of contingency, however, is not quite the same thing as to speak of luck. That there was no serious fascist or communist threat to constitutional politics in England in the 1920s and 1930s was not a matter of 'mere' luck but also a matter of political culture. Again, historical experience rather than character or institutions can explain much about those attitudes. The American political scientist, Richard Rose, long resident in Scotland, noted a consequent difference between continental European and English approaches to challenges to governing authority. The former had developed the tradition of 'the state defends itself' while the latter had developed the habit of conciliation and Rose believed that habit had dominated policy in, for example, Northern Ireland. He argued (presciently) that there was no certainty that challenges to authority would always be confined to one part of the United Kingdom. 'An English voice may protest: "But surely, it can't happen here!" To which an Ulsterman can reply in a voice loud and clear: "But it has"' (1982a: 131). Even when it has, from IRA (Irish Republican Army) to Islamic terrorism, the English assumption is still that it hasn't and it is tough to convince people otherwise. If this reveals the complacency of the civic view it also identifies one of the strengths of English patriotism: self-confidence about the resources of English common sense to deal with most threats. Though some may think both the complacency and the self-confidence are misplaced both remain vital elements of national life. If it is difficult to state precisely the source of that prevailing tone of English politics most sensitive observers at least have made a note of it. Even the metaphysical philosophy of Idealism, fashionable at the end of the nineteenth century and beginning of the twentieth, had a habit, as one scholar noted, of taking on a Whiggish or liberal tone in England (Burrow 1988: 152). It is traceable to a political tradition that is neither immemorial – Crick (1991: 93) for example, puts its beginnings in the eighteenth century – nor unchanging – it has been obviously modified in the last twenty-five years – but which has bequeathed a distinctive form of political discourse that is familiar still.

Dialogue in the English idiom

It is important to stress that this is not an exclusively conservative attitude. The radical historian E. P. Thompson argued that 'England is unlikely to capitulate before a Marxism which cannot at least engage in a dialogue in the English idiom'. Empiricism 'which for various historical reasons has become a national habit' set much of the tone and Thompson did concede that it could 'favour insular resistances and conceptual opportunism' of the sort despised by European intellectuals such as Voegelin. It could also be, in its popular versions, unconstructive and even reactionary. However, Thompson did think that it also contained 'acute intelligence and conceptual toughness' and a dismissal of it was tantamount to a 'dismissal of the English experience' itself (1978: 63–4). What that idiom might mean for politics was explored further by Thompson in his collection of occasional essays, *Writing by Candlelight* (1980). These essays considered a distinctive political inter-relationship and a common framework of assumptions within which the conversation about the nature of English identity took place. Thompson examined that inheritance and gave it a radical twist. For him institutions were also traditions but not every one was of equal value and some were sustained only by privilege and class, a view that Thompson and Mrs Thatcher would have shared. But there were others of a different order and around those traditions had accreted valuable precedents. They had become traditions defining the sort of people the English had become. 'They are rules which sometimes seem to trammel and limit us, but at the same time they limit the powers of those who would rule us and push us about. They are at one and the same time rules of conduct and the places where we fight about those rules' (Thompson 1980: 231). Thompson's ease with the bequest of history confirmed Colls's observation that the story of England can make conservatives into radicals and radicals into conservatives and echoed something of Oakeshott.

In defending the rule of law, in maintaining the accountability of police, in securing trial by jury, in preserving constitutional procedures, Thompson put himself on the side of this political culture, 'a constitution that is alive in the conjunction of memory and practice'. Here was a radical tradition that was not alien to the familiar language of 'English liberty' but conversant with its idiom. And rather like Kitson Clark, Thompson thought that though the 'freeborn Brit was full of self-congratulation' and, like Mr Podsnap, a bit of a hypocrite and a bore, nevertheless, 'it does so happen that we *are* their posterity and they *did* hand something down'. For this Thompson felt a duty of care and since 'we have had the kind of history that we have had, it would be contemptible in us not to play out our roles to the end' (255–6). Here was a very different understanding of tradition from the one normally associated with left wing discourse and it was clear that Thompson thought of it as the living stream of English experience. It formed a very stable patriotism that was also the basis of his international civic outlook.

The essays in *Writing by Candlelight* represented an attempt to save that very specific idea of tradition from the condescension of the New Left's theoretical sophistication and from the challenge of Mrs Thatcher's conservatism, both of which appeared unsympathetic either to conventions or to dialogue in the English idiom. However, it was also possible to read such a defence in another light. This required sympathy for English experience could be understood as an erudite expression of the parochialism which formed the common ground between, for example, Sir Arthur Bryant's conservatism and Jack Lawson's socialism (Stapleton 2001: 151–4). This defence of English political culture could also be understood as too narrow a field of intellectual reference, one which 'sometimes encouraged an uncritical attitude towards these traditions and a rhetorical exaggeration of their significance' (Kenny 1995: 184). If such criticism was an accurate description of politics in the style of the exemplary exception, a sensitive understanding of political tradition could acknowledge the pitfalls of parochialism, narrowness and national self-regard but still find something of inestimable value in the English inheritance. In very different works representing very different political perspectives a sort of Anglicised version of the cunning of reason in domestic history can be detected at work. For Thompson, those 'exhibitionists and hams' who waxed lyrical about the virtues of the 'pristine purity' of the British constitution would be laughed out of court today. Yet he admitted that they had 'a point of sorts' and the point was 'that the state was for them, they were not for the state' (1980: 255). From a different angle, J. H. Plumb wrote that Churchill's 'English history was a progression, a development of inherent national characteristics, a process whereby the Englishman's love of liberty, freedom, and justice gradually, by trial and error, discovered those institutions of government which were apt to his nature' (1969: 120). The professional historian, of course, could not take the claim seriously but for Plumb this tradition, if not its 'history', was certainly far from nonsensical. The English may have acquired and maintained political liberty 'not for the reasons Churchill would have given, but acquire it and maintain it they did' and this had been no easy achievement, not even for a modern European state (1969: 139). That English idiom today may not be as persuasive as it once was, the Whiggish tradition of politics it expressed may have become exhausted and the patrician tone it encouraged, on both the left and the right of political life, may no longer fit a more democratic age. However, before one can identify the tone of modern England it is necessary to appreciate the old, for the two, as most intelligent commentators acknowledge, are not entirely discontinuous (see Colls 2002: 380–1). Perhaps the most subtle appreciation of dialogue in the English idiom and its political effect can be found in Herbert Butterfield's celebrated *The Englishman and his History* (1944).

Butterfield's text was a synthetic statement of the English political tradition, so reconciling in its ambitions that Maurice Cowling described it as the promulgation of a 'positive doctrine' (Cowling 1980: 233). His doctrine came close to anticipating A. J. P. Taylor's old quip: 'History is no doubt best conducted, like the British constitution, on the principle that Whig plus Tory equals eternal truth'. But Taylor added that this principle only worked so long as it remained clear that Toryism was only half the truth (at best) of a complex reality (Taylor 1976: 21–2). Whig *incorporating* Tory, however, would be a more accurate description of Butterfield's thesis since his message was that 'the real Tory alternative to the organisation of English history on the basis of the growth of liberty' – the story of imperial expansion – was an alternative no more by the middle of the twentieth century. It had been swallowed into the Whig system (Butterfield 1944: 81–2). Butterfield, whose reputation had been made on the basis of his criticism of the Whig interpretation of history, distinguished between the truth of that system and its political effect. English respect for the past was actually combined with 'what one might call a sublime and purposeful unhistoricity' and the past that had been clung to was one 'conveniently and tidily disposed for our purposes'. Wrong history became a precious cultural asset and 'whatever it may have done to our history, it had a wonderful effect on English politics' (1944: 6–7). The wonderful effect revealed 'the happier form of co-operation with Providence' than the continental tradition of revolution and reaction. Butterfield was prepared to praise the 'reconciling mind' that had learnt from the experience of extremism – 'the dreadful consequences of wilful and high-handed action in the world of politics' (1944: 85) – and an echo of this very idea of reconciliation continued in the thought of writers like Crick (1991: 93).

The idiom of English politics in this view was not consensual in the sense that that term came to be understood in post-war British politics, namely agreement on *policy*. It was consensus on the *form* of politics rather than the detail and one that could be called a public, rather than an elite, disposition. The ballast of the English system, according to Butterfield, was to be found amongst the rank and file of the political parties 'who repudiated desperation politics or fanatical doctrinairism whether of the right-wing or the left' (1944: 94). In sum, 'Liberal, Conservative and Labour, schooled in the English practice, have mitigated the evils of party cleavage, and prevented the disruption of the state' (1944: 101). A stable and relatively consensual society can accept political manoeuvring within limits generally understood and the spirit of this style of politics was captured in Arthur Balfour's introduction to Bagehot's *The English Constitution*. Here was a politics that presupposed 'a people so fundamentally at one that they can safely afford to bicker; and so sure of their own moderation that they are not dangerously disturbed by the never-ending din of political conflict' (cited in Schwab 1985: vvii). This very English political game, as R. A. Butler once put it, was the art of the possible and until the shock of Mrs Thatcher's 'conviction politics' thirty-five years later (the Heath experience of 1970–74 appeared to have confirmed the rule), Butterfield's assessment of 'Whig plus Tory' would have been accepted as a truism. 'We must not forget that the virtues of the whigs have been distributed through all the great parties of this country; that they have liberalized English politics generally, and given a colour to all our progress; standing in protest equally against die-hard-ism on the one hand and mere lust for overthrow on the other' (1944: 136–7). Since this is an idiom of self-understanding it is almost impervious to subversive counter-example though it is very susceptible, as Butterfield admitted, to convenient bouts of amnesia and flexible re-interpretation. Or as Crick was later to put it pithily: 'If the Irish remember their history too obsessively, ordinary English people forget theirs too easily' (Crick 1989: 24). Of course, the English are not alone in this but in their case, Grant has suggested, there may be a deeper historical and cultural reason at work. The pursuit of the transcendent or absolute – politically this would entail a disposition *not* to make do – would overshadow everyday life and a kindly English God had bestowed upon them 'the gift of instant oblivion, so that they forget that they have ever seen him'. There may well be a worldliness in this disposition towards amnesia which could be 'a symptom less of materialism than of profound gratitude for the existence we already have' (Grant 1998: 31). If radicals and conservatives recollected the English past differently, generally they did so gratefully (Grainger 1986: 19).

If it remains true that nations 'are as happy in what they forget as what they remember' the English had a habit of forgetting what was inconvenient to their idiomatic self-understanding and at odds with its genteel tone (Watson 1973: 26). And forget they did, of course, about the profound tensions over issues like Home Rule or the class conflict of the National Strike. Rather, those tensions could be blamed on

Celtic passions that had temporarily infected Anglo-Saxon moderation and the class conflict of 1926 could be neatly revised as an example of English good sense and gentlemanly behaviour. This has had a wonderfully comforting effect and it became one of the broad-bottomed wisdoms of English politics that revolution was counterproductive. Rather, English wisdom maintained that only a paradoxical conserving revolution was productive, like that propounded in the mythology of 1688 and Butterfield, like Barker, carried an essentially Victorian attitude into the modern democratic age (Soffer 1996: 14). The key to this attitude was the distinction between progressive change and revolution, a distinction sharpened by hindsight. 'Reform is the guarantor of continuity. It offers a chance, even a probability, of moderating the shock of change and controlling its tempo. That was the prudent, even the conservative view. But liberals and radicals too came to see how lucky they had been to adopt legislative rather than revolutionary methods' (Watson 1973: 43).

Here was the irony: revolution promoted rigidity. The idea of revolutionary transformation was as much despised by reformers as it was by conservatives and for that reason Edmund Burke was a common reference for liberals as well as for conservatives. Whereas, argued Dicey in his *Lectures on the Relationship between Law and Public Opinion in England* (1905), England was popularly thought of as the land of constancy and France the land of revolution, in fact the reverse (in the progressive sense) was true. The Code Napoleon had remained essentially unaltered throughout the nineteenth century whereas English law had been substantially altered. As Watson described the consequent judgement, the 'line between reformation and revolution, after two French failures and a host of lesser ones, was forever drawn' (1973: 45; see similar comments by Butterfield 1944: 114–16). Even when political contest was at its most divisive in England between the wars, and despite the flirtation of some intellectuals with communism and fascism, the narrative of progressive stability continued to play a vital role in the English political idiom. Regardless of the deep tensions of the time, here was a political tradition that strove to remain conversational in a Balfourian sense rather than confrontational in a Leninist sense. 'When all the great states of the Continent were shaken by revolution and disorder,' wrote Herbert Read, 'England alone stood firm and preserved an unbroken continuity with her past.' This he attributed to the English concern for practice rather than abstract principles however admirable they may be (Read 1933: 131). Even when long-standing critics like Arthur Bryant launched their own attacks on Whig history in the 1930s, they too retained in a kind of 'Tory

Whiggism' the familiar 'narrative style and conception of a unified nation as the life-blood of British history' (Stapleton 2004: 230). The image of intellectual life in England during the inter-war years as one of intense ideological struggle has been rather overdrawn for the paradox of conservatives coming to believe that the safeguarding of liberal England had fallen to them and of progressives such as Bertrand Russell, appreciating the stability of traditional English attitudes in politics was a fact of life. Here the uniqueness of the English political inheritance had become the common factor and its forms were advanced not as principles but as sensibilities, as 'a style of political action appropriate to the English political world', one that offered 'critiques of the movements and intellectual currents by which that world seemed threatened' (Stapleton 1999a: 272–4). Of course, this was a very selective vision but its English idiom was familiar, comforting and sustaining. It was to become a more popular vision during and after the Second World War, one that has been difficult to displace from intellectual and cultural life even today (Stapleton 2000b: 810).

Barker called this the 'habit of compromise which the process of our history has infused into our political temper' and he believed that when the English failed to compromise they also failed to succeed (1927: 157). Or as Santayana observed in his *Soliloquies on England*, compromise is odious to passionate natures because it appears to be a surrender, to intellectual natures because it appears to bring confusion but to the English nature it appeared to be 'the path of profit and justice' (1922: 83). This was something that Naill Ferguson noted with shock sixty years later when he arrived at Oxford University to discover that the English 'see argument as a failure of manners' (cited in Farndale 2001). And for J. C. D. Clark this attitude defined the middle ground of English life, one that did not fit properly into the neat oppositional labels that both passionate and intellectual natures find so convenient or that classic nationalists find so desirable. Here was a social order that presented itself as 'both constitutional *and* royalist, libertarian *and* stable, tolerant *and* expressing religious orthodoxy, innovative *and* respectful of what was customary' (Clark 2000: 17). That Victorian inheritance survived remarkably well into present times. The Russian artist Wassily Kandinski once proposed that in the course of the twentieth century the index of modernist achievement would be the triumph of 'and' over 'either/or'. In its own idiomatic way, then, English politics was modernist before its time and its political leaders took this implicitly as a measure of its civilisation. This may help to explain, as Clark thought it did, why ethnic nationalism in others appeared to those leaders to be 'misunderstandings which could be easily cleared up' rather than 'evidence of an ineluctably different mindset which would have violent consequences' and this illustrates why the English found it so difficult to understand the political idiom of Northern Ireland (2003: 108).

Dialogue in the English idiom, then, may perhaps best be understood in terms of a Lampedusan paradox. This paradox is the *leitmotif* of Giuseppe Tomasi di Lampedusa's novel *The Leopard* (1972) and it proposes: 'If you want things to stay the same things will have to change.' When applied to *conservative* politics in England, it was a process by which 'Conservatives not only offend their more conservative associates but end up by changing themselves' (Fforde 1990: 43). In a striking phrase, Fforde argued that this (Whiggish) process had 'a vampire effect: it drew out the true Tory blood'. Hence the irony that 'the Conservative Party came to be an integral part of the means by which Liberalism and Socialism progressed – it was a political carrier of previously resisted proposals' (1990: 165). This was something of which Butterfield also made much. Contemporary academic research here repeats one of the enduring complaints about Conservative policy, one that may be traced back at least as far as Disraeli – Tory men and Whig measures. Lord Coleraine, for instance, thought that the problem for the Conservative Party was never that it would prove too reactionary but that it would be carried too far along the road of change and in the process lose the capacity to make its distinctive contribution to national life. Indeed, for most of the twentieth century, he thought, all the Party had to offer 'was a reformulation of the fashions of the day' (Coleraine 1970: 63). With his delicate register of Tory sensibility, T. E. Utley asked: 'Is it not the great merit of English Conservatism that it comes to terms with reality and the great merit of the Tory party that it confines itself to the role of a midwife to history?' For Utley, this represented 'a kind of sophisticated timidity', an attitude that led a politician to decide 'what he loves best and then consider how he can preside most elegantly and judiciously over its destruction, making that process as painless as possible, saving what he could from the wreckage'. He acknowledged, on the other hand, that it was far from being a 'contemptible creed' and accepted that its practical wisdom had often stood the party in good stead (Moore and Heffer 1989: 73–4, 88).

Concession, surrender and transformation may have been the lot of conservatism but that was only one side of the truth and not the whole truth of English experience. As Fforde himself conceded, much of 'the British "liberal tradition" is rooted in Conservatism and its political sense', an assessment which neatly inverts the conclusion of *The*

Englishman and his History (Fforde 1990: 166). Indeed, the Lampedusan paradox would be of little interest if it only illuminated a process of change. By contrast, from the perspective of *radicalism*, the remarkable thing about British politics is the extent to which conservative interests have survived. It was the traditionalism of English political culture that puzzled many, especially Marxist, commentators and the reason appeared to lie in the timidity of the Labour Party. Here, if conservatives cared to look, was the dividend from faithful subscription to the paradoxical idiom of English politics. The Conservative Party had helped to fashion an opposition that believed: 'if you wanted things to change, things would also have to stay the same'. The Labour Party, as one critic put it, became committed 'to the fundamental civic values of British political culture' which just happened to be very conservative, a 'manifestation of the institutional integration characteristic of British society' (Jessop 1974: 76–7). Another was absolutely convinced that British political culture '*is* a Tory culture' and the Conservative Party is a '*necessary* embodiment of the central core of this Tory culture' (Johnson 1985: 234–5). This was written in the 1980s, not the 1880s, and it goes to show how many on the left accepted conservative myths as political truths. Of course to Conservative Party activists most of this was academic nonsense since few of them really felt comfortable with modern Britain and for one of them it was luck, rather than a dominant Tory culture, that made the Conservative Party the 'Great Survivor'. And like all good Tories he felt its luck would soon run out (Bulpitt 1991: 7).

The acceptance of their respective sides of the Lampedusan paradox by the political parties does help to explain the distinctive experience of right versus left in British politics, an experience very different from continental Europe's in the first half of the twentieth century. No ruler, as Schopflin neatly put it, is going to share power 'if he thinks that those who are to be newly assumed into power will use it to string him up from the nearest lamp-post' (2000: 304). The conciliatory intelligence of English politics, at least as it was conveyed in Butterfield's description of it, meant that power was ceded but that no one was lynched (in Great Britain at any rate, if not in Ireland). The spirit of Coleridge, of the balance between the forces of progress and of permanence, had had its effect and, in a very English way, reconciled change and innovation with social harmony. One could argue, then, that conservatism had an equally vampiric effect, drawing out the true Socialist blood from the Labour Party, making it a political carrier of previously resisted proposals, Whig men and Tory measures. The criticisms made of Tony Blair's premiership, therefore, formed part of a venerable tradition of national criticism. Butterfield was aware, as indeed was Thompson, that this was not a tradition that appealed to those who 'cannot be happy if by remedying the condition of things a little in our own day, we postpone the end they have set their hearts upon' (1944: 107). But this tradition, argued Butterfield, helped to explain the shape of English national identity because it blended character and institutions. Customary acceptance of institutions and the common sentiment invested in them provided 'the basis for at least a minimum of national unity'. There was no need for the English 'to go hunting for our own personalities' and the English were fortunate in not having 'to set about the deliberate manufacture of a national consciousness, or to strain ourselves, like the Irish, in order to create a "nationalism" out of the broken fragments of tradition, out of the ruins of a tragic past' (1944: 114).

Of course, the implication of Butterfield's argument was not that the English thereby lacked a national identity but that theirs was so present as to be self-evident. There was no need to invent a tradition since people knew they were already part of a living one. Butterfield's sense of the identity of England appears to confirm Ian Buruma's measure of national sentiment. Commenting on Bavaria's 'traditional' dress, Buruma noted that it was mostly a nineteenth-century invention designed to sustain an identity whose political form was being steadily eroded: 'There seems to be a rule of thumb: when political identities weaken, native costumes get louder' (1999: 290). Buruma's observation was in the context of what he thought to be a contemporary uncertainty amongst the English, an uncertainty that provoked some into vocal anxiety about England becoming a mere province of Europe. However, Butterfield was not given to any such *Weltschmerz* about the persistence of English nationhood and he had no sense of it weakening. On the contrary, and in the conditions of war, he felt that England had rediscovered itself. This theme of 'return' or 'recovery', from which rather different sets of conclusions can be drawn, is examined further in Chapter 5.

On being English

This is also the idiom of Oakeshott's very revealing but frequently misunderstood essay *On Being Conservative*. That essay ranged much wider than the title suggests and was, in effect, a meditation upon the English political tradition. Indeed, Oakeshott himself was an individual whose own political character could be taken as an example of Whig plus Tory, libertarian but also respectful of convention. He was someone, rather like Macaulay before him, who thought nothing of symmetry and much of convenience. And that is possibly why Oakeshott tended to be misunderstood by those who thought in terms of neat oppositional labels. What one finds in Oakeshott's reflections is the lingering trace of Barker's Victorian sensibility that institutional tradition provides the familiarity of form 'which frees you from worry'. What one also finds is the acknowledgement of the English paradox so evident to A. L. Rowse. According to Rowse, who was here following in the tradition of Dicey, people think of English history 'as a very conservative affair' but this was a very one-sided view: 'What makes the inner heart and rhythm of English society difficult to understand, and what is at the same time the clue to it, is the paradox of outward conservatism with a continuing capacity for inner change and development.' The casual observer was often confused by the retention of older forms like the monarchy and so failed to notice both their changed circumstances and even their changed function. 'English history,' thought Rowse, 'has been as dynamic as that of any country in modern times' albeit with the inestimable virtue of being less bloody and unstable (Rowse 1945: 23). Oakeshott's essay provided a sophisticated explication of that particular English paradox.

Some commentators have been seduced by his description of conservatism as a preference for the familiar to the unknown, 'the tried to the untried, fact to mystery, the actual to the possible, the limited to the unbounded, the near to the distant, the sufficient to the superabundant, the convenient to the perfect, present laughter to utopian bliss'. However, there is frequently a failure to note that Oakeshott thought this conservative attitude was actually inappropriate 'in respect of human conduct in general' (Oakeshott 1991: 415). Moreover, he believed that modern citizens were more than likely to be disposed in the opposite direction and there was no point starting 'in the empyrean, but with ourselves as we have come to be'. Everyone's desire was to follow a course of their own 'and there is no project so unlikely that somebody will not be found to engage in it, no enterprise so foolish that somebody will not undertake it'. In other words, it is the privilege of humans to dream and to pursue their dreams. Sometimes people will come into collision with one another, cut across one another or disapprove the conduct of others. But, thought Oakeshott, conduct usually consists 'of activity assimilated to that of others in small, and for the most part unconsidered and unobtrusive, adjustments' and most people learn how to be at home in this commonplace world without difficulty. This is what most people took their culture to be, not a collection of artifacts but a homely mode of social intercourse (and it is vital that people *do* feel at home). It is possible, of course, to imagine a different condition and it is true that life was not always this way. The modern condition, thought Oakeshott, was an 'acquired condition' and not a force of nature being 'the product, not of human nature let loose, but of human beings impelled by an acquired love of making choices for themselves. And we know as little and as much about where it is leading us as we know about the fashion in hats of twenty years' time or the design of motor cars' (1991: 416).

It is an order of freedom, and here Oakeshott expressed a Tory understanding of English individuality, a sort of philosophy of being let alone to enjoy the multiplicity of activity and the variety of opinion (Aughey 2006b). One of the conditions of this enjoyment is that politics should be neither too emotional nor too passionate since that would confuse the public with the personal. The English idiom was nothing if not formally measured and Oakeshott admitted that the present condition and its circumstance of complexity can intimate a vast concentration of power in central government to organise and plan for common needs. That some such organisation and planning had become a necessity in the twentieth century was a fact of life but Oakeshott was wary of *politics*, as opposed to individual desires, as the 'encounter of dreams' and thought that a limited style of politics was appropriate to those who appreciated their liberty (1991: 436–7; see also O'Sullivan 2004: 36–40). In this he expressed a Whig understanding of the office of government. It did not suppose that government should do nothing but proposed that it should 'preserve peace, not by placing an interdict upon choice and upon the diversity that springs from the exercise of preference, not by imposing a substantive uniformity, but by enforcing general rules of procedure upon all subjects alike'. In this understanding of the English tradition (for Oakeshott in all his references reveals that it is England he is writing about) conservative politics and a liberal society were intimately bound together. 'Political conservatism is, then, not at all unintelligible in a people disposed to be adventurous and enterprising, a people in love with change and apt to rationalise their affections in terms of "progress"' (1991: 416). Indeed, he thought it pre-eminently appropriate for those who wished to live their own lives as freely as possible and this attitude may also be the core of the celebrated English eccentricity. The paradox, insofar as it is one, was resolved in the shape of a living English tradition. The civic patriotism of historical legend presented itself here as the reconciliation of political stability and personal freedom. Until quite recently, such an understanding was generally interpreted to put someone on the right of British politics. Things have now changed and as Colls noted, Oakeshott's explication of the English paradox is 'defensible from both left and right points of view'. It was not about nostalgia or about conserving the status quo but 'about what living communities knew they knew and thought was worth keeping'. The tradition – or practice – it explored sustained a politics that was understood precisely because it was familiar, requiring governments to respect 'common arrangements, encourage them, and let the people get on' (Colls 2002: 374).

The forms and formalities of English liberty expressed that paradox of outward continuity along with an inner capacity for change and development because the dynamism of the latter required the stability of the former and vice versa. The character of traditional English individuality, one can suggest, has been bound up with English conformity. Or in Oakeshott's own case, respecting the formalities permitted a personal and charming bohemianism. In short, observing public rules of behaviour allowed one to be as privately eccentric as one wished. 'A potentially anarchic tendency had to be subordinated to the demands of a disciplined national character, without sacrificing that "energetic individualism" which, according to the apostle of Self-Help, Samuel Smiles, "has in all times been a marked feature of the English character, and furnishes the true measure of our power as a nation"' (see Langford 2000: 300). The character of that individuality is changing and it would be a misreading of England to argue that things remain the same. But as things do change they also exhibit continuity. One historian claimed that these characteristics were detectable in what became known in the 1980s as 'authoritarian individualism' and that Thatcherism, far from being an exotic creation, embodied deeply-rooted and persistent traits in English culture (Clark 1990b: 44). Perhaps this was also the clue to a very distinctive English form of toleration in which rights and liberties fitted with the perceived deferential character of English political culture. Religion may be one guide here since the attitude towards doctrine of any kind was pragmatic rather than dogmatic and this itself was taken to be very characteristically English. It was history and not just geography that helped to explain the difference between English and American experience: 'Thus toleration in America allowed a wider variation of religious communities, whilst sheltering more intolerance within them, resulting in Tocqueville's well known paradox of greater cultural diversity with more personal conformity.' The small world of England permitted an alternative relationship: 'Whilst England without the luxury of space, permitted a narrower range of tolerance, it did so within more heterogeneous communities, allowing greater tolerance of disconformity between proximate individuals' (Hampsher-Monk 1995: 234). The English exemplary exception in this interpretation reveals its difference from the American version where Anglicanism, muddled as it may have appeared and continues to appear to more puritanical minds, provided the spiritual basis for what was to become a hallmark even of English secularism. Compromise, comprehensiveness and concession had become more than a policy. They had become a habit, answering to something in the acquired character of the English in modern times (Rowse 1945: 28).

An insightful historical examination of this matter but one with contemporary significance can be found in the recent work of Julia Stapleton who explored not only the tension but also the interaction between two rival conceptions of political society and argued that, for all the intensity of belief on either side, there was significant continuity throughout the twentieth century. The first was 'generally wary of the emotive language of nationhood, emphasizing instead the importance of democratic, liberal, and civic values based on reason'. The second 'emphasized the primacy of the nation over the state and the impossibility, indeed incoherence, of a world in which national ties had been significantly loosened'. However, as familiarity with the English idiom would lead us to expect, 'both cultures were informed to varying degrees by a broad-based liberalism that cut across the boundaries of conservatism and socialism' and, as a result, 'polarisation of the two cultures on Left-Right lines has been limited' (2005b: 152–4). If the former were emotional in their rational citizenship the latter were also rational in their patriotic emotions. An impressive intellectual cast lined up on opposite sides of this national debate. In Stapleton's narrative, philosophical Idealists such as Green, constitutional lawyers such as Dicey, historians such as Bryce and sociologists such as Marshall championed civic virtue over patriotic sensibility while writers such as Chesterton, historians such as Bryant and politicians such as Powell challenged the dominance of this liberal vision. In conceptual terms there has continued to be a tension between these two senses of political community and this has been deeply embedded in English nationhood. Here is the contemporary tension. If, on the one hand 'English national consciousness fails to develop into full-blown political nationalism, the visceral patriotism that has been its moving force hitherto remains a significant obstacle to citizenship in many of its contemporary forms: multicultural, cosmopolitan, and associationalist'. On the other hand, the 'ideal of citizenship risks becoming exclusive and ineffective' when it loses touch with the

English nation and the patriotism supporting it (Stapleton 2005b: 178; see also Bryant 2003).

Paradoxes are not usually associated with the empirical frame of mind. The conclusion one might come to, then, is that traditional English empiricism actually rested upon the political resolution, however contingent, of paradoxes that were un-resolved in some other countries or which there found passionately divisive political expression. At a very basic level this was something to which the English privately used to give thanks because their own, if limited, tolerance had meant fewer communal bloodbaths than elsewhere and this was a deliverance truly worthy of self-congratulation (Stapleton 1999b: 129). What that tradition may have lacked in philosophic power it was thought to make up for in 'a practice of mutual respect and tolerance for diversity and individuality' (Dyson 1980: 201). If writers like Oakeshott gave that civic patriotism a conservative inflection and writers like Barker gave it a liberal inflection both of them wrote in a common idiom that was recognisably English. This idiom could suggest sometimes that there was nothing for which the English might be criticised, where England is '*Othello* without Iago' and untainted by the baser motives of humanity (Eagleton 2002). But that was obviously a misreading and one purely for the children, the naïve, and faithful Ulster Unionists. It is tempting to define that idiom in an exclusively historical sense and to assume that it no longer resonates. In one sense that it is self-evidently true since contemporary secular intellectual discourse can no longer accept the thought of English providentialism and a more diverse intellectual community can no longer accept the 'organic tendencies' that discourse often assumed (Langford 2000: 7). The English, according to Elton, used to be ruled by two attempts to provide anchor-points of moderate certainty in a dangerous world: 'These instruments were religion (reassurance in the hereafter) and law (reassurance down here).' Both of these anchor-points have lost their force and even the story itself no longer has the claim it once had upon the popular imagination because most English people 'know very little and care not greatly about their history' (1991: 122–4). In short, 'the Stubbs-Pollard-Neale-Norstein-Morley-Arthur Bryant tradition is dead and should remain decently buried: the whigs have had their day' (1991: 115).

With that accustomed lack of *Weltschmerz* he had picked up from his adopted homeland, Elton admitted that he could see no purpose 'in telling a tale of demonstrable error' for the sake of interesting people in the past if the times were against it. Nor could one make the distinction any longer, as Butterfield had done, between history and serviceable myth. The problem as Elton saw it was that the crumbling of the power of the old legend of civic patriotism had left the field clear for a critical legend in which the English must don sackcloth and ashes, 'expiating for past arrogance'. Wrong history in this case would not become, as Butterfield had once thought, a precious cultural asset but would have a baleful effect on English politics since it would give play to a combination of contempt and self-loathing. It has been claimed that 'no one has found a late-twentieth-century idiom' to replace the legend of civic patriotism and the result 'is a vacuum – a vacuum of language reflecting a vacuum of feeling' (Marquand 1995: 189; see also Marquand 1993). If one accepts that there is some truth in those views, they need to be qualified in two ways.

First, they need to be qualified by reference to the moderating scepticism of English attitudes that continues to set the tone of political debate. This may no longer be the expression of a grand narrative but it has still significance in particulars and one of these particulars is the nation. A very illustrative case can be found in Crick's review of writing on national identities within the United Kingdom. What was needed, he thought, were 'more subtle ways of considering national identity', ways of looking at things that could 'modify passionate bad arguments in difficult situations like Northern Ireland'. The danger that Crick identified in present trends was that of opposing Britishness to other identities within the United Kingdom and in a classically English idiom Crick argued that 'middle positions are available. The fallacy of the excluded middle is only good for fights', a principle he also extended to the United Kingdom's relationship with Europe. The pragmatism of circumstance must always qualify whatever political principle has been abstracted from historical experience and it was in this sense that Crick described his politics as 'a brand of left-wing Oakeshottism' (2003: 23). And in his summary of what the new Englishness should be like Crick expressed the classic balance of the English idiom for he believed that any 'new Englishness' would need to 'recall that there was a radical tradition of positive citizenship as well as an establishment tradition of the loyal subject and law and order'. This new Englishness should not abandon 'the distinctive gentry belief that the good life includes both town and country (phenomenologically, artifacts and nature)' but most importantly it should grasp 'that toleration means, as the best English and Scottish political thinkers have long seen, the understanding, acceptance and at times even pleasure and pride in differences between national and ethnic communities, not a mistaken zeal for their diminishment' (Crick 1995: 180). As a liberal version of civic patriotism this was exemplary but it also contained a conservative element more concerned with appropriate outcomes rather than with some grand ideal and it assumed that the best way to deal with difficult issues was to defuse rather than to inflame them. Second, they need to be qualified by the insight that nothing in a tradition of behaviour as deeply-rooted as the English one is ever quite lost to it (as Oakeshott was at pains to point out). The world of historical sensibility that Elton believed had vanished irrevocably continued to show its resilience especially following the terrorist attacks in London on 7 July 2005. The integrative potential of the Whig interpretation was seized upon by government ministers keen to promote 'social inclusion' and keen to avoid political disintegration. The liberal think-tank *Civitas* argued that the Whig interpretation of history was a vital cultural resource, the teaching of which allowed schoolchildren 'to grow up loving their country' because to participate fully in public life citizens also need patriotism. It republished that old standard H. E. Marshall's *Our Island Story* and public interest in the text suggested, to *Civitas* at least, that the national story was far from over (Conway 2005: 10).

It has not been the contention of this chapter that the English idiom remains unmodified. It is constantly being modified but perhaps not as radically or as comprehensively as some might imagine. One radical historian has argued that although the narrative system has collapsed, 'in more fragmentary form the emotional truths it bequeathed are still evident' (Schwarz 1999: 203). Another conservative historian, in an examination of stadial assumptions in the history of ideas, has criticised the view that assumes: 'first one meaning was prevalent; then the intellectual landscape was transformed, and another took its place'. These assumptions make redundant attempts to trace the survival and influence of older usage and it is often the case in history, as in politics, that 'powerful survivals rather than tenuous origins' are what are interesting (Clark 2003: 102–3). The simple contention of this chapter has been that there are powerful survivals of self-understanding in the case of Englishness, that they continue to inform contemporary national identity and that they have a future as well as a past. It is the interpenetration of changing circumstances and idiomatic continuity that sets the tone of contemporary understanding. Capturing that relationship is the way to specify the limits to which the politics of contemporary Englishness may be confined but also to identify the hopes and anxieties that may be found within those limits. Before that examination can be undertaken it is necessary to consider the most influential of the recent legends about the nation, the critical form of which took shape as the persuasiveness of the older narrative began to wane.

4

Dead centre of inertia

Chapter 1 began by noting that a major theme of many recent studies in political Englishness has been the notion of a 'lack'. This chapter examines the most politically influential expression of that notion and traces its influence in the debate about English identity. It is an expression that anticipated the conclusion of Kumar's study and was a powerful revision of the legend of civic patriotism, one which inverted (but did not completely subvert) the English/British exemplary exception. In this reading England was indeed exceptional but it was exceptional only in its backwardness and if England was exemplary, it was exemplary only of offences against the modern world. The nature of the argument constituted a sort of 'anti-history' or 'inverted whiggism' and affected thinking about not only economic performance but also about national identity (Edgerton 2005: 98). In this legend, the English idiom represented nothing but the suffocation of political and cultural possibilities. 'A frustrated radical,' as Richard Rose once observed, 'might proclaim that by his or her values, England hasn't become modern yet' (1985: 16). From the early 1960s that is exactly what frustrated radicalism did proclaim and it did so with passion and intensity. The positive inheritance of the Second World War – that English constitutionalism had provided the one beacon of civilisation in a Europe destroyed by fanaticism and ideological extremism – still remained strong but it was of diminishing effect in the face of the 'multiple discourses of crisis' that informed post-imperial British politics. These discourses of crisis were institutional, economic, racial, class-based but also national and it was tempting, since the 'discourse' of exceptionalism was so familiar, to assume that the condition of England was exceptionally debilitating. As academic studies became more pessimistic in the course of the 1970s, so the political and journalistic tone also tended to become more apocalyptic (Howe 2003: 292). The mood has been defined as one of 'declinism', a pervasive sense that things were wrong with Britain and getting worse.

Economic difficulties, in particular industrial unrest, mapped on to constitutional worries, the rise of 'Celtic' nationalism, to raise insistent questions about the condition of England/Britain.

The proposition was quite straightforward. There was a direct link between economic and political decline and the English cultural idiom – its constitutional conservatism, gentlemanly capitalism, insular intellectual elitism and a misplaced superior self-understanding. Whereas the paradox discussed in Chapter 3 implied a positive relationship in English experience between continuity and change (or at least suggested that the relationship was a complex one), modern theories of decline understood the relationship to be entirely negative because it was a consequence of an England frozen into social and political rigidity (see for example Wiener 1981). This interpretation appealed to some on the right of British politics who blamed decline on the stultifying effect of the welfare state but it appealed mainly to those on the left who saw tradition and convention as obstacles to a modernised society. Significantly, the narrative of decline challenged the political beliefs that had underpinned the English/British exemplary exception. 'What a change this was,' observed Dennis Kavanagh of the political problems of the 1970s, 'from the Whiggish assumption that the British had an unmatched capacity for government, and from the almost universal admiration for the British system. From being an exemplar of stable representative democracy, indeed the exporter of institutions, Britain was widely regarded as a country on the verge of political breakdown' (1985: 537). The sense of British decline was not historically exceptional of course, and Kavanagh's interpretation, if not his conveying of the mood, is a misreading. These issues have been revisited and the complexity of the different arguments re-thought. English and Kenny's judicious assessment concluded that decline 'has been a concept central to late-twentieth century discussions of British economic performance and national identity alike'. They were doubtful that decline was the appropriate framework within which to understand modern British politics since close inspection of declinist arguments 'might lead one to be sceptical about their ultimate value' but they were convinced that the thesis of decline was deeply rooted in the culture of modern Britain. Balanced academic judgement would not, they thought, prevent influential figures and a wider public audience being persuaded by declinist arguments because they seemed to measure so starkly the country's loss of world status. Perhaps the most considerable contribution to the debate about decline from within the left of British politics was the series of articles published in the 1960s in the Marxist *New Left Review* by Perry Anderson and Tom Nairn.

These articles complemented that 'second nature' of British popular culture, a psychological expectation of failure (see English and Kenny 2000: 74, 284–96) and they influenced a whole generation of cultural historians and political commentators who wrote, and in some cases still write, 'as if Britain was all welfare, empire, decline' (for a critique see Edgerton 2005: 111).

Anderson and Nairn attacked the legend of civic patriotism in the English idiom, though the way in which they did so also helped to sustain the notion, albeit by inversion, of the exemplary exception. Both captured accurately a mood of change frustrated, that despite the many democratic transformations since 1945 the resistant culture of class remained in place. Anderson and Nairn explored that mood politically in the way in which John Le Carré's novels explored it artistically. As one character put it in *A Small Town in Germany* (1968): 'Much kinder to look *back*, I always think. I see no hope at all for the future, and it gives me a *great* sense of freedom.' Le Carré's is as good a description of decadence as one can get and he attributed it specifically to English class and snobbery, as did Anderson and Nairn. They wrote in the idiom of absences and one of the major historical absences in the English case had been a 'proper' revolutionary movement. The positives of civic patriotism became the negatives of a grand historical failure that had become so visible in the final half of the twentieth century. The Glorious Revolution of 1688, formerly the foundation of the English civil tradition, was re-interpreted as a 'failed' bourgeois revolution. The cherished continuities of the civic legend became the deformations of this critical legend which defined the English experience as one of 'increasing entropy'. The national culture, formerly an object of self-congratulation, was re-described as 'philistine' because there was a lack of substantial critical thought (in particular, there was 'no' sociology, never mind an 'intelligentsia'). British culture was 'organised about an absent centre' and lacked 'an overall account of itself'. This was not so much a case of *trahison des clercs* because the intelligentsia never took the field. It was a case of *absence des clercs* and the Anderson and Nairn view tallied with the old saying that if the Parisians laugh at bad manners, the English laugh at intellectual, especially theoretical, sophistication. In particular, they argued that English society was a product of 'arrested development' and its measure was 'the visible index of a vacuum' (Anderson 1992: 103). There was a certain heroism about the thoroughness of this critique which was reminiscent of La Rochefoucauld's maxim that those who obstinately oppose the most widely-held opinions do so because of pride and intelligence: 'They find the best places in the right set already taken, and they do not want back seats' (La Rochefoucauld 1981: 68). Anderson and Nairn certainly did not want back seats either.

What was perhaps most distinctive about their critique was its hostility to any 'flow of sympathy' with English culture and its erection of an index that measured only exceptional national inadequacies against a European, specifically a French, (exemplary) model. Life, it appeared, was elsewhere and this was unusual in the history of British radical thought since those who usually drew on patriotic myths for historical sustenance 'were at least as likely to be on the political left as on the right' (Evans 1994: 242; see also Cunningham 1981). If this sort of patriotism had not been so evident amongst intellectuals in the polarised politics of the inter-war years (a condition which was famously the focus of Orwell's wrath) a vernacular, non-Tory version was still available to those who cared to find it (Lawrence 1998). To take just one example, patriotism was central to J. B. Priestley's 'populist vision of national unity' which challenged the assumption that only a reactionary would want to be English (Baxendale 2001: 109). The new perspective, by contrast, proposed that England's was a 'distinct hermetic culture' without much to recommend it and its congealed traditions were a block to modernity: 'In the face of so much dense mass, it was hard to imagine options' (Colls 2002: 188). Indeed, the adaptability of the English ideology, the source of so much pride in the legend of civic patriotism, was here transformed into a fatal inheritance. It was hard to imagine options because, for Anderson and Nairn, English history was a bad infinity of repeated failures. As the focus of this debate shifted in subsequent decades from class (the conditions for radical social change) to nation (the conditions for the break-up of the United Kingdom) and as Marxism itself terminally declined as a political tradition, then Nairn's particular ideas about neo-nationalism established a template for critical analysis. As Anderson acknowledged, this was because his ideas addressed 'that historic reality which had been most neglected by Marxism – the nation'. Here was a very different radical possibility that had opened up in the 1970s and this 'conceptual transformation – the institution of a genuine dialectic of the singular and the universal – allowed Tom Nairn to return to the fate of contemporary British society from a quite new angle, as multiple national conflicts broke out within the United Kingdom at the turn of the seventies. The fruits were the series of remarkable essays – on Scotland, Northern Ireland, Wales, England, and the all-British Union clamped over them – published in *The Break-up of Britain*' (1992: 6–7). It is necessary to define the components of that conceptual transformation more precisely, specifically in the English case, since they became so persuasive for so many subsequent commentaries on Britishness in general and Englishness in particular.

The missing popular

As Anderson admitted, if any recent writer can claim credit for having first specified the conditions for the emergence of a self-conscious popular Englishness but also the conditions for the historical frustration of English nationalism it is Tom Nairn. *The Break-up of Britain* (1977) specified the character of England's national 'peculiarities' with insight and intelligence and appeared to indicate the necessary trajectory of the United Kingdom's disintegration, out of which a new England would emerge. The interpretation was logical, schematic and polemical and this explains its long-standing appeal amongst those for whom schematic logic and linguistic virtuosity are important. That book provided a framework within which influential critics, mainly on the left or centre-left of British politics, have continued to understand the question of English national identity and it has penetrated popular understanding as well.

From Nairn's arguments developed a digest of assumptions that were to harden into accepted wisdom and received truth. In more recent works, Nairn has added little to his original thesis though he has shown impatience that the logical conclusion to his argument – not only the break-up of Britain but also the emergence of a 'classic' English nationalism – has not happened yet. The failure of history to match schematically the logic of Nairn's argument should not detract from his seminal contribution to the debate about Englishness. It is a stimulating misreading, and not a simple catalogue of errors, mainly because its intent is practical rather than academic. It derived from the feverish debates in the 1960s within the New Left and between the New Left and the Old Left about the nature of the supposed (generic) crisis of legitimacy in the United Kingdom. What was distinctive about Nairn's contribution was its comprehensive negativity because the British crisis revealed no positive features of national politics. There was no impression that, as Orwell once put it, the country was sound, only that the wrong people were in charge. The crisis was so intractable because it was the consequence of an absence, a lack, in English politics and what was specifically lacking was a national imaginary that had the people at the core of it. Not just certain particulars were decayed but the whole system was rotten. The political and economic difficulties of the 1970s appeared to confirm the final bankruptcy of the old order and Nairn helped to capture the moment, making sense of it for a new generation of radicals. For example, Patrick Wright acknowledged how impressed he had been by Nairn's analysis when returning to England in 1979. He felt as if he 'had stumbled inadvertently into some sort of anthropological museum' and a society that seemed to be making 'not just a virtue but a new set of principles out of hindsight'. Nairn's framework helped him to put things in context and opened Wright's eyes to the regressive culture of nostalgia in 'deep England' (1985: 1).

According to this interpretation, the problem for England and the English in modern times has been the absence of popular nationalism. 'There is no coherent, sufficiently democratic myth of Englishness – no sufficiently accessible and popular myth-identity where mass discontents can find a vehicle' (Nairn 1977: 294). To modernise Britain, to sweep away the 'deformations' of the old order, an idea of the people was needed that permitted democratic mobilisation. Without popular mobilisation, the system was fated to permanent crisis and this sort of nationalism, argued Nairn, 'is not only a matter of having common traditions, revered institutions, or a rich community of customs and reflexes'. England already had these in abundance but popular Englishness of a radically transforming kind had been 'precluded by the main characters of English history since 1688 – precluded, above all, by those features of which English ideology is most convinced and proud, her constitutional and parliamentary evolution' (1977: 295). In short, what England lacked was the modern principle of *political* nationality that had originated in the French Revolution and so long as it was lacking the country would continue to decline. English recovery and, in a profound sense, the recovery of England depended upon altering the political climate but that was not possible while the old, rotting constitution remained in place: 'Without such a change, however, the economic formulae and tactics occupying 90 percent of English political thinking are still-born: they will return to a dead centre of inertia.' Nairn thought that this inherent decadence had 'always been obscurely acknowledged in government appeals to Dunkirk spirits and ghostly "teams" rowing in unison: the tribute of patrician vice to a missing nationalist virtue' (1977: 299). Every initiative was still-born because the British state had experienced a form of arrested development precisely because of its frustration of the egalitarian idea of the people. France, the 'Other' of Linda Colley's *Britons* (1992), had become the embodiment of this alien principle and its alienness had helped to secure the old corruption of a monarchical constitution throughout the nineteenth century. If the English had defined themselves against the French, here was a definition of English culture which adopted the prejudices of the other side of the Channel – that the English were philistine, barbaric, perfidious and money-grubbing. And like the revolutionaries of 1789, Nairn clearly believed that the people of England were in need of constant instruction as to their patriotic duty.

The catastrophe of mass politics in inter-war Europe had only given renewed life to this anti-democratic British *ancien regime*, blunting in its course the radicalism of the inter-war generation. Unfortunately, English dedication to institutional stability was not the secret of England's greatness but the condition of its long-term decline. Nairn here neatly reversed the old legend and its self-satisfied celebration of a distinctive English style of politics. It was succinctly captured in A. V. Dicey's observation that the success of English liberty lay in the fact that it did not indulge any romantic national idea (cited in Stapleton 2005b: 155). For Nairn, on the other hand, this meant a system without democratic substance. The civic legend celebrated English exceptionalism but this was an elitist stratagem designed to hide (everything had a negative design) what was truly remarkable – a political system that was inhospitable to the modern: 'The patrician political state and *mores* became permanent: an odd, transitional form petrified by primary and external success. The modern principle of political transformation (nationalism) was haltingly evolved every-where else, until it became near-universal' (1977: 297).

But it did not evolve in England and the 'patrician political' state had evaded this universal national evolution because it believed itself to be, as Dicey thought and as the tradition of civic patriotism proclaimed, the exemplary exception: 'The illusion that this system can persist for ever, in unending accommodation, is absolute: the only absolute of English politics.' That, one might say, is the English idiom's fantasy of continuity. What sustained the contradiction between the British state and the emergence of English nationalism could, accord-ing to Nairn, be summed up in a single word: class. This was nothing other than the decadent 'government by gentlemen'. Nationalism, by contrast, required equality and in England equality was 'unattainable without a radical *political* break'. Nationalism represented the path to democracy and was the basis of modernisation, although at this point, while the Marxist lineage of the argument remained in place as an ornament, the substance was now very different. The primary chal-lenge for radicals was not to modernise the *economy* but to modernise the *constitution* and this modernisation would depend 'on some restoration of the English political identity'. Upon the character of that transformation depended the future of British politics though its necessity would not be advanced 'by the constitutional grovelling' endemic to traditional Labour Party attitudes (1977: 300).

However, Nairn did detect in the England of the 1970s the stirrings of a new English identity, 'a cultural nationalism which has not yet come to consciousness of its own nature and purpose' (1977: 304). If this coming to consciousness required them to act only as Nairn prescribed, he was quite prescient in his observation that the English variety of 'left-nationalist popular culture' would begin to shift from socialism to 'ideas of England' – even though he did not predict that this would happen because of the collapse of socialism's intellectual and political appeal. The purpose of *The Break-up of Britain*, then, was to provide not only an analysis of the problem but also to promote a national-popular strategy which the left should adopt. Rather conveniently, Nairn could corral all the negatives of nationalism – racism, demagoguery, narrowness, 'Little England', reactionary – into another historical 'deformation', the English nationalism of Enoch Powell (see Chapter 7). Moreover, the spectre of Powellite nationalism was a useful incentive for the left to listen more attentively to Nairn's own nationalist advocacy: if you fail to choose the good variety you will end up with the evil one. In other words, the object was not only to describe but also to hasten the inevitable end of the United Kingdom. *The Break-up of Britain* had been designed as an appeal to 'those who care for England and strive to see her free of the old harness' of the British constitution. Nairn specified the future in the following terms. Much more than a scholarly rediscovery of the *Volksgeist* was at stake and to proclaim the English national popular required political action as well as bookish research. The purpose was to restore 'the People to the liberal-constitutional universe of the patriciate, labouring to supply the data and conviction which popular mobilisation against the old state will one day need' (1977: 304). Nairn's own bookish contribution, explicitly and implicitly, also became part of a common platform of understanding that would help to sustain the intellectual objectives of English nationalist thought.

This argument and this agenda were essentially rephrased in Nairn's later polemic against the monarchy in *The Enchanted Glass* (1988). The survival of the monarchy and its prominence in the popular imagination was another result of the corruption of modern (or classic) nationalism that passes for civic patriotism. The Royal Family had become a substitute for an authentic English national consciousness and its existence attenuated the ability to think seriously about the capacity of the popular will. It represented a 'strange a-national nationalism' that served to convince English people that their own patriotism is uniquely beneficent (1988: 127). In his summary contribution on this 'royal romance' in the third volume of Samuel's *Patriotism*, Nairn argued that the cult of monarchy once made the English feel that they were above nationalism: 'The vein of truth here is of course that the English are not above but below "that sort of thing". They have not got there. Empire, crown, establishment and Labour party have prevented them forging a modern democratic national identity, and this obstruction itself has become a revered proof of superior civilisation and tolerance'(1989: 84). Nairn's critical legend did not so much develop as use every opportunity for restatement and what was restated was the legend of British decadence. This interpretation has been ably sustained by Nairn but only at the expense, as he himself has admitted, of *déjà vu* since the arguments had become very familiar. For example, in *After Britain* (2000a), Nairn re-employed the theme of Robert Musil's *Kakania* – taken from his trilogy *The Man Without Qualities*, exploring the spiritual decay of the Habsburg monarchy – which he had used first in *The Enchanted Glass*. It had there been translated by Nairn into the term *Ukania* to describe the collapsing authority of the Union, a political order that was both 'insanely pretentious' and a 'pseudo-democracy' (2000b: 154). All efforts to prop up the regime would come to nought just as the fond hope of Austro-Marxists came to nought that they could save the integrity of the Habsburg Empire from nationalist challenge. New Labour's constitutional reforms, for example devolution of power to Scotland, Wales and Northern Ireland, merely replayed the old Austrian saying '*es muss etwas geschehen*' (something must be done). However, the fatalistic end was already implied in that action – '*es ist passiert*' (it just happened). And what will just happen is the dissolution of Britishness. We know what the future of the Union will be because we know already the fate of Austria-Hungary. Here is the *real* paradox of Englishness. On the one hand, a multinational union like the United Kingdom is on dangerous ground if allegiance is given to its component national identities. On the other hand, its multi-nationality is contradicted by an exclusive allegiance to a transcendent, institutional identity. Here is a paradox to which the British state can no longer find a workable solution – just as the Austrians failed to do. The critical legend proposed that as Britishness dies, popular, republican self-government would come inevitably to life. Even dear old England, with all its monarchical absurdities, could not hold out for much longer and that is why it *must* become nationalistic *before* the old order collapses ignominiously. In the new millennium, the English did seem to be getting there and in *Pariah* (2002) England had now become as a country 'not only conceivable, but now bearing down rapidly upon its inhabitants and knocking upon its own historical door, so to speak, in a way unlikely to be long denied' (2002: 102). For Nairn, it was not flag-waving football supporters that were the harbingers of this new popular Englishness but the mourners at the funeral of Princess Diana – which goes to prove how treacherous can be the politics of the moment to a legend that relies for its persuasiveness on the broad, and hazy, sweep of generalisation.

Despite all the weakness in particulars, the critical legend proved attractive because it appeared to synthesise two apparently contradictory developments: nationalism within the United Kingdom and a new, post-imperial, global framework for British politics; one which also traced England's loss of universal, world-historical significance. Partly this legend ran in parallel with a significant academic development, the emergence of the 'New British History' or 'Four Nations History' which shifted attention from exclusively English matters to the interaction of the peoples and the nations of the 'Atlantic archipelago' (see Kearney 1995). This historical revisionism was also part of the cultural *Zeitgeist* and complemented a generation of change in British universities, and intellectual modification of the former dominant Anglocentrism seemed an appropriate diminishment of the hubris of historians like A. J. P. Taylor who believed that British history really was English history, the rest being mere embellishment and detail. The critical legend presented itself as the companion political thesis, proposing that as the Anglocentric narrative of Britishness waned, then England, formerly first among nations, should now be described as the laggard of historical destiny, the political equivalent of the Beatitudes. The first (the English) had become last and the last (the Celts) had become first. Here was *Schadenfreude* indeed, a transition from a Celtic fringe to an Anglian fringe and the invitation now was to pity poor old England rather than to emulate her. This was attractive not only to nationalists in Scotland, Wales and Northern Ireland but to some self-pitying intellectuals in England as well because it also suggested an opportunity: that the historical situation could bring forth a different England coterminous with the hopes of post-colonialists, neo-nationalists and multi-culturalists (see Ingelbien 2002: 149).

The polemical integration of a return to the particular (the end of Empire and the break-up of Britain), loss of the universal (English institutional decay) and political absence (no national popular) provided significant possibilities for an active culture of complaint. Referring to his former New Left 'style of radicalism', Nairn noted how he and Anderson used to decry the British state's 'illogicality' against its defenders who thought that no such logic was required in these matters. That defence had now gone, displaced by history but the problem remained for Nairn that the English did not fit neatly enough into the political destiny devised for them (2002: 86). They kept failing to do what was required and the fault seemed to be with the people rather than with their destiny. The sophistication of the rhetoric, the humour of the satire, the evocative power of the polemic could not hide the unsubtlety of that argument. Moreover, Nairn's radical legend had its own history in the fate of Tom Paine's *Rights of Man*: 'So unanswerable was Paine's analysis in 1792 that, in a rational world, the English constitution should have sunk without trace.' So too, should the illogical British state have crumbled before the logic of Nairn's critique. That this is not the case certainly does tell us something about 'rational worlds' and, for the radical critic, the wonder is not that the constitution 'fails to tell the truth, but that its fictions have been tolerated for so long' (Colls 1998: 114–15). The implications of this conclusion are far from congenial, however. As one critic put it, either the English who 'find themselves in the most need of a restatement of who they are and where power lies' are so spellbound by the glamour of backwardness that their condition is hopeless or the English need to be led to their own salvation by those few who do know who they are and where power lies (like Nairn) – but that is hardly compatible with the emergence of a vital authentic 'national popular'. It represented the conceit of the social theorist that the people are cultural dupes 'whose thought is constrained within an ideological frame of which we, ourselves, are free' (Condor 1997: 251). And yet this conceit of the social theorist does conform in both cases to certain long-held views about popular suggestiveness and which owe much to the Nairn legacy.

Throughout recent history, it has been argued, the English have been prepared to accept an identity focused on the Royal Family as the custodians of national symbolism. This peculiar 'deformation' has meant that the 'first principles of effective national identity – the "way we do things", etc – have themselves become major obstacles to the reform of that identity' and in that context, Englishness 'can offer no way out or forward' (Nairn 1997: 111). This is politics as fate for, according to this logic, any government *must* be Tory in practice so long as *Ukania* continues in existence. New Labour after 1997 was judged accordingly, which is why Nairn wished that the English would just get on with it and become classically nationalist like everyone else (2000a: 290).

The influence of this interpretative heritage should not be underes-timated, and with good justification, one sympathetic commentator has argued that Nairn's *The Break-up of Britain* 'has become the prevalent wisdom even when people do not know its source' (Ascherson 2000). That book's thesis, in other words, has been the ghost in the text of many subsequent reflections on the politics of England. For Ascherson at least, Nairn can claim to have won most of the arguments (except, one would have to add, the decisive one: the break-up of Britain). The persuasiveness of the argument depended upon the fascination with a narrative of disintegration and the appeal of that narrative – like the legend of civic patriotism before it – served a psychological as well as a political need for those who were impressed by it and was almost impervious to counter-argument (Aughey 2006a: 49–51). It *had* to be true because that is how the world *must* become. This critical narrative had developed into some-thing of a mantra and as such as much of a dead centre of inertia as the legend it challenged. Ironically, it too had become a venerable insti-tution of the sort that usually attracted the scorn of its advocates.

Stephen Howe demonstrated how the Nairn diagnosis influenced a whole generation of critics and certainly conditioned the response of the left to Mrs Thatcher's reforms in the 1980s. The latter effect is quite surprising since the *leitmotif* of the critical legend was that every-thing was hopeless, but after Thatcher it was no longer possible to argue either that the 'crisis of capitalism' was fatal or that English/British society was unreformable. Indeed, Mrs Thatcher's 'authoritarian populism' had only succeeded in wrong-footing her opponents and her greatest sin appeared to be upsetting the theory as much as the practice of her critics by reviving once more, albeit in a non-genteel voice, the claims of the exemplary exception. Thatcherism understood itself to be an exceptional achievement, its message exem-plary and here was a dialectic of particular and universal that did not fit the script of the critical legend of British decline. Almost by default, attention shifted (as Nairn had suggested it should) to the one thing that Mrs Thatcher had left undisturbed, the constitution, and the one thing she took for granted, nationality. So the utility of the critical legend was actually re-invigorated as the debate shifted 'from argu-ment over the futures of Scotland, Wales and Northern Ireland, through a dramatically renewed and often febrile attention to the nature of England and/or British patriotism and the future of national identity, to analyses of Britain's economic performance, governing institutions, and constitutional future' (Howe 2003: 296). For many years, Nairn 'was regarded in London as a Celtic-fringe fantasist or –

worse – as a traitor to socialist internationalism' but things had changed and changed utterly under Thatcher. Those 'Old Left voices which used regularly to denounce all forms of nationalism as the prelude to fascism, racism and war (except for noble anti-colonial struggles, of course) have fallen silent' (Ascherson 2000). One can trace the enduring influence of the critical legend in many recent works on the English Question and a few examples from a range of disciplines reveal its widespread influence.

One perspective was provided by Richard Weight's popular history of British experience since 1945, *Patriots* (2002). He had drunk deep at the well of Nairn and came to the conclusion that there was 'a crisis of English national identity'. England was a nation not popular enough, a crisis which 'was made worse by the fact that they [the English] had never developed a sufficiently democratic narrative of their national identity with which to launch themselves into a post-Union world'. The solution to England's sense of dislocation and the solution to the democratic deficit in English political culture were one and the same: independence as a nation state with popular music and football as the levers of cultural transformation (2002: 450).

The political scientist (and republican advocate) Stephen Haseler also proposed a familiar Nairnite thesis in *The English Tribe* (1996) in which the British system of governance had fostered a maudlin medieval nostalgia which sustained the snobbery of class and held the country back from modernisation. To describe this nostalgia, he appropriated Nairn's expression 'the glamour of backwardness'. Conservatism was too strongly secured within the institutions of the United Kingdom and only their collapse would energise the English people. Haseler posed the same alternative futures that we find in Nairn: either the degeneration of England into Ruritanian quaintness or its regeneration as a European republic. England/Britain was 'nothing less than the western world's only remaining *ancien regime*' (Haseler 1990: 415).

The political geographer, Peter Taylor, also used the Nairn thesis in an article which tried to explain the peculiarities of the English and their Englishness – as much to themselves as to others. His explanation began by identifying the 'missing people' of England and interpreted their national identity 'as a particular deformed nationalism hiding behind its self-ascribed patriotism'. In England, he claimed, a 'whole people seems to be excluded from its own nationalism' (Taylor 1991: 146–61).

The social theorist P. W. Preston adopted a simple model of modernisation that was drawn directly and uncritically from the work of Nairn and by this measure British backwardness along with English complacency were bound together in a culture of decline. A critical part of the problem was the effective demobilisation of the population such that policy remained in the control of a narrow political elite. A thorough transformation of the constitution of the United Kingdom along lines proposed by Nairn was required to overcome a century of decline (Preston 1994). However, Preston's interpretation really highlighted one of the unresolved tensions at the centre of the critical legend. On the one hand, the English question was merely a question of *structures* and 'structural change' made it inevitable that 'received ideas of Britishness/Englishness will change'. On the other hand, it was really a question of *identities* and the new structural space of the twenty-first century, as a result of changing national self-understandings, would open up the possibility 'of discarding Britishness in favour of a rediscovery of Englishness' (2004: 171). It was a tension that could be conveniently ignored.

Finally, and intellectually most impressively, the subterranean lineage of Nairn's polemic can also be traced in Kumar's *The Making of English National Identity* (2003a). For Kumar, on the one hand, the English problem was due to that lack identified by Nairn, the lack of classic popular nationalism. On the other hand, he also observed that calls for English independence did not appear to be as outlandish in the new millennium as they once did a few decades ago. Nationalism, he thought, had finally caught up with the English and to the external colonial argument – Britishness as an imperial construct – Kumar added the internal colonial argument – Britishness as an extension of English power. By creating and maintaining their 'inner empire' of Great Britain, the English secured a position of political dominance within the British Isles. The global extension of this dominance in their overseas empire encouraged the English to see themselves, like the Romans of old, as being engaged on a mission of civilisation (Kumar 2006: 4–9). That world had now gone. As Kumar put it, the race was now on for the English to come up with a suitably popular answer to meet this crisis of identity and the attraction of the critical legend was that it provided a ready-made response to this supposed crisis. For Nairn, the United Kingdom was a failed political entity well beyond its sell-by date and this was the conclusion that Kumar also reached, not polemically but sociologically. This was perhaps an unsurprising conclusion for a sociologist since the critical legend was presented in terms of a basic conflict between enlightened values – the 'new' nationalism – and archaic superstition – the decaying British polity. If, as Ascherson claimed, much of this legend is now taken for granted, what sort of purchase on the condition of England does it actually have?

After Nairn

The lifespan and influence of this particular critical legend is all the more remarkable since its main flaws were pointed out early on by E. P. Thompson in *The Socialist Register* of 1965. Thompson described the legend as one of 'inverted Podsnappery', one 'whose typological symmetry offers a reproach to British exceptionalism'. The polemical style favoured by Nairn used 'a shifting terminology whose treacherous instability is disguised by a certain metaphorical virtuosity' but this could only seduce those who wished to be seduced. To use an Oakeshottian expression, the critical legend provided the reader with history 'as the crow flies'. Thompson described it as a 'thirst for a tidy platonism' that becomes 'impatient with actual history'. The consequence was a misreading of history and the 'misunderstandings are so large that it is tempting to capitulate before them'. Obviously many have done so and continue to do so, which suggests that success is connected with something other than purely intellectual credibility. What particularly irritated Thompson was the 'ruthlessness' with which Nairn dismissed the English experience and ordered the complexities of that experience into crude categories of 'class power' or 'hegemonic aspirations'. Nor was there permitted in the legend any English contribution to intellectual life. 'It is not only that no one has ever been right; no one has ever been wrong in an interesting or reputable way' (Thompson 1978: 35–91). Thirty-five years after Thompson, another penetrating criticism of the Nairn version by J. G. A. Pocock also pointed to the impoverished nature of its limited understanding of Britishness in terms of monarchy and an antiquated, imperial class structure. In particular, this impoverished understanding was debilitating when it came to imagining England and the English. Pocock did admit that 'British' was often a word meaning 'English' in disguise but that only begged the question: 'Nairn's problem – which he thinks is an English problem – is that he wants the English to cease being British, but does not know whether they will or can, or how he wants them to go about it, or what they are supposed to become' (Pocock 2000: 46). The stratagem resorted to by Nairn, the politico-literary use of the *Ukania* satire, Pocock treated dismissively: 'All Nairn wants to say by these means is that it is absurd for the English to think they can bring about a multi-national politics.' However, Pocock thought that Nairn's easy dismissal of the future of multi-national politics was actually a concern about the substance of his own argument: 'The aim of his satire is to lessen their political will, not to transform it.' The heady promise of the English national popular Nairn set out in 1977 had become nothing more today than a farcical pageant but this would just not do: 'As for the English, not even their class structure reduces them to having been mere victims of themselves. Nothing will ever deliver them from having been an imperial people. There is no pre-imperial identity, lurking in the post-imperial thickets until it can emerge to redeem them from their history' (Pocock 2000: 47).

Jonathan Clark also criticised *The Break-up of Britain* as 'a work disclosing a secular, left-wing Scot's lack of historical understanding of the substance of Englishness' (2003: 74). Clark did concede the central point of Nairn's (and Kumar's) thesis that there was no 'classic' nationalism in England and he also admitted that 'nationalism becomes a key problem for historians of England, resembling the classic conundrum "why was there no socialism in America?"' However, this was all beside the point. The problem with the critical legend was that it measured the English experience against some ideological, or authentic, norm such as 'modernity' but as the modernist assumptions behind that ideological understanding came under question it was no longer credible to treat the term 'nationalism' as if it were a reified actor on the world stage striding like a dinosaur across the nineteenth and twentieth centuries (Clark 2003: 88–9). And as Howe put it in a penetrating challenge to the orthodoxies of the critical legend, 'being interesting does not make it true'. Life is more interesting if we believe in the Loch Ness monster 'but that is not a good reason for believing in it if, in fact, it does not exist' (Howe 2003: 29). The grounds for scepticism were legion, the most serious being those relating to the 'imperial polity' of Britishness. In Howe's view a whole raft of under-explained claims have been attached to this single argument in order to explain the United Kingdom's anticipated break-up. There was the decline of England's 'external empire', the weakening of England's 'internal empire', the eclipse of England's cultural authority, the slipping authority of the archaic features of the monarchical constitution and the disillusion with and disarray of the welfare state, itself a product of the old imperial polity. The critical legend insinuates all of these things and as a consequence, we are no further on in explaining anything. 'Questions about when things ended – or may yet end – and perhaps more importantly questions about what persists and remains formative of national experience, cannot be resolved while we remain so uncertain about what the most important 'things'

are, or how best to characterize the twentieth-century UK polity'
(Howe 2003: 31).

The literature deriving from the Nairn version does tend to make
these sorts of sweeping generalisations and to be based on questionable assumptions. The problem is not the partial insight of the colonial view of British/English or the distinctiveness of English national
identity. The problem is partial insight presenting itself as the whole of
political understanding, predicting the future accordingly and not only
predicting the future but also asserting the logical necessity of English
national separatism. As Crick admitted, the New Left domination of
intellectual discourse did not mean that it had any deep effect on
working class opinion or even 'Middle England' but he did think that
it 'helped create among historians and political commentators a
miasma through which it was difficult to see clearly some aspects of
our national past'. In this regard, it was as much of a 'deformation' of
historical understanding as the civic legend that it criticised. The 'arbitrary construction of history' in the doctrine of the critical legend
blinded a generation of intellectuals to the complexity as well as the
commonality of English/British identity. Patriotism and nationalism
were the common property of all the major parties precisely because
this was indeed *popular* and *not* absent. Moreover, the 'patriotism of
the left' was far more like that 'of the rest of the country than zealots
or enemies liked or were wont to portray' (Crick 2002: 368–70).
Absolutes such as nation versus class, patriotism versus socialism or
Britishness versus Englishness do not properly capture the complexity
of attitudes in the history of popular politics.

The assumption of the critical legend, so long sustained by Nairn
and his admirers, has been that the absence of a self-conscious popular
nationalism in England denotes a failure of the English to understand
themselves. This too is questionable. It was Orwell who observed in
The Lion and the Unicorn that Englishness was less politicised in that
sense and was to be found in 'the pub, the football match, the back
garden, the fireside and "the nice cup of tea"'. Genuinely popular
culture 'is something that goes on beneath the surface' and to share in
it does not require subscription to any particular political ideology or
project but to 'take into account its emotional unity, the tendency of
nearly all its inhabitants to feel alike and act together in moments of
supreme crisis' (cited in Gervais 1993: 178–9). English writers might
feel uncomfortable about using such language today and perhaps it
was poetic licence to assume that even the 'supreme crisis' of the
Second World War had created such an 'emotional unity'. However,
the insights that popular patriotism is not absent, that it is neither

exclusively conservative nor lacking in self-understanding remain valid.

Nairn argued that the absence of a democratic myth of Englishness was 'the source of the disconcerting lurch from a semi-divine Constitution and the Mother of Parliaments to the crudest racialism' (1977: 294). A quarter of a century later and the alternatives appeared to be different but no less hopeless. On the one hand, there was 'the idea of reversion to an irrecoverable rurality' of a post-British culture. On the other hand, there was the longing 'for a virtual dissolution of identity into multiculturalism or "Europe"' (Nairn 2000b: 102). Those stark alternatives were, however, determined not by the realities of English politics but by the requirements of the critical legend. Because of the supposed absence of political nationalism amongst the English it was assumed that there could be no resting place between either the comforting lies of the civic tradition or the apocalyptic predictions of right-wing demagoguery. These are hardly flattering alternatives, the one characterised by deferential subordination to myth and the other by anxiety and xenophobia. Here is a bad infinity of eternal recurrence though it is not the way things necessarily are. The absence identified by Nairn and others meant that they have been inattentive to the English people's story because they have been determined that the people should have played some other role in history. It is a legend in which the task of defining has easily given way to the attraction of redesigning; one in which the mask has been confused with the mirror. The logic of the Nairn version, as Pocock stressed, is that it appears to require the English to abolish themselves before they can become fully nationalist. The English need to emancipate themselves not only from the old political system (Britain) but also from their old cultural selves (imperial, racist, superior, insular). The redemption must be found in something far greater than merely institutional or constitutional change. As Ingelbien noted, the void in Englishness 'will always remain a scandal to those whose thinking is shaped by identity politics, and who can only read it either as the absence left by a defunct British Imperialism or as an emptiness that must urgently be filled with new national myths'. That there may be an alternative reading rarely detains those in search of the missing centre (Ingelbien 2002: 219–20). That there are alternative readings are considered in the chapters which follow and which try to explore the ambiguity of the *Zeitgeist*.

Part II
Anxieties of Englishness

5

English before they were British

Jeremy Paxman began his popular book *The English: A Portrait of a People* with the line: 'Once upon a time the English knew who they were' (1998: 1). This knowledge had been the efficient secret of the country's success and the hidden reservoir from which all the distinctive characteristics of the English people were drawn. However, Paxman's use of the fairytale expression 'once upon a time' was perhaps significant because such confident self-knowledge is, as the expression implies, mythological. After Borges, it is yet another mask and not a mirror. 'Once upon a time' is not even the remotest of historical moments but is a current state of mind. Thus, at the very time when Paxman assumed the English did know who they were, Mathew Arnold was asking in his lectures *On the Study of Celtic Literature* (1867): 'And we, then, what are we? What is England?' (cited in Watson 1973: 200). If Paxman does not describe a past of which any historian is aware he does refer to a nostalgic present. The 'once upon a time' is an exercise in nostalgia and as one critic put it, nostalgia has a habit of telling it like it wasn't. There always appears a time when 'folk did not feel fragmented, when doubt was either absent or patent, when thought fused with action, when aspiration achieved consummation, when life was wholehearted; in short, a past that was unified and comprehensible, unlike the incoherent, divided present'. The only thing missing in this past, of course, is its own nostalgia for an undivided, coherent past (Lowenthal 1989: 29). 'Once upon a time', then, is a term which prefaces a description of the perceived failings of today, and the sensation that self-knowledge has been lost may provoke a melancholic or elegiac disposition (the longing for a golden age). It may also provoke a romantic evocation of a changeless centre from which the people have supposedly drifted and to which they should anchor themselves once again (an eternal England). Both of these forms of nostalgia represent impossible quests for authenticity. When the English lost their self-knowledge an inevitable 'descent into anxiety' has been assumed, a descent into a state of inauthenticity (Aslett 1997: 19). Today the English, according to Paxman, are in the process of recovering the past (not *a* past) that was for centuries buried and hidden from them. In concluding in this vein he implies a magical idea of 'return' and though critics may dismiss this idea of return as a fantasy it is one that continues to have a popular resonance (Gilroy 1999: 57; see also Adair 1986).

One of the familiar themes of return in English literature is the attraction of rural life, and the attraction of rural England was the possibility of discovering the permanent and the underlying. For the English to lose their sense of place was tantamount to their losing Englishness itself and this was the central idea in the work of a writer like H. J. Massingham (Palmer 2002: 27–31). However, one should be careful how one interprets the meaning of rural, 'eternal England' for it is too easy to fall into the trap of labelling it as simply reactionary. It was true, as John Lucas argued, that in the modern age to be English in this sense meant not to be English at all and that the romantic rejection of industrial, urban England was a rejection of what was truly real about the country. Imagining England, then, often meant not imagining it at all (Lucas 1990: 205). That is only a half truth since this interpretation was both an exaggeration and a misreading. English experience has been more complex, even for those normally associated with the cult of the rural and the traditional. For example, in his 'historian's testament', *The Lion and the Unicorn* (1969), Arthur Bryant wrote an evocative essay on the magical topography of 'that little corner of earth where Wiltshire joins Dorset'. In recapturing how his childhood imagination peopled this landscape with a cast of English history from Cavaliers and Roundheads to Alfred the Great, Bryant invited the reader to share not only in the unchanging constancy of the English soil but also in the continuity of English history. And yet the conclusion was somewhat different to what one might have expected – that here was yet another invocation of the virtues of the old against the new, of the traditional against the modern. Bryant thought that the dreams of his Edwardian boyhood seemed certainly far away from modern England of the Swinging Sixties but the one (the past) did *not* stand as a rebuke to the other (the present): 'There are times when one wonders whether the world of sixty years ago was an illusion or whether the world today is, for they seem so incompatible with one another that they cannot both be reality.' The past and the present are both real and both illusory but the measure of these transient human strivings is the eternalness of nature: 'The contours of Wessex hill and plain and the clouds from

which the great Dorset and Wiltshire trees draw their life-giving mois-
ture will still be there when the age of Joseph Chamberlain and the age
of Harold Wilson are equally memories of a remote and seemingly
unreal past' (Bryant 1969: 30–1). The landscape for Bryant was not
the metaphor for a 'golden age', be it that of King Alfred or Cavaliers
and Roundheads. It really stood for the robust virtues of the English
people and its evocation was an exercise in contemporary patriotic
self-regard. If the author intended his readers to take any message
from the description of rural beauty it was that there will always be an
England so long as England meant as much to them as England meant
to Bryant. For Bryant, as it was for Ernest Barker before him and as it
was to be later for Benedict Anderson (whose phrase had all the force
of supposed novelty) the nation was an imagined community, not only
of the moment but also through time (see Anderson 1991). It was an
exercise in sentimental, even romantic, education and it was a schooling which appealed to many English (but not just English) readers and
it helps to explain Bryant's enduring popularity for those who lived in
towns and cities as well as in the countryside.

And if one believed that patriotism slumbered, as the landscape also
seemed to do, then it was also possible to believe in its re-awakening
and that was something in which Bryant did have faith. Out walking
on a post-war St George's Day, he reflected on the 'grass, trees, blos-
soms, flowers, even the very weeds' which modern industrialism had
failed to eradicate. In England there was loss, yes, but also something
which redeemed and transcended it: 'that which is lost shall be found
again, that which is broken shall be repaired, that which is grown old
and worn shall be made new'. A nation that endured a challenge such
as the Second World War – and here one can substitute *any* challenge
– 'has the power to renew itself from the ashes of its own past' (1969:
150). When it does renew and awaken, another inspiring historical
chapter beckons and here eternal England and golden age connect in a
seamless national imagination. Bryant hoped that 'the people of this
country, who inherit the instincts and aptitudes which formerly made
her great and honoured, will again produce leaders, both in action and
thought, who will re-inspire them with the sense of purpose and faith
they have lost'. Resuming under new forms (this is not a *literal* return)
the country will become again strong and stable (recapturing a golden
time) and take up its 'ancient precedence' to be a guiding light to
others (England's civilising mission) (1969: 223). Bryant's turn of
phrase may no longer be popular and his presumption no longer credible but the concept of enduring, but hidden, virtue and the possibility
of its rediscovery are far from unusual in the English political conver-

sation. It may be bad form to overstate the case but the case is frequently stated and, of course, this belief is not unique to England. Some notion of the eternal may necessarily attach to all identities in which the homeland helps to naturalise the nation and in which the characteristics of a people find their metaphorical reference in the features of the landscape. 'In simple terms,' as one group of social scientists have argued, 'the nation is a route to immortality in a secular world' (Reicher, Hopkins and Condor 1997: 84; see also Smith 1995: 160).

It may be a commonplace 'that those who appeal to bygone ages for the way, the truth and the life, are often those who know least about them' (Porter 1992: 1). But that sort of appeal is not only a habit of the un-historically-minded public but also a temptation for the professional historian. One example of this temptation can be found in an article by David Starkey which discussed the manuscript collection of the Tudor Archbishop Matthew Parker. What has been lost, argued Starkey, 'at the beginning of the 21st century, in the reign of Elizabeth II, is the confidence of the 16th-century England of Elizabeth I'. In this view, old self-assurance had given way to contemporary shame, despair and uncertainty. Starkey's object was polemical rather than historical because his purpose was to call for an intellectual re-foundation of England, towards which he felt the spirit of the Parker Collection might contribute (Starkey 2001). One other example was George Kitson Clark's reminder to his readers (1950: 40), at a time of relative national self-confidence, that when the ancient constitution faltered, the English had been English before they were British and an English identity could be found beyond, or perhaps behind, the institutions of the United Kingdom. One interpretation of recent British history suggests that the diminishing authority of the old institutions has indeed provoked a re-assessment of Englishness and as one literary critic suggested, some of the drive towards this re-assessment has come from authors attempting to reclaim Kitson Clark's promise of 'Englishness before Britishness'. The very act of 'naming' England, in other words, has been an attempt to bring it back to a virile existence after decades of 'decline' (Cowley 1999: 29). There may be some exhilaration in the pursuit of the authentic England since pursuit of the authentic is a sort of romanticism in politics and its appeal to some is that it provides a poetic alternative to the prosaic tradition of English empiricism. This romanticism is rarely a *Weltanschauung*, more a turn of phrase or mood. Every generation will have its own 'once upon a time' and it is important not to get the contemporary version out of perspective but what, if anything, is distinctive about present concerns?

The point of return

The urgency of contemporary cultural Englishness has been attributed to the widespread political impatience with either a sense of the country's 'disconnectedness' or with a sense that England is somehow without meaning (Easthope 1999). There has been a tone of self-pity in the thought that 'Englishness found itself marooned in the modern world' and that it had become much easier to think of England 'in terms of its past rather than its future' (Gervais 2001: 159). But what if that glorious past is also understood as a fabrication? What is to become of the English, asked Elton, when they discover that the history they once believed in was also an invention of the dream-makers (1991: 44)? In that case, not even nostalgia can provide proper solace, nor can it provide any sense of retrospective pride because it implies that perhaps the biggest illusion of them all was to believe in England's greatness in the first place. Some critics assume that even expressions of English self-confidence should be taken as a deeper manifestation of national uncertainty and ailment (Spiering 1992: 168). Here, it seems, is a clear case of moral vulnerability matching the material insecurity of the country's diminished status in the post-war world (see Green and Whiting 1996: 388). One can detect in these remarks the lure of *Weltschmerz*, a state in which the past is discounted, the present is sadly debased and the future can only be worse. To be English, then, means to live amidst the ruins, a constant reminder of past guilt and present failure in which things are blocked at every turn, a realisation of a very Nairnite nightmare. But as Barker reminded his readers, the English are not often given to *Weltschmerz* but inhabit a culture of 'make do'. Thinking in terms of return or of recovery is always present in any political culture, it has its own vitality and it is one that pays little attention to intellectual blockages. The popular attraction of eras of historical veneration 'once upon a time' when things were certain, when people had real and virtuous choices to make, is that they intimate 'a voyage of return to the past' as a political act of recovery (Baucom 1999: 18). Recent reflection on Englishness has been frequently defined by proposed voyages of return though it should be clear what this does *not* imply in England's case. It does not mean, generally, a reactionary objective to recreate the past in the present. Return in this case has a very English meaning, recalling Oakeshott's view that a political tradition involves a 'swerving back to recover and make something topical out of even its remotest moments; and nothing for long remains unmodified' (1991: 59). Romantic authenticity is usually qualified by pragmatic utility and this is typical of the English idiom (see in this case the judicious remarks of Elton 1992: 230–5). It is a characteristic that is evident even in the most romantic of contemporary texts about England (Ackroyd 2002).

Return or recovery, then, can have a number of different meanings. In the most commonly understood meaning it has involved a contraction of power now that Britain/England, whose influence was spread across the globe, had returned to the condition of a medium-sized European power. Not only had political power contracted and been returned to more limited ambitions but also the power of English cultural attraction had weakened, returning it to the parochial when formerly it was international. At first sight this is an unrelieved tale of political retreat which has been the *leitmotif* of important studies of post-war experience (see, for example, Barnett 1972) and Englishness as a legend of return can often be discussed 'as though this shift implied a humiliating diminution' (Ingelbien 2004: 160). Yet there is another meaning incorporated in this legend which is also a tale of rediscovery, one in which the incredible vagueness of being English – a vagueness that is not authentic but a product of its imperial accretion of Britishness – is dispelled in the achievement of self-recognition. This possibility may be clarified from an unusual, non-English angle. The Ulster writer Robert Johnstone noted how, in his childhood, the map on the school wall was coloured half in red, including Northern Ireland, with London as the capital of it all. Relatives lived across the globe in the largest bits of red like Canada. On the television, British Prime Ministers appeared to be dictating the course of world events in tandem with American Presidents. Johnstone concluded that the horizons of his (Ulster) people were not narrow but that, perhaps, 'like England's they were too broad for us to be able to see ourselves clearly' (1987: 251). What is implied in these reflections is that national authenticity requires a limited focus and a new sharpness of vision, that only when the fuzziness of imperial extension has gone is it possible for a people to (re)possess real self-understanding. This notion of return, of course, inverts the 'once upon a time' of Paxman and proposes a course from past distortion to current clarity. Both are mythological but they do hold out in their different ways the prospect of recovery. Langford thought that it was a matter of regret for some that the identity of England had been absorbed so fully into the vagueness of Britain and its empire. 'Who knows,' he asked, 'what vigour Englishness might exhibit if for the first time in many centuries the English find themselves speaking only for England?' (2000: 319). If that was then (imperial Britishness) and this is now (a more chastened but also more self-consciously realistic Englishness), the voyage to now has meant self-discovery, though self-discovery may either be for good – the emancipation from myth and illusion – or for ill – the recognition of the depressing ordinariness of all things English. The two can also be one and the same.

The modern political context for these reflections can be, in part, traced to the character of the United Kingdom polity itself. The concept of the Crown meant that the political association was not conceived of as a specific state but as an infinite domain (Rose 1982b). The empire was an attachment of territories overseas just as Britain was an association of territories within these islands. What had been attached could be also detached, what had been associated could also be disassociated and this is one way of understanding the fate of the imperial adventure, internally and externally. Whether this fate was a public trauma or not is a large question and the opinion of imperial historians remains divided. P. J. Marshall argued that the British state 'developed its own trajectory with very little regard to what was happening in the empire' and Britain's political leadership rarely allowed the supposed needs of empire to upset the requirements of domestic politics (1994: 382–3). Marshall concluded that whatever 'one's view may be about the institutions of the present British state, it is unlikely that empire has had much to do with shaping them' (1994: 393). J. G. Darwin was of much the same opinion. In other European countries, the retreat from empire had contributed to serious political upheaval and social convulsion. In Britain it had left few visible traces and had never threatened the viability of British institutions. Even the bombastic imperialists, found mainly, but not exclusively, within the Conservative Party thought that 'empire was meant to serve the party and not the other way round' (1986: 33). Because of the reluctance to mobilise opinion on imperial issues it has become difficult to gauge the force of popular sentiment but public opinion appeared to receive the death of empire with equanimity and the reason for this may have been the priority given by political parties to domestic strategies. Others, of course, have claimed that this prominent 'minimal impact thesis' conveys neither the depth nor the extent of the imperial legacy (see, for example, Webster 2005). Perhaps the most judicious comment has been from Linda Colley who has argued that the popular approach to empire was always 'bifurcated'. Treating empire and the nation as separate entities was not an indication of guilt but a way of investing in empire 'to a conspicuous degree while simultaneously drawing a mental line between it and themselves is what large numbers of Britons have always done' (2001). In this attitude the public behaved with the same detachment as most of their public representatives and of all the

British nations involved in empire. Elton speculated that the English were perhaps the most indifferent to the ending of that expansionist era which they had demonstrated by their almost immediate forgetfulness of it (Elton 1992: 234).

In a highly intelligent study of twentieth-century Englishness, Jed Esty provided one account of this process of return which involved significant cultural consequences. He entitled his study *A Shrinking Island* (2004) and by choosing the word 'shrinking' rather than 'sinking' (the title of a previous study by Hugh Kenner in 1987) to describe England's recent history, Esty counterposed a mixed tale of both contraction and consolidation to a straightforward narrative of cultural decline. The 'shrinking' of English experience was a return of sorts in which the grandeur of the imperial idea of exemplar became displaced by a prosaic post-imperial confrontation with the limits of modern circumstance. It involved a process of re-invention which followed from the discovery that England was not a providential exception but only one unique culture among many. In other words, the shrinking was defined by the transformation of English self-understanding from being universal to being particular or, to use another of Esty's terms, this entailed in England's acceptance of 'becoming minor'. He detected in this process a historical irony: 'the fact that native intellectuals in England confront the problems of cultural revivalism that are comparable with, if not parallel to, the problems confronting writers in former colonies, from Ireland to Nigeria to Jamaica to Pakistan, who must negotiate between the liberating and stultifying effects of celebrating national essence'. What Esty observed was the return 'to historical supply lines' that promised to give to Englishness a potentially new national cohesion. However compelling this interpretation may be, the transition between the universalist cultural principles of the metropolitan era and the particularism of contemporary England is often framed too confidently and can be cavalier with historical complexity. That there was a move to recover 'a vital English core from a crumbling British exoskeleton' may have been true for some but it was not true for all (Esty 2004: 199). Moreover, to take Irish experience as a comparison for the English is rather wide of the mark because the Republic of Ireland has defined itself *against* England in a way that England cannot define itself against the other nations of the United Kingdom. Nor is it accurate to say that the definition of an exclusive English identity became the motor of devolutionary politics in the United Kingdom since claims to devolution were of much longer standing. Nevertheless, Esty captured well the difficulties facing English politics: 'that of steering language and culture between the Scylla of rote nativism and the Charybdis of liberal elitism, of keeping nationalism apart from populist xenophobia, transnationalism apart from solipsistic anomie' (2004: 224–5). Again, as we have argued, awareness of those difficulties is not new and it has recurred in English thought during and after empire, on both the left and the right. Indeed, one could argue that the English idiom itself was – and remains – a product of that awareness and identification. If it has been anything at all, it has been a 'steered' discourse between the claims of formal citizenship and patriotism.

The sense that Englishness had lost universal significance provoked one response that seemed to invert its relationship with the other nations of the United Kingdom. This was a universal development that was welcomed by that astute reader of the times, Tom Nairn, who detected a shift in the balance within 'the incredibly shrinking state' towards the nations of the United Kingdom and away from the epicentre of English domination in the Home Counties (Nairn 1996: 29–34). Anglo-centrism, as noted in Chapter 1, had promoted two anxieties within the other British nations. The first anxiety was the anxiety of provincialism (and England was the metropolitan measure); the second was the anxiety of influence (provincial talent would be absorbed into English culture). There has been a noticeable tendency for this flow of anxiety to be reversed recently and for the English to worry more insistently about their own *British* provincialism (there always was a cosmopolitan tendency that abhorred England's cultural parochialism) and the influence others, especially the Scots, have in their public life.

Upon such anxieties, of course, the politics of identity thrive since they provide intellectual space for all sorts of historical and cultural revisions. For most English people, these anxieties may be nothing more than what H. V. Morton once called the 'vague mental toothache' of Englishness, a disquiet more often based on the feeling that one *should* feel anxious rather than the state of actually *being* anxious (1927: 46). For others, the vague mental toothache has become acute and needs to be addressed urgently (see Chapter 10). The claim has been made that the English are now traumatised, alienated, unsure, aggrieved and displaced. In short, the question of English identity today is bound up with the new complexity of British governance and with the novel uncertainty, especially in the post-devolution era, of how England fits into it. G. K. Chesterton's words about 'the people of England, that have never spoken yet' have become a constant refrain in reflections about that English condition but those words too are ambiguous. On the one hand, they are often interpreted positively to suggest that calling forth a self-conscious Englishness is an invitation to complete the constitutional settlement within the United Kingdom. As Vernon Bogdanor observed, England is hardly mentioned in devolution legislation though it is probably the key to the success of the whole enterprise (1999: 264). The realisation that one's country is no longer exceptional in the burdens it carries for and the gifts it bestows on civilisation might make that enterprise easier. On the other hand, these words can be interpreted negatively as a threat of self-assertion, one that intimates England, *our* England and those who are not English may be more sensitive to its tone (see McCrone 2002: 313).

Rodney Barker noted one change that had taken place in political debate in the course of the 1980s. When it was assumed that people shared broadly similar needs then politics was mainly argument about policy but when the assumption of homogeneity was challenged by devolution then a rather different sort of concern emerges, one that worries about difference rather than sameness (Barker 1996: 11). An essential ingredient of devolution was thought by its supporters to be the promotion of a benign form of English identity politics. 'We English,' Crick wrote, 'must come to terms with ourselves.' It was time to stop infusing 'everything that is English into the common property of Britishness' and the answer to such anxieties was 'not less English nationalism' (1991: 104). On the contrary, the English, like the Scots, the Welsh and the Irish should develop 'a self-confident and explicit national feeling' (1995: 180). If English national identity was becoming an urgent matter of dignity it was so by being defined by what it *lacked* on the (questionable) assumption that everyone else already possessed a dignified and proud national identity. As the editors of *Political Quarterly* noted, it was now time for England to engage in identity politics. The English, they argued, 'have begun to look grumpily insecure in the face of the external pressures of Europe and the internal pressures from Scotland and Wales'. Now, however, England was on the move, twitching and stirring 'as if awakening from a prolonged period of slumber'. Devolution meant, as Barker thought it would, that the politics and economics of territory was 'returning with a vengeance' and it was important to think through England's place within Tony Blair's New Britain (1998: 1–3). One of those editors, Tony Wright, wrote (more grumpily) two years later that the English were the 'silent and uninvited guests at the devolutionary feast' (2000: 11). An even grumpier Kenneth Baker objected to the idea that the people of England should be treated as 'the residue of constitutional change', inverting their true significance within the

United Kingdom (1998: 15). In short, one can indicate a mood of English discontent that politicians were beginning tentatively to detect, to express or to promote, though it is wise to be cautious about attributing depth to that mood. Here appeared to be a condition of contemporary Englishness in which the politics of identity, predicated on the notion of a lack, intersected with the politics of territorial institutions, now also predicated on the notion of a lack. Together they suggested that Englishness was being denied and, even if *what* was being denied remained rather vague, this sense of denial can be traced in a number of English anxieties.

States of anxiety

How have these anxieties been expressed? What is the provenance of these anxieties? One persuasive, historically contextualised, suggestion has been provided by Clark who argued that the great historical schools which dominated British discourse for almost two centuries – imperialism, liberal constitutionalism and socialism – had now disintegrated. The imperialist school had collapsed by the beginning of the Second World War, the liberal constitutionalist school, by far the most influential, had lost confidence in its explanatory framework by the beginning of the 1970s and the socialist school disintegrated during the 1980s, dealt a crushing blow locally by Mrs Thatcher and globally by the collapse of communism. 'Now that the old overarching ideologies have been deconstructed,' thought Clark, 'it seems likely that *all* cultural images will look as if they are regionally and culturally specific' (1990b: 95). This represented a distinctive alteration in public understanding because if *everything* was regionally and culturally specific then the one thing remaining, now that the old universal gods had departed, was national identity. The effect may not be as thorough-going as Clark implied but he had identified a turn with the potential to be profoundly disquieting in the post-devolution era. 'There is an anxiety about what it means to be English today,' argued Paul Gilroy, 'that has reached a level of intensity in the past five years' and modern English anxiety has taken a number of forms (cited in Hill 2004).

The first is the anxiety of absence. In his consideration of *English Imaginaries* (1998), Kevin Davey's objective was to bring 'England's national imaginary' up to date and this was an urgent need, he believed, because the English 'are experiencing with a new intensity long-standing fears of engulfment, evanescence and separation' (1998: 10). Davey's sense of evanescence and separation as a product of the dissociation of the national and the popular provided a strong echo of Nairn's critical legend. However, the problem in this case appeared to go much deeper than even Nairn envisaged. Davey cited the joke of the French Neoist Alliance: 'Since the English do not exist we won't bother to reinvent them' and while Davey's was a manifesto of re-invention, the joke illuminated a deeper anxiety. For the fear expressed in the anxiety of absence is that Englishness has indeed become nothing, that the English do not exist and that they may never be rein-vented. For example, one *Guardian* report referred to a study by the Joseph Rowntree Trust, based on interviews with 600 school children in four English towns, which found that for most 'white kids' being English meant nothing. It cited other studies which had found a deep degree loss even in some middle-class districts. Insecurity, it was argued, had become 'the elephant in the room in the identity debate' and that there was a growing school of thought which felt that this particular anxiety – 'the absence of a strong, meaningful sense of Englishness' – had become a real cultural handicap (Bunting 2005). Other countries have experienced similar disturbance so why should this English anxiety be felt so acutely?

Its English particularity may be traced to the assumption, as Paxman illustrated, of notable self-possession: that Englishness was of universal, not just local significance – an exemplary exception – and so did not have to adopt, to use Buruma's illustration, the Bavarian stratagem of cultural distinctiveness (see Chapter 2). Here was a double English tragedy since the sense of world-historical significance had been lost but the cultural inheritance of this legend remained as a crippling cultural absence. The other side of being everything turns out to be being nothing. Englishness had few cultural barriers against first Americanisation and now globalisation and according to Roger Scruton, globalisation had been felt more keenly in England than else-where because 'it has induced in the English the sense that they are really living nowhere' (2000: 246). The nation of shopkeepers has refashioned itself into the nation of shoppers, its identity defined by patterns of consumption rather than by patterns of belonging. Whereas someone like Bryant understood patriotism to be a compound of faith in British justice and voluntary subordination of the individual to this larger purpose, today it is understood as spend-ing more on credit to sustain economic confidence – or at least, that is what the anxiety of absence suspects. Nor is this an anxiety that is confined to conservatives. Martin Jacques lamented that the country had failed to become cosmopolitan as the old Empire collapsed in upon itself and 'substance has been replaced by vacuity, grandeur has given way to self-absorption, historical destiny to an obsession with celebrity' with the result England had become deeply parochial (Jacques 2004). Of course there are those, especially novelists, who seem to take pleasure in an anxiety that feeds English self-contempt. According to the novelist J. G. Ballard – unselfconsciously part of a venerable tradition of inverted Podsnappery – the problem is that the English continue to think of themselves as a great nation when they are so obviously not: 'We're just beginning to suspect that we're not even great in the way the Italians are great, or the French or the Germans.' Ballard's vision of modern England is the M25, with its 'car rental shops, business parks and video shops where most people live' and, like those in the Massingham tradition, he finds the prospect appalling. There is no virtue in Englishness at all and Ballard falls willingly into the void of the anxiety. 'Even though we're obsessed with leaving the country and talk of nothing but holidays abroad, we react with xenophobic terror to the thought of losing our national identity. If only we had an identity to lose ...' (cited in Wakefield 2001: 23). This is a mischievous un-truth, of course, but the un-truth does express the truth of a notable anxiety. A sustained presentation of the anxiety can also be found in Julian Barnes's novel *England, England* (1999) which rather contemptuously posed contemporary England with a choice between the vacuity of national heritage and the vacuity of backwardness. Presenting the choice thus is a creative misreading of English possibilities but an accurate reading of a self-indulgent English cultural melancholy.

The second anxiety is the anxiety of silence, an anxiety which explicitly or implicitly involves the suspicion of conspiracy and this anxiety can be found in even the most sober of commentaries. For example, one judicious assessment of England's place in the devolved United Kingdom contained a rather revealing line: 'Until and if it becomes inescapable, England's role in the UK may well remain bound by the same virtual conspiracy of silence as for most of the twentieth century.' The conspiracy here is intent either on keeping the 'English question' out of political debate or confining it exclusively to 'issues of efficiency of government' in order to avoid raising the issue of national identity (Sandford 2002: 790). More obviously, Richard Weight concluded his survey of post-war British history with reference to England's sense of national dislocation. He had little time for the 'Celtic elites' whose interest after devolution now appeared to be that of suppressing the potential of English people and denying them their proper due. He had even less time for those on both the left and the right who had been traditionally dismissive of their own people. At the beginning of the new millennium, the English were therefore faced not only with a stubborn, self-serving political elite, but also with a myopic intellectual elite, unwilling to weave England's 'many-splendoured features into a coherent, progressive picture around which the country could unite' (Weight 1999: 27). In short, 'England, the last stateless nation in the United Kingdom, was leaderless and adrift' (2002: 726). Weight's was partly an exercise in self-pity, but only partly, since there was sufficient evidence to confirm his criticism of some in the English elite, political and cultural. When mixed with a sense of deprivation, of course, this is the basic stuff of nationalist grievance. The emphasis of this argument has been to highlight what the English are being denied and what apparently is being denied to them is what the non-English always thought the English had in abundance – self-confidence. One touchstone for some has been the silence of the political elite on the proper commemoration of St George's Day. This may be a legacy of England's former universalism which rendered such particular commemoration redundant but it has become a mark of the perceived conspiracy of political leaders against the 'many-splendoured' identity of England. As Sandford concluded, much of this subterranean anxiety can be attributed to the fact that 'virtually no public debate has taken place on the governance of England' (2002: 791).

The anxiety of silence intimates an even deeper national malaise. It is that young people are no longer told the story of England and the educational system has been designed 'to leave them with, at best, a belief that they have nothing to be proud of because they are English, at worst that they should be thoroughly ashamed of the fact' (Henderson 2004). The anxiety imagines a generation that has little knowledge of anything beyond the present, a generation that has become effectively deracinated. Scruton thought that this process constituted the 'forbidding of England' and here his conservative instinct connected with the radical criticism of Weight. Both of them hold that national pride has been relinquished by English opinion makers who 'laugh at the culture and institutions that might have been theirs' (Scruton 2000: 250). Because of this silence about the positive achievements in English history – and this is one of the consequences of the exhaustion of the liberal constitutional school – people are that more susceptible to the empty attractions of the three-minute global culture. This culture is just a greater silence because it has nothing meaningful or lasting to say and here the anxiety of silence and the anxiety of absence complement one another. If the English language has spanned the globe the cultural consequence is that the former exemplary exception of English culture has been rendered mute.

A third anxiety is the anxiety of anticipation. It is a premonition of abandonment that resembles Kipling's lines about empire, where 'the beginning of the end is born already' and as 'men count time the end is far off; but as we, who know, reckon, it is to-day' (1898: 41–2). The anticipation in this case is not the end of empire but the end of the United Kingdom or the anxiety that, while the other nations are coming out from under the 'safety blanket' of Britishness, the English will be smothered under its folds. This is thought to be not so much a political as a psychological problem. The confusion of English and British is no longer just a failure to acknowledge the proprieties of nomenclature in a multi-national Union, but a failure to acknowledge the world the English are now in. If historians and critics had decon-structed Anglo-centricity there had been a failure to re-discover Englishness before *and* after it was British. There is expressed a longing to define clear lines in order that England will avoid becoming 'some sort of British rump' (Bragg 1996: 15). What is being given voice to here is a mood of identity-sickness, a sense of the nauseous quality of things as they are in England today. That mood can be captured best by the Russian word *skushno*, a word that is difficult to translate into English but may be understood to convey 'a spiritual void that sucks you in like a vague but intensely urgent longing' (von Rezzori 1984). The void is the absent popular and the urgent longing is to fill it with a beautiful vision of a new England. There is a sense of living amidst the ruins of an old country, amid the decay of an old state and the fear is the fear of becoming historically superfluous, of being left behind, of failing the test of modernity or even postmodernity. It has encouraged some on both the left and the right of politics to propose that the choice for England is between remaining within a decadent Britishness and recovering a popular Englishness long suppressed by elitist snobbery.

A fourth anxiety is the anxiety of imitation. Following a weekend in which the televising of the rugby Six Nations had attracted a large audience, the *Daily Telegraph* correspondent Jim White commented on a remarkable discovery: 'Question any collection of blokes in a London bar,' he wrote, 'all of them living in England, all with English accents, and at least half of them will support Ireland, Scotland or Wales.' However, there appeared to have been an interesting transfor-mation in national allegiance: 'For a while this year everyone was Irish; now suddenly they've all turned Welsh.' The whimsy of the article suggests that what continues to be distinctive about Englishness is the lack of interest it has in itself, at least insofar as that interest would translate into classic nationalism. The English do not worry about what national team to support because it is irrelevant to their self-esteem (White 2005; for a very different view of the 'universe of white Englishness' see Hickman et al. 2005). However, the anxiety of imitation takes this apparent insouciance to mean a lack of self-esteem and possibly lurking beneath the tolerant surface is a very different culture of envy and resentment. In other words, the anxiety holds that this condition is a product of self-loathing, a condition for which even Weight's Englishness provides evidence. For half a century, he claimed, 'English society had been profoundly racist' and the greed of the Thatcher years made it harder for the English to claim that 'they were a people with a social conscience'. Partial redemption was to come from an unusual source, football, for years one of the major causes for national self-loathing. In 1996 it was to help transform England 'from a vile antithesis of a nation' into one 'trying to rediscover itself by synthesizing the cultural changes of the postwar years' (1999: 26). If the anthem of Euro96 for English fans was the song 'Football's coming home' then the significance of the tournament was the intimation that England was coming home to itself. This was one sort of return at least and what the English needed to do, according to the anxiety of imitation, was to assert themselves – but in a self-confident and agreeable way. This anxiety assumes that other national identities are cuddly, likeable and fun and the linkage of this certain idea of England to comparisons of international football support is obvious. The world seems to love Irish or Italian supporters because they are _not_ English. The English must try to become as cuddly and likeable and fun as the others (so long as one does not bother to look too deeply into their cultures).

There is another material dimension to this anxiety. In the more transparently national bargaining system for resources within the United Kingdom, there is a call for an end to English reticence. The other nations are taking advantage of England's lack of corporate identity and the English must advance their own identity politics if they are to protect their interests (Kundnani 2000: 15). Self-esteem is to be re-discovered in self-promotion and even though most English people might not feel particularly anxious 'yet they have noticed that, nowadays, nationalist whingeing seems to pay off'. The English have decided that they should begin to play the identity game, though even this rather ironic form of self-assertion is freighted with a conspiratorial sense of the anxiety of silence. The left-wing elite wishes either England was Irish and 'hates its fellow countrymen for their stubborn refusal to embrace ideological correctness' or wishes it was Italian and 'despises its countrymen for their vulgarity and stroppiness' (Cox 2002). That *New Statesman* view found its companion in the *Spectator* view. 'Britain's self-loathing is deep, pervasive and lethally dangerous,' argued Anthony Browne, and the 'only thing we are licensed to be proud of is London's internationalism – in other words, that there is little British left about it.' The time was ripe for a new, self-confident story of the Churchillian sort about the nation (Browne 2005a: 10). These are half truths but again the truth of the anxiety is to be found in these exaggerations of national self-loathing. Taken together, these four anxieties re-enforce and draw upon one another but do not necessarily promote the adoption of any single political option. The mood is the message. That mood can be described as 'irritable growl syndrome', a complaint of varying intensity against present conditions.

A more balanced view (in the English idiom) can be found in the remarks of Paul Laity. He thought that neither the British in general nor the English in particular felt particularly favoured any longer and that the 'cult of island freedom has fewer and fewer followers'. People 'are reconciled to the loss of Empire, are less sure than ever that their constitutional arrangements are uniquely valuable, and understand that their nation is not too grand to be contained within Europe'. In short, they 'seem to have realised that God may not, after all, be an Englishman'. However, none of this should be a cause for *Weltschmerz*. In that familiar manner of English scepticism, Laity thought that just 'as announcements of the deliquescence of Britain seem premature, so talk of a more specific English identity "crisis" is surely hyperbolic'. Moreover, England will continue to persist as a political community and (in his wish-fulfillment prediction) the 'majority of English people will remain, well ... very *English*, even after the monarchy has been abolished, MEPs are household names and Britain has had a black Prime Minister' (2002). Yet in the engagement with the present, these anxieties and anti-anxiety reveal the trace of Baucom's historical supply lines and should be considered within a long tradition of reflections about the character of English politics. For all the reasons suggested in this chapter there has been something of a turn towards recovering a sense of Englishness and distinguishing Englishness from Britishness. However, it was also the contention of this chapter that this turn has provoked a number of anxieties, ones that are more likely to be found amongst intellectuals, who worry professionally on behalf of others about questions of national identity, than they are amongst the English public. These present anxieties are intimately connected with contested visions of the character of English nationality and have deep roots in the national imagination. The great success of the legend of civic patriotism was that it provided a reasonably stable accommodation, if not reconciliation, of those visions (Freeden 1998: 765; Stapleton 2000a: 268). The attraction of the critical legend has been its ability to specify where the instability and the anomalies of that accommodation can be found. Chapters 6 and 7 explore the ambiguous and ambivalent outworking of these anxieties in contemporary engagements with the 'particular' of Englishness. The first is a left/liberal version of the English 'particular' that celebrates a civic, liberal, multi-ethnic idea of Englishness, an idea that it struggles to reconcile with concerns about native populism. The second is a conservative version of the English 'particular' that celebrates – if not unreservedly – a more populist idea of England, an idea that it struggles to reconcile with civic, liberal and multi-ethnic values.

6

England.co.uk

In 1999, Richard Weight announced that the 'English left has a great opportunity: to become, for the first time in half a century, the party of patriotism' and if they were only to raise their heads from theory and to look more sympathetically at their own people 'liberals and socialists might see that the development of a radical patriotism is still possible in England' (1999: 26). The task was one of recovery *and* modernisation, a task which the left once thought it had achieved in 1945 (see Ward 1998). Yet this positive case for Englishness derived from familiar concerns. In November 2004 an article in the *New Statesman* with the title 'Reclaiming England' exhorted its readers to embrace a new radical patriotism while also expressing a deep cultural anxiety. The English, it claimed, had become a 'lost people' primarily because what formerly had distinguished the country was being transformed by global capitalism into 'soulless non-places'. Consequently, and with disturbing rapidity, 'England is becoming a one-stop shop on a road to a global market peopled by citizens of nowhere'. Echoing the sentiments of inter-war critics of urbanisation, ribbon-development and road building (see Matless 2001), here was a horrid vision of an England in which the local pub had been lost to the giant pub chain, where the high street had become a multinational mall, where villages had become commuter suburbs, where orchards had been grubbed up and farms become agri-businesses and where town centres atrophied as corporate mega-stores took up residence on the ubiquitous ring-road. For good measure there was a lament for the landscape in which authentic English culture used to be glimpsed whereas in the new despoiled England resided now 'a people anxious about their identity'. Since it had contributed to the shameful 'deculturisation' of the English people, the left bore some of the responsibility. The only positive message in all these negatives was that the left had the chance to become patriotic again. 'We need a new declaration of Englishness', was the conclusion, 'one that takes our country back from the sneerers on the left and the bigots on the right' (Kingsnorth 2004). Like Richard Hoggart's more intellectual lament, the message was to 'realise how far we have fallen' before considering what to do next (Hoggart 1998: 464).

Here was a patriotic appeal at odds with a recently widespread perspective amongst left intellectuals. Two decades earlier, Stephen Howe observed the tendency to distinguish good nationalisms from bad ones 'and that of England is irredeemably "bad"'. It was irredeemably bad because it had been forged in a long and disreputable imperial history whose cult of supremacy had become constitutive of its very character. Therefore, radicals 'cannot realistically hope to turn self-images thus moulded' to their own very different objectives (1989: 137). That perspective, however, suffered from what Susan Condor called 'the presumption' of radical social theory, the presumption being that its interpretation alone could draw on qualitatively superior visionary resources when reflecting on national identity. This has all the qualities of a misreading since in her experience social theorists assumed their intellectual task to be the exposure of the conservative and probably reactionary nature of popular 'commonsense' and this overlooked the ability of people to be as critically reflective as the intellectual on their own nationhood (Condor 1997: 251). Until very recently the contest for left intellectuals appeared to be between universals such as conservatism and socialism and from this perspective, Englishness was just 'a peculiar conservative nationalism whose construction has led to an exclusive rather than inclusive identity' (Taylor 1993: 139). For now, at least, this attitude has waned, though it would be foolish to claim that it has disappeared entirely (see, for example, Steele 2006). The trend has been towards the recovery of an older and ethically dramatic sense of Englishness, a secular version of the religiously-informed radicalism of former times. As Stanton Coit put it in 1900: 'There are two Englands just as there were two Israels – one worshipping Baal, the other serving God' (cited in Geoghegan 2003: 510). Today's radical patriots also claim that they are on the side of God's England, albeit the God of liberal democratic inclusiveness, and in the formulation of their concerns they confirmed Oakeshott's notion of a tradition, one capable of swerving back to recover and to make something topical out of even its remotest moments. If there was an ambiguity in the faith it lay in another familiar divide. Was the new England already in existence on earth, although hidden beneath the remains of imperial Britishness; or was the new England a destiny unfulfilled, a project to be achieved by political struggle and social reconstruction? This distinction between the *already is* and the *not yet* can be traced in the recent debates about the character of radical patriotism and this distinction is much more important politically than the distinction between that minority, like Weight, who want to promote England's political independence and those, like Crick, who want to promote cultural self-confidence amongst the English people, though of course these two positions may shade into one another. It is the lineage of this approach which can be revealing.

Becoming English once again

In an essay written in 1964, the novelist John Fowles wrote that his Britishness was a mere superficial conversion of his fundamental Englishness. 'In all the personal situations that are important to me,' he wrote, 'I am English, not British' and he repeated the radical trope that the authentic English ideal was always a subversive one: to live in a country that was not the strongest in the world but the most *just*. This 'often puritanical obsession with justice' was for Fowles 'the quintessence of Englishness' and he explained the expansion abroad of the English partly in terms of this 'mania' for justice: 'The *reason* for the emigration has often been nationalistic ("British") or individualistic (selfish), but the *quality* of the emigration has depended and still depends much more on its Englishness (that is, on the spreading and maintaining of our concept of justice) than on its Britishness (the desire to spread and maintain imperialistic and master race ideals) or its individualism (the desire merely to live abroad)' (Fowles 1998: 83). In this radically Whiggish formulation, Englishness represented the spirit of Robin Hood not that of John Bull. Fowles symbolically called this spirit 'green' and the essay was a powerful statement of the idea of a radical English *return* from the British red-white-and-blue – and it is interesting to note that Paxman used more or less the same formulation when he argued that for the English today 'the red-white-and-blue is no longer relevant and they are returning to the green of England' (1998: 264). Like Sir Ernest Barker before him, Fowles thought that the English were psychologically averse to *Weltschmerz* because they could be neither Spenglerians nor martyrs and he also thought that their philosophy was one of 'make do', one which was devoted 'to reform justly, or at least to ensure that just reform is always a possibility' (1998: 88; see also Ingelbien 2004: 161– 4). If this may be thought a rather curious and dated way to understand the English radical tradition, a variant of it can be found in many other reflections on radical patriotism. In Jonathan Freedland's *Bringing*

Home The Revolution, for example, the Robin Hood qualities of justice and popular assertiveness that informed Fowles's spirited Englishness had indeed been exported, in this case to the United States. 'The founding principles of the US,' argued Freedland, 'were British ideas of liberty and democracy, which somehow slipped out of our hands and drifted across the Atlantic' (1998: 14). Freedland's message, rather like Fowles's a generation ago, was that it is time for the country to become green again in spirit and for the 'revolution' to be repatriated. His 'nationalism of ideas' was faithful to an earnest tradition of justice and popular improvement which distinguished itself from – as Fowles distinguishes the (eternal) English green from the British red-white-and-blue – the corruptions of the established order, both British and American. Thomas Paine and others, who in the eighteenth century had formulated the principles of American democracy, 'were the British left of their day'. At the beginning of the twenty-first century, 'the British left should reclaim those dreams for our own time' (Freedland 1998: 26). Here is a very literal return and Freedland is only unusual in that, unlike the prevailing consensus on the left, he continues to hold American ideals and practice in such high esteem (2005). If Freedland's was a statement of the *not yet* others were frustrated by the denial of the *already is*. Weight's survey of British history since 1945, *Patriots*, concluded that there was 'a crisis of English national identity' and this crisis 'was made worse by the fact that they [the English] had never developed a sufficiently democratic narrative of their national identity with which to launch themselves into a post-Union world'. The solution to England's sense of dislocation, the solution to the democratic deficit in English politics, required dismantling a decadent Britishness and confirming the vibrant Englishness that was already welling up beneath the political surface. The British state was a product of external colonialism 'primarily established to further the quest for Empire' and was not an authentic expression of the English national popular. Now that the external prop of imperialism had gone, it was time for England to acknowledge itself as a nation once again (Weight 2002: 725–7). In short, what the old Union flag represented 'is becoming a foreign country' to most English people (Weight 1999: 25). Weight's English patriotism would be inclusive (there will be black in the flag of St George) and it was already detected by him in the culture of that most maligned group, England's national football supporters. This is what Pocock once dismissively called 'that populist, soccer-fan Republic of St George' which occasionally has taken shape in recent radical imaginings (2000: 46).

It is worth summarising the constituents of this radical view of

English nationality and that nationality's supposed British 'deformation'. The argument relies upon a simple opposition between what Britishness *has been* and what Englishness has now or will *become*. On the one hand, traditional Britishness is taken to mean imperialism, monarchism, conservatism, hierarchy, racism, masculinity, militarism and xenophobia. On the other hand, an emerging Englishness (though not necessarily English *nationalism*) is taken to herald multiculturalism, egalitarianism, democracy, radicalism, international (specifically European) cooperation, modernism and openness to other cultures. Here are the lineaments of a new project, detached from old-style socialism and attached to the cause of national regeneration. Here is a discursive framework that would seem 'to guarantee the emergence of an Englishness unblemished by either the Empire or backward-looking little-Englandism' (Ingelbien 2002: 218). At its centre is a modern populism and, as Margaret Canovan has argued, populism is not just a reaction against established structures of power but also an appeal to a recognised authority: the people. This style of politics distinguishes between two forms of democracy, the 'redemptive' and the 'pragmatic'. Pragmatic democracy stresses rules and practices and above all it means institutions, 'institutions not just to limit power, but also to constitute it and make it effective'. Redemptive democracy, on the other hand, is one of a family of radical visions holding out the promise of secular transformation. Ultimately, 'the romantic impulse to directness, spontaneity and the overcoming of alienation' lies at its heart. Without the power of the redemptive, pragmatic democracy becomes an empty shell and a 'recipe for corruption'. In such circumstances, the populist must appeal 'past the ossified institutions to the living people' and this is what some of the radical literature on Englishness seeks to do (Canovan 1999: 8–10).

One interpretation holds that we are witnessing the growth of a new style of popular politics because, paradoxically, one pillar of democracy – the popular one – has been under-developed while the second – the executive one – has been strengthened. This has contributed to 'the progressive isolation of governing elites from people's pressures' and it has become the basis of institutional alienation (Meny 2002: 4). Another interpretation traces the emergence of a 'new populism' to the crisis of legitimacy in 'the political agenda, institutions and legitimacy of the modern welfare-state model of mixed-economy capitalism' (Taggart 2000: 73–84). Yet another finds the attraction of populism in a better educated and more emancipated electorate: 'As a consequence of the egalitarianism of the 1960s, citizens today expect more from politicians, and feel more competent to judge their actions. This cognitive mobilisation has led citizens to stop accepting that the elites think for them, and to no longer blindly swallow what the elites tell them' (Mudde 2004: 554). This implies an historical shift from the *quantitative* democracy appropriate to an industrialised society to the *qualitative* democracy appropriate to a post-industrial society and the shift is supposed to be related to a new democratic self-understanding that demands 'rational accountability' (Cooke 2000: 967). Since we are, or think ourselves to be, better educated, better informed, more sophisticated, more critical and intelligent consumers of ideas than previous generations then the activity of politics must be made to correspond with our sense of 'who we are'. The radical motivation is to develop what Young calls 'deep democracy', an active engagement to widen the political conversation (2002: 50–1). As Haseler described the case in England, popularity in a democratic age imposes democratic demands upon politicians, demands which challenge the old deferential English system. 'A beguiled democratic people are not slaves to the fantasy of antiquated authority; rather, they are increasingly instrumental in their public fantasies, wanting of them what *they* want, not necessarily what is on offer' (Haseler 1990: 424). Here is a democratic alternative intimating the emergence of new forms of social co-operation and it is one which stresses inventiveness, reconstituting politics around the dynamics of an engaged public discussion. In short, it represents an attempt to make democracy operate explicitly on the basis of what it implicitly is for modern *people like us*. The emphasis of some current thinking is to suggest that this is most appropriately and effectively done in re-imagining Englishness, either inside or outside the United Kingdom (for a radical interpretation of this idea see Wainwright 2004).

In this regard, the long-standing attraction of Nairn's critical legend is obvious since it made exactly that contrast between the cult of formality, the empty ritual of British institutions and the will of the national popular with its radical democratic potential. As Rodney Barker argued, there has developed a widespread assumption that within the United Kingdom one is witnessing a movement of the people against the state and the most consistent element 'is that national and ethnic groups are popular, democratic communities, in which the ordinary citizen plays a full and powerful role'. Barker was suitably sceptical of this assumption, believing it to be another misreading of Englishness, but he did acknowledge the attraction of the contrast between the 'populist phenomenon' of community and a governing elite which allegedly holds the state together 'in artificial uniformity in defiance of their national or ethnic character' (Barker

1995: 209). In the particular case of England, this contrast is thought to be all the more tragic since now the Scots, Welsh and Northern Irish have their own (potentially) redemptive, devolved democracies. The English, on the other hand, are for the moment condemned to live in the rotting hulk (or 'sweaty sock' as Billy Bragg once called it) of the old imperial system. Post-devolution, 'England's governing institutions are Britain's governing institutions, leaving expressions of English nationalism very little alternative but to remain within the previous discourses of empire and nation' (Wellings 2002: 107).

It is this fate that the new, *already become*, radicalism wants to change. Pragmatically, the old order, especially the Queen if not the Royal Family, may retain some residual respect amongst the people but for those who proclaim the national popular the system is ulti-mately irredeemable. Populism requires, as Nairn foresaw, a project of political mobilisation if it is to be anything more than the emotional outpouring of the soccer fan republicans. The problem for the left in England, it has been thought, is the distinctive conservative colonisa-tion of the patriotic mind. R. W. Johnson once argued that the national popular was undermined linguistically by the fact that the term 'public' and not 'the people' is used in English political discourse and 'public' has a more restricted and reserved meaning, confining the people to a subordinate position within class society (1985: 230–4; see also Wright 1985: 87). The popular in the political sense had been rejected in English political history because democracy *en masse* was considered to have no will or if it was considered to have a will, that will was conceived to be anarchic or self-destructive (Tannsjo 1992: 3–4). Indeed, two standard British academic texts on populism had little or nothing to say about England at all (Ionescu and Gellner 1969; Canovan 1981). As a disposition within politics, if not a periodic feature of historical experience, populism appeared to be decidedly un-English. 'I do not suppose,' argued Donald MacRae, 'that there has ever been a genuine English populism' even if there had certainly been English *populists* (1969: 161). Post-1996, it was assumed that things had changed, that liberal academics had been inattentive to the rise of radical patriotism and that the English had already begun to transform themselves. Popular trends had undermined the fabric of traditional Englishness and now that the old barriers to national redemption had begun to fall, the radical task was to make sure that the England which emerged from their collapse was progressive, inclusive and representa-tive of what that (progressive) people the English, in their diversity, *had now become*. Two decades ago that opportunity would have meant replacing conservatism (monarchical, imperialistic, hierarchical, unequal) with socialism (republican, meritocratic, egalitarian, internationalist). Now it meant replacing Britishness (still monarchical, imperialistic, hierarchical, unequal) with a recovered Englishness (already become republican, meritocratic, egalitarian, inclusive, internationalist). And despite the apparent novelty of the argument it too has a history for this identification with an Englishness both authentic *and* radical is a tradition that goes back (at least) to Milton and the Diggers (Collini 2003).

The formula, in short, was this. When it is considered regressive, or conservative, populism is 'the antagonistic construction of the people in opposition to an imaginary liberal elite' but when it is considered progressive, even if the language sounds very like its conservative *alter ego*, populism is the positive construction of the people in opposition to a resistant institutional elite (Reyes 2002: 19). Conservative populism does not want to change the people or their values or their way of life but radical patriotism *does* want to emancipate people fully not only from the old political system (Britain) but also from their old cultural selves (imperial, racist, superior, insular). That redemption must be found in something greater than merely institutional or constitutional change and current conditions appear ripe. Nairn's prediction that the English people would come to elbow their way past the political elite jealously guarding the privileges of the old order had come (partly) true. If we have witnessed the slow death of 'gentlemanly' democracy along with 'gentlemanly' capitalism – the final blows, ironically, having been executed by Mrs Thatcher's Conservative Governments – then here is a double death to the deference which held back the English people (Collins 2002). The positive populist *Zeitgeist* meant, firstly, the end of the snobbish deference that sustained the Conservative Party. It meant, secondly, the end of the class deference that once sustained the Labour Party's embrace of old Britannia. Both were part of the cult of Britishness – no longer credible to modern English *people like us* – and two contrasting illustrations of this simple opposition of British/English may suffice to give a flavour of the intellectual style.

In their exposition of a 'cosmopolitan Englishness', June Edmunds and Bryan S. Turner made the distinction between a 'malign' and a 'benign' identity. The malign version is an Englishness bound up with the old myths of Britishness and its attributes are familiar. It is closed (resentful of Celtic nationalism), insular (threatened by European integration), earnest (believes in a distinctive cultural basis of the nation), masculine (sanctions the imperially militaristic value of dying for one's country) and reactive (tends to be nostalgic, even elegiac). The benign version is open (tolerant of Celtic nationalism), cosmopolitan (open to European integration), ironic (aware of both the contingency and construction of national identity), feminine (peaceful in international affairs) and creative (its values are civic and liberal) (2001: 92–4). Of course, an historical understanding would have made these writers aware that the values of their wished-for cosmopolitan Englishness would have sounded very familiar to liberal stalwarts of the old identity they seek to replace. Moreover, in the way in which Edmunds and Turner described the acceptable parameters of this Englishness – it must be 'ironic' and 'contingent' for example – one wonders why national identity is worth having in the first place. This is nationalism without tears, certainly nationalism without passion, and it suggests a partial misreading of both nationalism and Englishness. The Edmunds-Turner thesis requires the English to be serious about Irish, Scottish and Welsh nationalism, and about the values of ethnic minorities, but not to be serious about their own Englishness. Of course, this lack is the very thing of which Nairn complained and the very thing which had frustrated the emergence of a self-consciously *nationalistic* Englishness in the first place. By a long circuitous theoretical route, Turner and Edmunds appeared to endorse the very ideal of 'traditional' Englishness they set out to challenge and this suggests an original misreading of the question on their part (for a different criticism of the 'tendentious' character of their argument, see Bryant 2003: 406). The problem lies in the failure to note the incompatibility between 'irony' and 'contingency' in national identity. If irony there is, surely it lies in the thought that only when national identity is relatively solid and secure can the people can afford to behave as if everything is indeed contingent and constructed. That luxury is the consequence of the stability of Englishness and not something that emerges as its alternative. A profound sense of the 'enduring' of England in history ('There'll always be an England', even a radical England) appears to make English*ness* more open to the 'difference' they both desire. In other words, the proposals of Turner and Edmunds are unselfconsciously English and assume a vast hinterland of historical experience. According to Colls, the English never did lose their desire to belong but at the same time 'for all of the modern period', they put themselves in positions of 'extraordinary openness to the cultures of other peoples' (2002: 380). It is what cannot be seen when most of the flags of St George are taken down that remains a better guide to the politics of Englishness. The lack of an overt nationalism does not mean the absence of nationality and the truth has been and continues to be quite the reverse.

A more popular and engaging consideration of these questions can be found in the lyrics and journalism of the singer Billy Bragg. He faithfully reproduced the Nairn formula for English emancipation when, in his song 'Take Down the Union Jack', Bragg announced that Britain 'isn't cool' and not 'really great' it is just 'an economic union that's passed its sell-by date'. Britishness, for Bragg as it was for Fowles, is represented by the Queen handing out MBEs with all the discredited trappings of a lost imperial heritage and the English should take their cue from the Scots who have turned 'an abstract notion' of identity into 'nationhood'. As the song advised, it was time for the English to take down the Union Jack and learn how to become 'an Anglo hyphen Saxon in England.co.uk'. The 'hyphen' represents the virtue of the 'mongrel' quality of Englishness, an idea as old as Daniel Defoe (1997) and '.co.uk' the requirement to make English identity conform to the contemporary needs of modern *people like us*. Bragg developed the political logic of these lyrics in a number of newspaper articles and interviews. Reflecting on the appearance of the ubiquitous Cross of St George along many English streets, he invited readers of the *Daily Mirror* to ask themselves which flag, the Cross of St George or the Union Jack, best represented the country as it is today. The first, he thought, symbolised the country as it already is 'vibrant, multicultural and forward looking'. The second 'always seems to be in the hands of those who wish to look back to our imperial past'. Britishness, this imperial construct, was an identity whose time has gone because the time for England had now come. 'To my mind, British culture identifies too strongly with the monarchy, the Union Jack and the Empire. That narrow definition is mirrored in the Royal Family itself. Compare it to the England you see out there representing us in the World Cup. Which group best reflects the make-up of the country?' (2002a). Bragg thought that the task for the left (as Weight also thought) was to reclaim the notion of Englishness and to wrest the idea of patriotism from the hands of the right. By 'attempting to distance ourselves' from Englishness, he thought, radicals only allowed 'the far right' to dominate the debate. 'Are we in England,' asked Bragg, 'going to sit by and watch the Scots, Welsh and Irish struggle for devolution, unable to join in because we are squeamish about hoisting the flag of St George?' We English 'deserve our independence too, from the imperial state that we live in' (1995: 14). For too long the left 'has tip-toed around the notion of Englishness' but now it must directly engage with the new populism (1996: 15). 'What I want is a compassionate society. I think we can build socialism through accountability. Yes, we can build it around philosophers such as Marx, but that language is dead, we need new ideas and a new ideology' (2002b). Bragg was demanding here, as Nairn had suggested a quarter of a century earlier, that English cultural nationalism should now come to a sharper awareness of its own nature and purpose and that finally the English variety of left-nationalist popular culture should shift from ideas of socialism as an *alternative* to Englishness to ideas of Englishness as a path to what socialism once promised. One of his solutions was for the English to find a communal way of celebrating itself, an alternative, radical St George's Day that stressed cultural diversity rather than the ethnocentric stereotype of Morris dancing. As one astute commentator remarked, 'Bragg clears his "mantelpiece" of all the rubbish other people have put on it and puts on it whatever he feels is characteristic of a multicultural, liberal, patriotic Englishness' (Reichl 2004: 217). This may be an appealing display but Bragg's mantelpiece only demonstrated the difficulty and did not solve it.

One of the long-standing problems for English radicalism has been the tension in this analysis between the politics of inclusion and the politics of the national popular, the resolution of which has been assumed but never fully reasoned through. To what extent, then, was the English nation that Bragg desired actually a very complex – if unequal – social reality (*already is*) or a specific project of the political imagination (yet to *become*)? To what extent were the traditional elitist reservations about populism the very condition of liberty? Radicals themselves were never too sure and it has been the source of another profound anxiety. On the one hand, there has long been disenchantment with the aristocratic embrace of the Labour Party and its acceptance of constitutionalism, disenchantment that led some to look favourably upon extra-parliamentary measures. On the other hand, there was the suspicion that English people actually were more reactionary (and racist) in their opinions than either the Labour or the Tory establishment. In other words, English radicals may continue to be romantically attached to the cause of the people but only insofar as the people behave as they ought. And what has troubled their conscience is the unpredictable quality of the nationalism that may be called forth during the fall of the rotting British constitution. As Schopflin has claimed, English identity was never primarily ethnic and English identity was 'intimately bound up with class'. Whereas continental Europeans 'have ethnicity, the English have class'. For Schopflin the reason why attempts to change the class basis of Englishness have foundered is because class status has given the majority of English people 'a very clear and very secure identity' and this applied as much

to the working class as to the middle class. The subtle English snobberies and inverted snobberies were actually conducive to social and
political stability. They also appeared to have had one important and
positive effect: since England was actually rare in subordinating
ethnicity to class 'this has helped to make the country relatively open
to migrants, exiles and other foreigners' (Schopflin 2000: 323). This
may be a conclusion arrived at by a different route than the reasoning
of Colls but it is one that is remarkable in its consistency. However,
politicising the 'national popular' of Englishness risked ethnicising
those attitudes often 'cognitively blanked out' by the old snobbery.

Though it is a misreading of Englishness if left unqualified,
Schopflin's argument did capture one thing brilliantly and that was not
so much the conservatism of English identity as the dilemma of radical
Englishness. He captured well the frustration with the survivals of the
old class-ridden culture but also the anxiety that popular Englishness
may not be so respectful of 'difference' as radicals would like. He
captured the radical hostility for hierarchy that is thought to be
geographical as well as social but also the hesitation about reconstituting Englishness in regional form (see Chapter 8). The decline of the
'cult of the gentleman', itself a metaphor for Englishness-as-class, may
not be an unmixed blessing and this was something acknowledged by
the more astute sympathisers of a 'new Englishness' (Crick 1995: 179).
The old Englishness of class may have offended the egalitarian spirit
but this analysis suggests that it could be replaced by a nationalistic
offence to the spirit of tolerance. In other words, there has often
existed a subtext of mistrust for the very English identity that is being
proposed and rather like the German left's support for European integration, the radical version of Englishness often appears to incorpo-
rate a revulsion against the very thing it desires. This can be fear, as in
Mike Marqusee's declaration during the 2006 World Cup that the only
result which mattered was that England did not win because it would
'ignite an orgy of nationalistic celebration' as if that sort of celebration
would *not* take place anywhere else, a declaration which again
revealed a peculiarly English attitude. It can also be loathing, captured
succinctly in Paul Gilroy's radical horror at 'the "two world wars and
one world cup" variety of belligerent, alcohol-fuelled nativism'. This
revulsion was also one of the driving forces of post-colonial, multicultural politics that demanded a turning away 'from the morbidities' of
living in England. 'The distinctive mix of revisionist history and moral
superiority' that has often informed the radical embrace of the
national popular in England 'offers pleasures and distractions that
defer a reckoning with contemporary multiculture and postpone the

inevitable issue of imperial reparation' (Gilroy 1999: 67; see also 2005). Here was an 'incorrigibly primitive beast' best kept locked up in its cage of guilt and self-loathing, irrespective of the culturally inclusive flag-waving of the Cross of St George. That attitude has been a more authentic expression of the attitude of the English (intellectual) left in recent history and as Crick remembered it most of them 'used to regard any discussion of their own national identity as subversive of the purity of the Word and a distraction from the Good News of the class struggle'. Most of his adult life he had found, like the subject of his biography George Orwell, 'that most of my fellow left-wing intellectuals' were suckers for other nationalisms but 'contemptuous of (and what is sometimes even more dangerous, ignorant of) their own' (Crick 1989: 27).

The paradox for radicals, as Canovan observed, is that they appear to be saying to the people (at least, in some theoretical formulations): '*We* are in charge of humanity. *We* will consider authorising you to run your own affairs, provided we are convinced that you will do it in our way, not in yours' (2001: 209). Popular Englishness must have no hint of 'nativism' and if it does, it cannot be permitted. This is an attempt to domesticate the prowling beast and can lead to the further paradox of those who, like Turner and Bryant, look for salvation to a cosmopolitan Englishness. The paradoxical fact here, argued Canovan, 'is that although in some future state of the world the doves of universalist humanitarianism may roost in some kind of non-national space-station powered by its own sources of solidarity, for the moment they take flight from the bounded and exclusive havens provided by nation-states' (2001: 213). In contemporary form is played out here yet again Stapleton's historical contest between citizenship and patriotism in English discourse.

Multi-cultural and national

As Stapleton has shown, the intellectual appeal of multiculturalism for the left was grounded in the decaying plausibility of its traditional statist approach. Multiculturalism implied the mobilisation of civil society in the cause of a radical form of citizenship which involved 'active political participation, on the one hand, and diversity, on the other' (2001: 190). Diversity for some may be universally individualised as a result of the variety of modern existence and nationality here is merely one aspect of a person's identity, no more important and possibly less significant than others. One may be English by birth, but so what when everything else meaningful in one's life, from French

food to Austrian scent, happens to be 'foreign' (Bywater 2000: 11).
The individual citizen consumes not only products but also cultures.
An editorial in the *New Statesman* asked its readers (echoing,
consciously or not, the view of that celebrated 'icon' of pop
Englishness, Malcolm McLaren) to spend 'a morning at an English
country house, move on to a Caribbean carnival, relax in an Irish pub,
round off the day with a Chinese or Indian meal (bearing in mind that
none of these will be nearly as "authentic" as they pretend), and then
ask yourself what Englishness is supposed to mean, and whether you
really need to know' (1999: 5). Personal identity is discovered through
consumption and constructed from a bazaar of possibilities which, in
turn, has deconstructed any notion of Englishness apart from the
empty vessel of 'inclusiveness'. While this understanding may be
appealing, especially to those attracted to the idea of a 'cosmopolitan
Englishness', it has been far from convincing and often superficial.
This is a species of *anti*-patriotism and it has been used mainly as an
argument against thoughtless national assertiveness rather than as a
coherent statement of an alternative. According to George Monbiot, if
'you want to defend liberalism, then defend it, but why conflate your
love for certain values with love for a certain country?' Here was a
classic instance radically opposing the universal of citizenship and the
particular of patriotism. Monbiot did not hate his country and was not
ashamed of his nationality but he had no idea why he should love it
more than any other (Monbiot 2005). Critics of this cosmopolitan
view thought that it only 'conspired to get rid of the real world as a
category of perception, while social science and cultural studies
conspired to get rid of human nature as a category of understanding'.
And so, by 'rejecting all that was determined and centred in favour of
all that was indeterminate, inchoate, messy' they had difficulty coming
to terms with the autonomy of national sentiment (Colls 2002:
352–3). It should be said that Colls did not subscribe to ethnic homogeneity as the basis of English national sentiment, only that in seeking
a new national popular *modus vivendi* 'the nation's propensity for
seeing itself as diverse should not be allowed to outstrip its propensity
for seeing itself as united'. Popular patriotism and the national culture
have been traditionally bound up with questions of origins and tenure
and what was needed, Colls thought, is neither ethnic nationalism nor
centreless pluralism but an engagement to increase 'the number of the
points of origin, and loosening the terms of tenure' but whatever it
became it would never become that mythical beast, exclusively 'civic'
nationalism (Colls 2002: 371). Most serious thinkers, then, have
subscribed neither to postmodern super-individualism nor to commu-

nal exclusivity but have tried to negotiate a way between the two and that has been as true of the right as it has been of the left.

Bhiku Parekh, perhaps the most articulate advocate of the citizenship approach, has written consistently of the inter-relationship of two contrary trends in modern politics. The first is indeed an identity of consumption derived, ironically perhaps, from the homogenising global reach of corporate capitalism. The second is its particularist twin, a return to specific cultural roots. Parekh was optimistic enough to believe that these trends were not necessarily incompatible, that there was no reason 'why one cannot be true to one's own way of life and remain open to the influences of others, choosing and integrating whatever outside elements one considers desirable into one's own way of life'. Multiculturalism was one creative solution to integrate the universal, in this case the 'nation' state, and the particular, its constituent ethnic, religious and cultural groups (1995: 147–9). A state needs some shared view of its identity, yet every such view has the potential 'to demean those outsiders who constitute its acknowledged or unacknowledged point of reference'. Every nation needs to modify its identity according to a redemptive vision of what it ought to be and Parekh set out the criteria necessary to address this paradox of national identity in the United Kingdom. It should be as inclusive as possible and open to revision, acknowledging its history not for the purpose of nostalgia but for the purpose of imagination. It should not inspire collective loyalty alone but also inspire critical reflection on that loyalty and it should encourage a solidarity which links different social groups even if this solidarity was *political* – an association of citizens – rather than *cultural* – a nation of patriots (2000: 7–8). For Parekh, then, modern national identity must be capable of embracing a complex society which contained a significant proportion of citizens who would fail the 'Tebbit test' and who would feel no obligation to cheer on the English cricket team. (That this is not peculiar to the 'ethnic minorities' can be seen in the refusal of the Scottish First Minister to support England in the 2006 World Cup.) Perhaps that radical style of multicultural politics reached its height with the publication of the Parekh *Report on Multi-ethnic Britain* (Runnymede Trust 2000), and the rather embarrassed reception of it by the Labour Government encouraged a shift of emphasis from citizenship alone back to older notions of *patriotic* citizenship.

In the philosophical grounding of this Report, Parekh captured the problematic embrace of the cultural and the national. On the one hand, in demanding less of its citizens in terms of nationality, multiculturalism may expect too much of them in terms of civic virtue. On the other, in appealing to universal principles to defend particular cultural practices it risks contradiction. The ideal is one of 'thin Englishness', an Englishness without any of the comforting myths of unity. 'Let those who live here,' wrote one commentator, 'become a Runnymede nation – in the words of the Trust's Parekh report of 2000, "a community of communities", where identities are fluid and we can link ourselves to whatever group we choose' (Hewison 2003: 43). That was a rather individualistic interpretation that did not quite fit with the cultural pluralism of the Report even if it did correspond with an English tradition that tended to idealise both the tolerant spirit of its race relations but to agonise over the periodic eruption of race hatreds (see Favell 1998). However as one critic argued, the pluralism of the Parekh Report could not just be added to liberal values but was actually in conflict with them. Acknowledging that England (particularly so amongst the British nations) is a multicultural society has no necessary bearing on a policy of *promoting* cultural diversity. That is a political preference, not a logical conclusion, and the consequence of following that line of reasoning may be to 'thin' Englishness into fluid abstraction and 'thicken' ethnicities into rigid communal blocks: 'It is hopelessly inconsistent to call upon universal values as the basis for demands on the majority and not to hold minority communities to the same universal standards.' If the 'national' community has to make fundamental changes according to universal rights claims in order to address 'ethnic' demands then why should not minority communities also be reshaped in terms of universal rights claims (Barry 2001: 70)? One way out of this dilemma, of course, would be to redesignate the English/British as one ethnic community amongst others with no historic claim to cultural priority. The English would constitute one community of the communities that make up the abstract entity, the state. As Yasmin Alibhai-Brown argued, the problem with multiculturalism has been not its inclusiveness but its marked exclusion. It has excluded the English as a specific group and fostered public resentment, and the project now should be one of 'encouraging the English to be English' as part of an inclusive, progressive multi-ethnic British identity and this 'cannot be done unless the English are brought in from the cold' (2002: 47–50). Here was an optimistic invitation to engage in the therapeutic engineering of a radical Englishness but one cannot avoid the observation that there attaches to it something of the patronising or even paternalistic. Others who worked in race relations, on the other hand, thought that such a development would only open up the door to the worst sort of English populism and the proposition that 'the English must advance their own identity politics' was only a recipe for racist excess (Kundnani 2000: 15; see also 2001). However, the objective of multicultural advocates to promote 'respect' rather than 'tolerance' struck some as an absurd request to suppress all critical judgement, and to create another problem (see Crick 1999: 467). At the extreme, the danger was the evacuation of all that was commonly 'British' or 'English' and indeed, it became increasingly difficult to understand, how making tribalism an object of policy would assist the objectives of any radical agenda.

For instance, Harry Goulbourne acknowledged that Britain 'developed a civic culture which had contributed massively to notions such as the rule of law, parliamentary sovereignty, individual freedom, and certain common assumptions about individual freedom and group tolerance in a wider social collectivity' and that it was from these basic materials of the old Whiggish tradition that a new, fairer, more inclusive society could be constructed (1991: 238). What Goulbourne deplored was the rise of the ethno-cultural paradigm for he thought that style of politics would indeed evacuate the common ground upon which Britain's civic culture was founded. Similarly, in his British Academy Lecture, Amartya Sen took the Parekh Report to task not for its principles of anti-discrimination, with which the official culture of the country was fully attuned, but for the 'non-issue' of whether Englishness had racial connotations. That the English happened to be predominantly 'white' was a historical fact as was the cultural fact that it had a distinctive way of life. This way of life had strong roots in political and social tolerance as well as imperialism and to complain 'that the terms "British" or "English" were not historically pre-fashioned *ex ante* to take note of the future arrival of multi-ethnic immigrants would surely be an exercise in futility'. It was an exercise that distracted attention from the necessary patriotic solidarity that made recognition of particular identities possible and the growing mood that this distraction was actually politically dangerous encouraged a re-examination of multicultural politics by significant voices on the centre-left of politics (Sen 2000).

In part this was a reaction to the al-Qaeda attack on the World Trade Center in New York on 11 September 2001 – but only in part. That event permitted a more open discussion of concerns and anxieties that had been current on the liberal left for much longer. John Lloyd also believed that the high-water mark of radical multiculturalism came with the Parekh Report which, he argued, saw the 'indigenous white community' as the bearer of deep-rooted racism. However, the subterranean tremors of concern had been there since at least the time of the *fatwa* declared on Salman Rushdie in 1988. The lesson of

Islamic extremism in the new millennium now appeared to mean that the country must be 'secure enough to maintain its human and civil rights' and that in turn meant 'no large enclaves of cultural exceptionalism'. The subsequent attack by terrorists in London on 7 July 2005 seemed to make that necessity even clearer as an object of national policy. Multiculturalism 'at its worst', according to Lloyd, condoned or tried to explain away the worst sort of prejudices and sectarian attitudes in the name of respecting difference. The new challenge for the liberal left was to propose a new sense of national belonging capacious enough for all who sought to live peacefully 'in an atmosphere of mutual tolerance'. If the accent was now on 'mutual' rather than 'tolerance', then that was all for the better and in phrasing his conclusion thus, Lloyd's judgement was rather harsher than Crick's only a few years earlier (Lloyd 2002). Critics considered this argument to be an example of white liberal loss of confidence in the face of tabloid scares about immigration, asylum seekers and moral panic about the threat of Islam (Kundnani 2001). That would be a misreading, however, for it was a judgement not confined to white liberals alone. For example, Kenan Malik wrote that, as a consequence of the Rushdie affair, he came to the conclusion that tackling the 'politics of difference' was as important as challenging racism itself. He thought this because multiculturalism had transformed the character of anti-racism, shifting the focus 'from political issues, such as policing and immigration, to religious and cultural issues' and this marginalised liberals in many ethnic communities, but especially the Muslim community. His own Bradford, Malik believed, had been turned into 'a more tribal city'. In present circumstances, multiculturalism threatened the very universalism of radical thinking because the idea 'that society consists of a variety of distinct cultures, that all these cultures should be respected and preserved and that society should be organised to meet the distinct needs of different cultures – these continue to be the hallmarks of a progressive, anti-racist outlook'. It was that simple message that the left had simply got wrong. 'The lesson of the past two decades, however, is this: a left that espouses multicultural-ism makes itself redundant' (Malik 2005: 56).

Malik published his essay in the journal *Prospect*, the editor of which, David Goodhart, had already declared a liberal manifesto that challenged the basis of that 'progressive, anti-racist' outlook. His was an anxious reflection on the erosion of a common culture in the United Kingdom in general and in England (where these issues are most acute) in particular. Goodhart did acknowledge the tension between patriotic solidarity and diversity of citizenship rights but he felt that the left's 'recent love affair with diversity may come at the expense of the values and even the people that it once championed'. Citizenship 'is not just an abstract idea about rights and duties; for most of us it is something we do not choose but are born into – it arises out of a shared history, shared experiences and, often, shared suffering'. Multiculturalism had the effect of promoting abstraction and attenuating what was formerly shared. Interestingly, Goodhart suggested a sort of Schopenhauerian explanation for the manner in which multiculturalism had developed in England. Schopenhauer had proposed, in his fable of the porcupines (a fable which Oakeshott found congenial to his own notion of Englishness), that it is only when people discover a moderate distance between one another that life becomes tolerable: mutual needs can be satisfied and, as far as possible, we can avoid pricking each other. Schopenhauer used in the original the English expression to define the wisdom of that association: 'Keep your distance' (1892: 142). For Goodhard the 'weakness of national solidarity, exemplified by the "stand-offishness" of suburban England, may have created a bulwark against extreme nationalism' but it also had encouraged indifference, especially on the left, to the consequences of multiculturalism 'because we don't care enough about each other'. It was a point of view also shared by some conservative critics (see, for example, the insightful criticism of English tolerance by Daley 2005). This attitude was embedded in the *laissez faire* approach 'in which ethnic minorities were not encouraged to join the common culture (although many did)'. That attitude and that approach should be buried and a new form of solidarity must be promoted by the left, one which would distinguish itself from 'the coercive assimilationism of the nationalist right, which rejects any element of foreign culture, and from multicul-turalism, which rejects a common culture'. Goodhart's rhetorical conclusion bore a striking resemblance to Lloyd's own view. 'People,' he argued, 'will always favour their own families and their own communities; it is the task of a realistic liberalism to strive for a defi-nition of community that is wide enough to include people from many different backgrounds, without becoming so wide as to become mean-ingless.' If it was extremely difficult today to foster a strong common culture some notion of commonality should be the underlying assump-tion of public policy (Goodhart 2004; for a bitter critique of the patri-otic 'self-righteousness of the new centre' see Hall, Massey and Rustin 2005). The mixed response to Goodhart's arguments revealed that there remains a lively debate about what definition of community *does* suffice to include as many people as possible without becoming mean-ingless. However, Goodhart's intervention was one sign that the terms of conversation were changing, that it was no longer required of those on the left to reject 'an instinctive sense of national belonging' and that it was now permitted to speak positively, as Colls had already done, of Englishness as a 'rather open ethnicity' (Goodhart 2006: 29) What national belonging should involve and how that openness should inform public policy remained imprecise though, after its first term, the Labour Government became keen to promote the debate (see Chapter 10).

It would be a misreading to suggest that the discourse of patriotism had displaced the discourse of citizenship but the tone on the left was noticeably different from that of the previous decade. What the current debate does reveal is a deeper concern with questions of nationhood and this concern has ranged from advocacy of English secession from the United Kingdom (albeit 'within Europe') to the fostering of a new British solidarity. If sometimes the language in which these concerns have been expressed appeared very similar to that of traditional nationalism, the substance of the politics remained different. Whether the choice of national community was English or British, the stress was now on the requirement for patriotism, that part of the citizen equation which the left had allowed to lapse in its recent seduction by radical identity politics. As Freedland admitted, many on the left were frightened of patriotism, 'fearing that it reeked of compulsion or white-only exclusivity' but what was now needed was a 'sense of kinship' so that 'we are able to see each others as members of a shared society' (Freedland 2005). The anxiety lay in the concern that it was more difficult than had been thought to strike a balance between citizenship and patriotism. Moreover, the anxiety was neither confined to intellectuals nor was it confined to the left in British politics because conservatives too, with a different sense of the required balance between citizenship and patriotism, had to engage with the English/British Question. The debate amongst conservative intellectuals has shadowed the debate on the left and together they constitute a vital and continuing national conversation.

7

Slow alchemy of centuries

Conservatives assumed, for most of the twentieth century, that they were in tune with the patriotic spirit of the country. Conservatives claimed to understand best the public interest because their instincts were naturally part of the fabric of national character. Harold Begbie once described conservatism as 'the very breath of English history' and 'an element in every Englishman's patriotism' (1924: 9). Lord Hailsham argued that conservatives believed in 'the underlying unity of all classes of Englishmen' and that unity of the nation was at the base of all their political thinking (1959: 35–6). The solidity of England was the condition for the stability of Britain and conservatism was the buckle which fastened together the collective national interest, one which owed more to stability than to the pursuit of abstractions. In the past what their opponents most feared, said David Willets (1998), was conservative understanding of 'the drumbeat of national identity'. National identity in this case supposed the people in their regional and social variety, their customary beliefs, particular affections and long-standing prejudices and it was this certain idea of the people with which conservatives identified. 'Unlike "the people", the nation is not an abstraction. It is a given historical reality' and one made particular and immediate 'in language, custom, religion and culture' (Scruton 1993: 21). Conservatives once believed themselves to be engaged in struggle with its opposite, a radically 'abstract' vision of the people that offends against history. The people in the radical 'imaginary' suffer from a double abstraction. On the one hand, radicals have an abstract idea of the nation and 'the moment abstraction enters the mind of politicians, the blood and substance of the people they govern is sucked out, and they decline into ideological poster-people'. These 'eviscerated subjects' then become the subject of state manipulation, to be persuaded or cajoled 'into the plans of their rulers' (Minogue 1996: 4). On the other hand, these eviscerated subjects are abstractions from a very particular and peculiar cultural milieu. When the 'modern liberal tries to make concrete the ideal of freedom that he proposes he finds himself always constrained to endorse (whether wittingly or not) the habits and predilections of a particular way of life – the way of life of the emancipated urban intellectual' (Scruton 1986: 44).

If this claims for conservatism a distinctively popular construction, it co-existed with a patrician intent. In this view, the task of conservatism has been to educate the nation in the necessity of limiting the effect of democracy. As Lord Salisbury candidly put it, the best form of government in a democratic age is one where the masses have little power, and seem to have a great deal. Public sentimentalism could subvert reasoned judgement and the decencies of civilised life could also be challenged by plebian barbarism. If the political class cultivates the wrong sort of public culture then it undermines its own authority and this has provided a constant refrain in conservative argument. 'If the political establishment,' observed one contemporary journalist writing within a venerable tradition of complaint, 'decides the people can do without the Serjeant at Arms, hereditary peers, the Lord Chancellor, the Royal Ulster Constabulary, etc, it can hardly be surprised that, increasingly, the people seem inclined to the view that they can also do without the political establishment' (Steyn 2004a). In short, a populist strain co-exists with very real fears (to use another of Lord Salisbury's expressions) of public disintegration. In the past, thought Peregrine Worsthorne, the conservative task was to make sure that that the job of governing the country was done by those with civilised ideas about what constituted a good society and the last thing true Tories wanted was for England to arise, especially if it meant pandering to working class louts in shell suits (Worsthorne 1998). Traditionally, then, conservative patriotism, like conservative democracy, was a patriotism that voted Conservative and the popular and the patrician together formed that formidable political force, the conservative nation, which for most of the twentieth century radicals believed was politically impregnable (see Gamble 1974). The worst possible thing for conservatives, then, 'worse even than intellectual decay, is for us to feel strangers in our own land; to come to feel that we are some "sect", possessing a special political insight hidden from the vast majority of the people' (Willets 1998). This rhetoric was often the political equivalent of whistling in the dark for, despite radical assumptions, conservatives have rarely heard the drumbeat of the nation as exclusively their own tune. They have been conscious of the fragility of the conservative nation and uncertain of the stability of their brand of civic patriotism.

Thus, when Richard Weight argued that to most English people Britain was 'becoming a foreign country', his proposition was formulated within a radical framework which assumed that things British represented the forces of conservatism while the new, radical Englishness represented the forces of progress and that he had history on his side (Weight 1999: 25). When the then Conservative Party leader William Hague used a similar phrase he meant dispossession rather than attainment. If the former was infused with the optimism of anticipation the latter was infused with the melancholy of anticipation. If a sense of frustration attached to the former it was the frustration of what ought to be; if a warning attached to the latter it was a warning against the careless loss of what used to be. If an anxiety of foreignness attached to the former it was that the dead wood of the old British order was stifling the flourishing of the new English one. For the latter, the anxiety of foreignness lay in the experience of a nation 'brought up in the culture and mores of one place' yet finding itself 'involuntary immigrants to another' (Hague 1999). Hague's remarks about the culture and mores of the people, those pre-political affections such as a sense of belonging upon which a stable political order depends, implied that the conservative nation, both populist and patrician, had been displaced and its character 'effectively demoralised' by the institutional vandalism of liberal cultural elites over years (see Heffer 2005). In her reflections on Hague's speech, the *Daily Telegraph* columnist Minette Marin claimed that English people were 'not really permitted to celebrate, or to mourn, the country that they have, metaphorically speaking, lost'. For those who valued the country's institutions and traditions, 'the present is indeed a foreign country, some of the time'. If this attitude could be partly attributed to the passing of youth and to the disenchantment of age, part of it must also be attributed to the chill of official attitudes (Marin 2001). Moreover, one response has been the emergence of 'a new and rather irritable sense of Englishness' fostered, she claimed, by the 'traditional left-wing contempt for patriotism; by the resulting suppression of national history; by the suppression of national traditions for fear of giving offence to newcomers; by aggressive multiculturalism and by fast mass immigration' (Marin 2006). Roger Scruton, as was customary, took the argument further, claiming that the patriotic sentiment people need to find reflected in the reporting of public life 'is constantly ridiculed or even demonised by the dominant media and educational system'. This he called oikophobia and it involved the repudiation of inheritance and home, finding its niche in state institutions that offer oikophobes 'the power base from which to attack the simple loyalties of ordinary people'. This permitted a sustained assault on national values and institutions, especially under the Labour Government after 1997 (Scruton 2004a: 36–7). The propagation of this prejudice had debased the national character, weakening it by generations of social engineering, progressive legislation and 'touchy-feely' mediocrity. As Charles Moore put it, this had resulted in 'the sort of people whose only skill is in getting something for nothing out of the state', a nation of 'selfish hedonistic pagans' who 'no longer possess recognisably conservative values' (Moore 2004).

This, at first sight, appeared to be a manifesto of despair. However, one should be cautious about taking that appearance to be the whole truth because, rather like the Italian poet Leopardi, there is a conservative disposition which holds that a state of despair is necessary to enjoy life, a tendency associated with those familiar English characteristics, Old and Young Fogeyism (Carsaniga 1977: 43). That disposition may be part affectation, part conviction but rarely the sum of conservative politics in England. Marin, for example, also thought that talk of alienation and foreignness had put into the centre of public debate possibly the key issue of contemporary politics. 'Who we are and what we will become does matter, very much, to all of us' and it was an issue on which conservative argument could have some effect since this was traditionally natural conservative territory (Marin 2001). The conservative hope lay in an act of recovery in which the people would return to their patriotic identity, a (metaphorical) return of a people who loved their country and despised the 'cultural nihilism' of the radical elite. Even Moore's despair could turn to hope because he could detect, like Disraeli before him detected those angels in marble, a people whose 'love of liberty is not a love of weightless freedom' but of responsible independence (Moore 2004). Beneath the manifesto of despair lurked the anticipation of national revival and the re-invigoration of patriotism. In the new millennium the characterisation of the nation and the content of its patriotism had indeed become key issues of political contest (see Lynch 1999).

However, if the mind of conservative patriotism was and has remained British, its heart was more often than not English. This was not the familiar *confusion* of England and Britain but was actually the *distinction* between what was English and what was British and it defined the 'Toryness' of British conservatism. In that sense T. E. Utley was not being completely mischievous when he wrote that 'there are absolutely no authentically Conservative Scotsmen, Irishmen or genuine Welshmen' (cited in Moore and Heffer 1989: 76). One outsider remarked that Toryism, this very English style, was a specific and locally rooted view of politics, one so specific that it was difficult for outsiders to feel it if not to understand it (Minogue 1996: 5–6). One insider argued that the advantage of the name Tory over conservative was that 'it is not a name for foreign imitation'. It indicated (despite being an *Irish* word) conservatism's English origin and made clear that 'Toryism is not for export' (Biggs-Davison 1952: 5). Once the programme of devolution to Scotland, Wales and Northern Ireland was put in place by the Labour Government it was felt by some that the only authentic conservative patriotism could now be found in England and that Britishness now frustrated its emergence. The conservative temptation since 1997 has been to drift towards Englishness, a temptation that has always been a current in the Conservative Party's history – that is, to treat the non-English parts of United Kingdom instrumentally – but one against which the leadership has always set its face. At the source of this temptation has been the idea of continuity (albeit one often suppressed or hidden) and its mystery informed the question once asked by Sir Arthur Bryant: 'How did we come to be what we were and, as I believe, despite all we have since passed through, still are?' (2001: 184). If there was something familiar about the contemporary embrace of continuity it was because this style of politics had formerly taken potent shape when an *English* politician speaking about *England* as *Britain* tried to make Englishness again politically seductive by making a romance out of its historical continuity and its emotional congruence.

The return of England

That politician was Enoch Powell who revealed the unresolved tensions of conservative Englishness apparent in subsequent attempts to define it: cultural authenticity and cultural diversity; constitutional wisdom and institutional alienation; the renewal of England and the decadence of England, the very conundrum that still confronted Charles Moore almost 50 years later. Ironically, like the view expressed in Salman Rushdie's *Satanic Verses*, Powell appeared to believe that because *British* history had happened overseas the *English* had lost their sense of selfhood. The imperial experience had waylaid the politics of England and sometimes corrupted the minds of its politicians. Only in coming home to itself could England discover that 'the continuity of her existence was unbroken when the looser connections which had linked her with distant continents and strange races fell away'. The romantic Toryism of the conservative outlook would provide guidance in this new circumstance. In his famous Royal

Society of St George speech in 1961 Powell had announced the end of this imperial 'Greater England' and argued that England would now need to re-attune itself to an older, pre-imperial England: 'So we today at the heart of a vanished empire, amid the fragments of demolished glory, seem to find, like one of her own oak trees, standing and growing, the sap still rising from her ancient roots to meet the spring, England herself.' Home from their distant wandering the English would come to find themselves as English, a nation once again, and able to recognise 'the homogeneity of England', one brought about 'by the slow alchemy of centuries'. Here was a familiar patriotic appeal to authenticity and this rediscovery of England intimated a re-awakening of the national spirit, something those on the left, albeit for different purposes, began to mimic forty years later. Powell's idealism traced authenticity from the soil of England, to the laws, disciplines and freedoms emanating from 'a thing called "Parliament"' which dispensed the same justice to all the people of the United Kingdom (cited in Heffer 1998: 334–40). But there was another, elegiac note to this romance and this was another characteristic of Powellite conservatism. If the rhetoric was able to enchant a wide constituency it was also capable of disenchantment, intimating not only England's return but also England's demise. What if those institutions that had served England (and the United Kingdom) so well had themselves become 'inauthentic'? What if they were complicit in the alienation of the alchemy of centuries? What if they had estranged themselves from England herself and helped to confound the homogeneity of the country? What if that most civilised and the most effective method of parliamentary governance had itself undermined Englishness? The disillusion implied in these sorts of questions presented a serious challenge for conservatives since the very thing that they desired to conserve was perhaps no longer capable, or even worthy, of conservation. The irony of Powell's Englishness was that in the pursuit of authenticity he seemed only to discover alienation, internally with immigration policy – and later multiculturalism – and externally with European policy and the 'special relationship' with the United States.

What Powell believed to be a failure of the English political imagination was thought by others to be no problem at all. Of the peoples involved in the Empire, suggested Elton, 'the English (not the British) may turn out to have been the most indifferent to the ending of an era'. Quite rapidly most of the imperial legacy had been forgotten since it was never a vital part of people's lives and in a remark recalling both Bryant's feel for the continuity of national identity and Kitson Clark's notion of 'England before Britain', Elton thought that the English 'lived on in their towns and shires, before and during and after the imperial phase' and would also do so when, or if, they were to 're-emerge from their British phase' (1992: 234). If this solid equanimity was an accurate description of the English character, then there was a further irony in Powell's impact on national life. Concern for the integrity, continuity and stability of national life had prompted his famous 'Rivers of Blood' speech on 4 April 1968 in which Powell had argued that the permissive policy on immigration was 'like watching a nation busily engaged in heaping up its own funeral pyre' (Powell 1968). The consequence of Powell's intervention was, as Bill Deedes believed, to encourage the authorities to pretend that there was no problem at all since 'to talk about prospective religious or cultural differences; to mention the danger of different races congregating in certain places, thereby paving the way to segregation, would be inter-preted by some as supporting Powell's thesis'. Better, then 'not to draw attention to such clouds on the horizon' (Deedes 2001: 20). The irony was that it made it difficult for conservatives – and until recently, anyone at all – to speak openly about concerns with immigration or multiculturalism for fear of being labelled either racist or xenophobic. To question the official consensus was to appear still, according to one alienated (English) Londoner in 2006, as either nostalgic at best or reactionary at worst since it could be dismissed as 'just a deplorable attack on multiculturalism, a bigoted refusal to join the universal acclaim for the all-smiling rainbow coalition that is the capital. Pure Powellism' (Whittle 2006).

If there is an element of self-pity in such a position, the criticism of modern England it expressed represented a deep current of political life. The continuing influence of the Powellite idea of England's return can be traced in contemporary reflections and it should be noted that his views, if not his conclusions, are no longer so peripheral to respectable discourse. Simon Heffer, for example, developed Powell's logic from its original British to an exclusively English conclusion and proposed that the Conservative Party should now proclaim explicitly what he believed it had become implicitly: the party of English nation-alism. It had shied away from this possibility only because English nationalism was thought to involve (and it was Powell's intervention, of course, that had helped to prompt that thought) 'bonkers theories of racial superiority' (1999: 91–3). This was now changing and the challenge for Tories 'would be to forge a nationalism that, while respecting and advancing the aspirations of the English, does not contribute to xenophobic feelings among the inhabitants of these islands' (119). The task was a populist one, harnessing a distinctive culture to majority and not just to elitist tastes in order to subvert what Heffer believed was 'the obsessive desire by much of the political class to eradicate the notion of nationhood' in England, a view that he shared, of course, with radicals like Weight (105). Like Weight, he also argued that the Union flag had become 'an ever more anachronistic symbol' since the English had 'resurrected another symbol of their own, developing patriotism: the red cross on white of St George'. British patriotism was now an illusion and English patriotism the new, if embattled reality. What these English patriots had to confront was 'the destruction of their way of life, their traditions, their values and their interests' (Heffer 2002a). Mimicking Hague, Heffer made distinctively Anglo-centric the fear of deracination and the resentment that the English had become foreigners in their own country (Heffer 2002b: 13). In this view, the New Labour government was 'probably the most anti-British and certainly the most anti-English in history' and it appeared dedicated, in its constitutional vandalism, to the suppression of England. The ancient institutions that conservatives revered, that the English had built and that had worked so well in the past were being 'wrecked in the interests of political expediency and democracy ha[d] been perverted' (Heffer 2002c: 15). In his animosity Heffer was not alone. Another journalist complained that whenever the 'Scots-heavy' New Labour Government spoke of England it set her teeth on edge since, she claimed, it had wiped 'the word "England" from official publications' (Woods 2006). So within these islands, in a ruthlessly logical extension of Powell's argument, the English would need to return from the *British* constitutional structure that now exploited them in the shape of an unjust devolutionary settlement. Heffer thought, as many Tories thought, that the anti-English bias of Labour governance was 'plainly and simply, revenge for Thatcherism' (2005). Moreover, he was also explicit about wanting to foster a 'conscious atavism' in order to rescue and revive the English tradition. Heffer's newly emancipated England would have to think seriously about the difference between a national society that tolerated various cultures, something that was right and proper, and one that encouraged multiculturalism, something that was very different. This would no longer be 'dear old, somewhat unsure-of-itself' England-within-Britain. It would be an England in which the object of state policy would be to encourage the English 'cultural continuum'. Diversity would be acceptable only so long as it did not violate 'legitimate English sensibilities' (Heffer 1999: 42–5).

Richard Body's *England for the English* (2001) repeated many of these themes and exhibited a direct lineage to Powell's romance of

England. Because he exemplified 'the virtues of a traditional Englishman', and for radicals he seemed to epitomise the disposition of the typical Tory squire, it was tempting to dismiss Body's views as a reactionary treatise on the times. However, this would be a misreading since a review of his previous publications showed how Body had anticipated emergent policy issues, such as environmentalism and agricultural reform (Cave 2001: 49). Though his reasoning could be challenged, his conclusions on the English Question were not too distant from some of the trends of contemporary debate (and here the title of the book may mislead). For Body, England had indeed 'returned' from its 'imperial interlude', one during which the English had become 'in their nature and behaviour a different people'. With the Empire gone, 'there is ample evidence that the English are going back to being and behaving as in their past', by which he meant freedom-loving, individualist and tolerant (Body 2001: 98). Body shared with radical critics like Nairn the notion that what made the English 'British' was the Empire, and that what British had meant was the intoxicating hubris of lording it over millions of subject peoples throughout the world. In short, the faults of Englishness could be conveniently attributed not only to the interlude of Empire but also to the interlude of Britain. Like Heffer and Weight, Body anticipated the 'demise of the United Kingdom' and concluded that 'the English will have no alternative but to come to terms with what will in due course be a fact of history'. What was required was not only return but also rediscovery and the main rediscovery would be Englishness itself. 'What matters,' thought Body, 'is that there are some distinctive qualities of Englishness that the English people themselves need to recognise' and the condition of that rediscovery was another act of return, the recovery of their right to govern themselves. When they had achieved that 'they can determine how to lead their lives according to their own inherited values and bequeathed to them down the centuries' (153–5). The subtext of Body's optimistic project was the familiar claim of deracination. If the English 'always have been a nation of immigrants, a prime example throughout their history of a multi-racial society', he was convinced that English tolerance would only survive in 'the context of a common culture to which all its people feel they belong and which, in all important respects, they accept'. And this could only be achieved if the 'indigenous people' *did* know of their own culture (and the conspiracy against such knowing by the cultural establishment finally ended) and if 'newcomers' were taught about 'the culture they are joining' (2001: 181). If Body's language and his premises fitted uneasily with radical Englishness, it is interesting to note that his concerns no longer did.

In the normal expectations of politics that pitched radical against reactionary, the assumption would be that the patriotic bias of these conservative reflections entailed another sort of return, a return to economic nationalism. This would be another partial misreading of the argument since these deep anxieties about national identity were often, though not always, combined with a thoroughgoing commitment to free trade and commercial openness. The historian David Starkey's views provide an exaggerated illustration of this combination. In an interview to promote his televised history of the monarchy, in 2004 Starkey repeated a familiar claim that England 'is now the country that dare not speak its name'. He thought that there was still a dreadful inhibition about English patriotism, despite all the football flag waving. 'England is a historic country which has shaped the world we are in. It is arguably the very origins of modernity. This is something we should celebrate, not be ashamed of' (cited in Hastings 2004). In an earlier debate in the online series *Chronicle of the Future*, Starkey had outlined his case in greater depth. The 'millennial crisis' for the English was 'a crisis of de-nationalisation' and this was a product of their former success. The anxiety was a familiar one, the evaporation of English distinctiveness in the universalisation of its culture which, in Starkey's understanding, was represented by English dress (the suit) and the English language: 'Without a dress and language to call our own, we stand inarticulate and naked among nations – as you will find out if you ask an Englishman to define his Englishness.' Rather than investing in 'cultural icons' (by 2006 something the Labour Government was actually doing), Starkey thought that the English 'revered their political institutions, such as parliament and common law'. If there was a common root to the present national malaise it was loss of confidence in the country's political institutions that had robbed the English of their sense of identity. The English are different, he argued, because their 'sense of Englishness is primarily political, not cultural. Take that away and you take away everything'. That was the reason why devolution and European integration posed such problems: precisely because they both threatened to remove Englishness from England. The country needed to re-invent itself outside both the British and European Unions and in Starkey's opinion, 'England should become an international marketplace in which people, ideas, wealth and trade all move freely – without taxes, tariffs, censorship or immigration controls.' The result would be a 'post-national England' taking the best from its past – political and economic liberalism – and the best from its present – tolerance and ethnic accommodation (Starkey 1999). What Starkey suggested, as one sociologist observed, was 'a huge shift in the national imaginary, away from the rural idyll and notions of landscape as marking something peculiarly English, to the social constituents of an English socialscape which is multi-ethnic, hybrid and culturally diverse' (Westwood 2000: 191; see also Baker et al. 2002). There were some who believed that this is what England had already become in its popular hedonistic desire for ever more materialism, 'a shop for internationally traded products on to which it can hope at best to affix some kind of national branding, seal of approval, or royal warranty' (Boyle 2004: 210). This was partly an accurate interpretation and partly a misreading. It was an accurate representation of the logic of Starkey's argument but it assumed that the logic was to be taken completely seriously. There is reason to doubt that conclusion since this England would have become merely a geographical expression, disconnected from the patriotic, and this was not his intention.

While superficially appearing to meet the requirements of cosmopolitan citizenship as set out by Bryant and Turner, on closer inspection Starkey has actually transgressed most of them. For example, he had no time for either Celtic nationalism, which he thought a backward-looking development, or for European integration, a lumbering construction unable to adapt to the demands of global competition. In this regard, his intervention shared much in common with that of Heffer and Body. What might appear shocking to conservative sensibilities – in particular, Starkey's position on immigration and cultural openness – was less so when read in the context of the popular requirement for this post-nationalism. Controversial interventions, at which Starkey has excelled, do not require logical consistency and the question haunting his argument, as it also haunted the argument of Bryant and Turner, is the 'why England?' question. If what Starkey said about post-nationalism is true, why then premise everything on the existence of England itself? Why, indeed, worry about a country that dare not speak its name? That he did indeed worry about England suggested that England was something more than a market state and a set of procedural arrangements. The return that Starkey had in mind seemed to be that the spirit of swashbuckling, Tudor times should become the animating spirit of contemporary England. He assumed sufficient popular continuity with those times that the fragments of tradition (as Oakeshott would have understood them) could be fashioned into a newly vibrant patriotism and this would involve something more spiritually satisfying than an idea of England as a supermarket (the success of Tesco as a great British institution notwithstanding). Speaking as an historian and not as a polemicist, Starkey argued forcefully that national memory is a vital ingredient of any society. One that loses its collective memory, he argued, has nothing and without 'an awareness of the need for collective memory any notion of community, value or stability vanishes and we become merely individualised flotsam and jetsam'. Without the definite connections of a specific way of life, was this not what Starkey's post-national vision intimated? To avoid that conclusion, he was prepared to make the case for the celebratory approach to the teaching of history since 'English history, in particular, has a fundamentally optimistic message' (Starkey 2004) and his concern and his recommendation found favour in a wider constituency in academia (see Henry 2005). Here, Starkey's position actually recalls the patriotic vision of Sir Arthur Bryant, and before him Froude, where England was an outward-looking, global nation based on sea-borne trade and not an inward-looking, continental European state, a nation capable of absorbing ideas from outside while transforming them in the light of its own tradition of law and liberty (see Stapleton 2005a: 262). Though Starkey argued forcefully that English nationalism had nothing to do with culture his own argument was itself a cultural repetition of that distinctive English mixture of exemplar and exception.

The loss of England

In these Anglocentric narratives, however, the actual case for English independence was not the point, even if it might be a sincerely held opinion for some, one of whom was formerly Director of the Conservative Research Department and a member of Mrs Thatcher's Number Ten Policy Unit. Like victims of prolonged misdiagnosis and maltreatment, the English might consider 'amputation' from the United Kingdom as undesirable but they may conclude that it is the only remedy for national revival (Harris 1998: 51). If support for English independence remains limited and is often a code for larger British concerns, the arguments of those like Heffer, Body, Starkey and Harris reflect a mood in tune with that English manner spoken of by Alan Bennett: joking but not joking, serious but not serious (cited in Paxman 1998: 18). There is political knockabout, especially in the combative 'Why, oh Why' style of Heffer and Starkey, but the deep-seated resentment about English disadvantage – real or imagined – is authentic enough. There are respectable arguments about how constitutional change has unbalanced the political shape of the United Kingdom but there is also the feeling that much of it is done without (absolutely) serious intent. And this too appeared to be characteristic of an English mood which itself had a history. As Peter Ackroyd once put it, one of the unique English characteristics is that you 'can't be in the presence of the sacred without wanting to be profane' (cited in Howse 2002). Intelligent conservatives are aware of that too and it usefully prefaces remarks about the elegiac tone of Roger Scruton.

Scruton has never doubted the importance of the nation – not as an ethnic or religious redoubt against change, but as a way to transcend the limits of both ethnicity and religion. Thanks to national loyalty, he argued, 'it has been possible for people to accept a common allegiance and a shared sense of community, and put old ethnic and religious conflicts behind them'. Citizenship and patriotism, according to this understanding, are not in conflict because in the English idiom the first assumes the latter and the latter sustains the first. The 'idea of citizenship, which confers such inestimable benefits on all of us, also has a cost' and this cost is loyalty (2004b). Fortunately, national loyalty is neither visceral like kinship nor uplifting like worship but it is suited to 'the modern world and to a society of strangers in which faith is dwindling or dead'. The English today are 'heirs to the deep historical experience of England as a homeland and a territorial jurisdiction, a place of uninterrupted settlement under the rule of a common law'. For Scruton, Britishness has centred on that identity of England since what has defined the history of England is that it has been permissive towards difference and allowed 'other loyalties to nest within it and around it' (2004a: 15). This confident expression of Englishness which Scruton believed to be the popular, if not the elite view, of the nation, sat uneasily with another understanding. For the very purpose of Scruton's argument was to point not to the dangers of nationalism but to the dangers of internationalism. Or, to put that more accurately, it was to point to the particular danger of England losing a certain idea of itself. Being English made it difficult for him to be a nationalist since, despite his former certainty of the country's enduring significance, he felt that 'there is no such thing as the English nation'. Scruton had come to this surprising position because (as Kumar had argued) England itself was never sufficient to encompass the ambition of Englishness. England 'is the metropolitan center of an Empire that has vanished'. Culturally 'it is everywhere and nowhere, the point of departure for the greatest experiment in international government the world has ever known' (2005: 29). Like Starkey, the argument is that England's present curse had been its historical success and like Powell, the suggestion is that the historical expansion of England meant that the idea of home has become lost. Like Oakeshott too, Scruton assumed that the measure of England's growing loss of self-possession was that its concrete rights have returned from abroad as a doctrine of abstract human rights, confounding politics and corrupting minds: in short, that English principles have returned, disguised in foreign dress and blurred by false theory (see also Oakeshott 1948: 490). This is no longer just a dissenting theoretical point but also a live political issue as the Conservative Party leader David Cameron's remarks on the need for a 'British bill of rights' to replace the Human Rights Act demonstrated (Woodward 2006). The English who are condemned to live in the amorphous multicultural environment that is being forced upon them are required to open their 'hearts and minds to all cultures and be wedded to none' (Scruton 1999). What they suffer is an experiment by intellectuals to discard the solidity of national loyalty for a vacuous political universalism. The agony Scruton recounts here is profoundly different from the celebratory tone of the deep historical continuities of England and its landscape that he otherwise retails.

Indeed, Scruton wrote of a 'disenchanted' England which the people no longer believe to be theirs and this disenchantment has also weakened national character. His is an England over which the Owl of Minerva has been hovering, a civilisation 'which is now passing from the world' (2000: vii). It is an England that has experienced disenchantment because the English have come to believe that the country is no longer theirs. This is now an alienated country and one element of this alienation has been the experience of mass immigration (2000: 8). Scruton's former England consisted 'in the physiognomy, the habits, the institutions, the religion and the culture' of a very distinctive way of life: 'Almost all have died.' They depended on 'England being somewhere and a home' but that 'somewhere' and that 'home' have been dismantled. His conclusion was that 'England has been forbidden – and forbidden by the English' and it has been a development orchestrated by the opinion-making elite (those whom he later called 'oikophobes'). The disenchantment has been all the more powerful since the enchantment of the patriotic story, for those still open to its charms, had been so strong for so long. Scruton dedicated himself to illustrating its charms but in the past, not the present, tense and he believed that no political enterprise necessarily followed from this illustration since to 'describe something as dead is not to call for its resurrection' (2000: 244). Critics thought that no political enterprise followed because the world Scruton described was an illusion. According to Stefan Collini most books in this mould never really rose above the level of 'dyspeptic grumbling' and their supposed critical force rests 'on a misty idea of "Old England", "the real England", or "essential Englishness", an implicit standard of social health against which the pathology of the present could be measured'. Scruton's elegy fell fully within that tradition and Collini pointed out the logical contradiction of the enterprise. Scruton, he noted, spoke insistently of the loss of pristine enchantment 'but a project of deliberate re-enchantment is bound to be artificial' (Collini 2001). Another critic, Will Hutton, wrote that Scruton's view of England 'holds that the essence of the country lies in the values of an Anglican Tory squire and that all else is a deviation from that happy cultural anchor'. Therefore, Scruton's elegy for this lost world could be rejected as 'little more than sentimentality' (Hutton 2002). However it is questionable if both these criticisms captured the real object of the book.

Scruton argued elsewhere that the 'sentimentalist may seem to grieve at the other's sorrow, but he does not really grieve' for he welcomes the excuse for tears, for 'another occasion to contemplate the image of a greathearted self' (2001). The sentimentalist is only playing a role and some have thought that Scruton himself has played the role of the conservative sentimentalist very well, albeit a role given to playful paradoxes such as for 'the conservative temperament the future is the past' (2002). Moreover, radicals are, as a rule, serious about politics but that is not always the case with conservative commentary. Intelligent conservatives can recognise that too and Scruton, Heffer and Starkey are nothing if not intelligent. In an insightful comment on Scruton which has wider application, the former Conservative MP George Walden wrote that his intellectual life was one of finding 'comfort in uncomfortable truths'. Here the elegiac disposition actually permits the politics of solace since being able to survive in this hostile world, to manage its burden of fate, can engender a form of self-esteem and a sense of nobility (see Aughey 2006b). In other words, elegiac Englishness can be as prideful in an inverted way as the most bombastic style of Englishness and again the argument is both serious and not serious. It is serious when it invites the reader to consider that some things of value have been lost (even if many think those things were worth losing). It is not serious when it implies that everything in England is going to hell. Beneath the veneer of doom the elegy helps the alienated to live with reality and find some comfort in their own discomfort (on such literary strategies see Nunning 2001). If this were not the case then Scruton would have failed Barker's *Weltschmerz* test, a test that some of his critics did indeed accuse him of failing (Palmer 2000). The political intent was rather more straightforward. Scruton argued in an interview that what thinkers like him had to do was to 'make people less ashamed of the prejudices on which the social order depends and make them less prone to be steamrollered by the half-educated opinions of the chattering classes' and in this objective he combined both the populist and patrician tendencies of conservatism (see the interview with Turner 1996: 5).

In another interview, Scruton admitted *England: An Elegy* represented an England reflected through his own ideals. 'I know ideals aren't realities, but they do influence reality – social, legal, cultural' (cited in Wroe 2000). Indeed, he believed that one day it would come to be seen how people like himself had influenced the agenda of national politics and it is interesting to note how the atmosphere *has* changed since 2000 when Scruton's book was published. Who would have expected that only a few years later a Labour Chancellor of the Exchequer Gordon Brown, in a major speech on national identity, would have quoted Scruton, neither to ridicule his sentimentality nor to dismiss his dyspeptic grumbling but to approve one of his central propositions: 'When people discard, ignore or mock the ideals that formed our national character then they no longer exist as a people but only as a crowd' (Brown 2004; the reference is to Scruton 2000: 67). And if he were approving the spirit in which it was written, then, Brown was moving onto territory of conservative resentment that despised the Labour Government for having no ambition higher than aspiring to abolish 'the House of Lords, hunting, the monarchy, or anything else that bears the genial expression of old England on its face', resentment that felt deeply the denial of English political identity, the repudiation of its national history and the herding of its people into a multicultural future (Scruton 2004c). As one astute commentator remarked, there now appeared to be a modified political idiom that spoke less of economic and institutional matters and more of cultural, 'even existential', matters (Kruger 2006). This idiom of national cohesion seemed to favour the dialect of conservatism rather than that of radicalism, and the bombings by radical Moslems in London on 7 July 2005 also gave hope to those who for long had been on the margins of the political debate but who now witnessed their concerns also becoming central to public anxiety.

Take, for example, the unapologetic nationalists writing in the journal *Steadfast* who declared that the English are a people 'bound together by common origins, culture, history, and all those things that a shared sense of belonging entails' and who subscribed to the view that the 'public culture of England should be that of the indigenous English'. There was no self-mockery in these contributions or any sense that chauvinism could ever be a bore. From this perspective, the myth of the English as a 'mongrel people', announced by Daniel Defoe and cited by the left as the truth of English identity, must be dispelled because the reality is that 'the English are an insular people who have ever been suspicious of foreigners' and they have remained remarkably homogeneous (Henderson 2003). Progressive education was a project designed to 'culturally cleanse the English' though there exists 'a generation of English children just waiting to be given their culture back. All it needs is the political will to do it' (Henderson 2005). The liberal elite, those hovering 'angels of communal death', had inflicted a nightmare upon recent generations and had tried 'to convince the English that the struggle is lost; that resistance is futile; that what has been done to us cannot be undone'. However, for those good people who have agonised for so long about the loss of England, *their* England, the tide has begun to turn and the important battle of perceptions is now starting to be won (Linsell 2003). Certainly, the positions of *Steadfast* on immigration, Europe and English nationalism represented the centre of gravity neither of conservative politics nor of public opinion, but it did share certain common characteristics – but not common intentions – that require summary discussion.

The recovery of England

The first characteristic of conservative patriotism is that the populist version of Englishness has become more prominent that the patrician. This is both a general and a specific aspect of contemporary politics. There remained fixed the general assumption that conservative instincts on immigration, patriotism and national culture continued to reflect the public mood. There was also a specific animosity directed towards Labour's, in particular Tony Blair's, usurpation of conservative themes and his occupation not only of Middle England but also of Middle Britain. What intensified the frustration of the first and the rancour of the second was the feeling that the authenticity of popular patriotic sentiment was being perverted by the truly subversive anti-patriotism of the Blair Governments. Was not Blair that 'curiously deracinated individual' with 'no historical sense' who, as Andrew Roberts believed, did not see the world 'in quite the same way as 90 percent of the British people see it' (interviewed by Turner 2003)? It was difficult to admit the truth that Blair had spoken convincingly in the English idiom, though it was one that David Cameron was soon to copy. The assault on the Blairite 'project' took the form of a traditional populist manoeuvre by setting the virtuous and honest people against the dishonourable and mendacious, in this case, liberal elite (Reyes 2002: 19). Blair, though presenting himself as the voice of the

English 'heartland', was really engaged in its betrayal (Taggart 2000: 95–8). Conservative critics could not understand why this was not obvious to everyone and the reason had to be the effect of cultural demoralisation. One of the most vitriolic critics, Peter Hitchens, thought the irony of the last twenty-five years has been that conservatives won the political battle – they had defeated socialism – but that they had not fought what was now the real war, the cultural battle, the one that their opponents believed was crucial: 'On the great battlefields of marriage and the family, education, morality and law, the Tories have been utterly outmanoeuvred and bypassed.' Though the heartland of the country thought that New Labour's 'metropolitan social liberalism' was repulsive, conservatives were unable to give political voice to their repulsion (Hitchens 2005). The second, and related, feature was cultural denial. There had been 'a contemptuous repression' of Englishness 'within cultural studies, in politics and among the right-on intelligentsia' and there had also been 'a determined exploitation of post-imperial guilt among people who, in truth, are entitled to feel proud to be English'. The English had been told consistently that they must celebrate an identity that now resides in diversity and this is another repression of the truth: 'Diversity, by definition, is at odds with identity; identity requires a critical mass of sameness among people.' In this cultural atmosphere 'of appeasement and nicey-niceness' people are oppressed by the weight of conformity to what is thought to be acceptable (Marin 1999). The third common feature was criticism of multiculturalism as an officially imposed ideology which threatened the necessary 'critical mass of sameness' that had made England what it was. Multiculturalism required 'a radical cultural makeover in self-identity' but significantly it demanded that the majority relinquish 'to the point of almost total evisceration, the salience their national culture and traditions have long enjoyed'. One consequence of this ideological strategy had been the undermining of traditional English liberties and the erection of a discriminatory bureaucratic edifice (Conway 2004: 1–3). Opposition to multiculturalism, then, combined as a rallying-cry both themes of elitist conspiracy and cultural denial.

In an accomplished conservative polemic that wove together these patrician and populist themes, Kenneth Minogue argued that multiculturalism had imposed a sort of Jacobinian 'dictatorship of virtue upon a previously free people'. The eagerness of the establishment to abandon British/English customs 'reveals the extent to which multiculturalism arises less from love of others than from hatred of our own form of life' (2005: xv). For some, this had been most clearly revealed

in the teaching of history in schools: 'Excessive contemporary deference to diversity, plus undue fear of excluding or slighting any minority, has resulted in a national curriculum for history that deprives
pupils of the wherewithal to acquire a sense of national identity that
gives them cause to feel proud of being British, irrespective of their
ethnic background.' The evil is not, as multiculturalists would argue,
the 'privileging' of national history. The greater educational evil is the
deracination of the country's youth and this has been the 'sad fate' of
all too many in recent years (Conway 2005: 7). One consequence of
this failure of education, it was claimed, was most dramatically
revealed in the London attacks on 7 July 2005. Those events awoke
the nation 'to the realisation that the real suicide bomb is "multiculturalism"' and to the elite-sponsored evisceration of the national
culture. It exhibited a horrible irony: the London bombers were 'to the
naked eye' assimilated but what they were not assimilated to was the
essence of identity, national allegiance. You 'can't assimilate with a
nullity – which is what multiculturalism is'. There could be no identity
with the nation because the nation had been denied its identity (Steyn
2005). The ghost of Powell haunted the debate and his biographer
noted, with a certain relish, that there had to be a recovery of national
spirit or the alternative would be 'rivers of blood' (Heffer 2006a).

If Hague's 'foreign country' speech was widely condemned at the
time as an appeal to British xenophobia, four years later the atmosphere was quite different. Patriotism, according to David Green, was
back in fashion and was making a comeback amongst the left intelligentsia (Green 2005). Another commentator observed that where once
'patriotism was seen as more embarrassing than pornography' people
were 'beginning to realise that it is vital to be proud of their heritage
and to be enthusiastic about what their country can achieve in the
future. Self-hatred only breeds more self-hatred' (Thomson 2005). The
opportunity to be patriotic and proud of it had re-asserted itself and
this had modified the character of political competition. The engagement of political leaders in this contest did appear to mean that today
the battle was on 'for a modern, patriotic political message that will
appeal to voters' (Helm 2006). There was no necessary policy conclusion to this change in the terms of debate but it did provide an opportunity for conservatives to restate more persuasively what they took to
be patriotically necessary – building a single community and promoting the common values of nationhood. In appealing to the popular
mood, conservatives required good judgement and not a return to
fantasy and the trick was 'to revive national confidence without
retreating into blimpishness – and we may just find that the present

danger gives us the chance to do so' (Kruger 2005). David Cameron was clear about one thing in the conservative tradition. Echoing Edmund Burke, he stated that our nation 'is not a blank sheet in which each goes his own way' since society was not, as the Parekh Report had claimed it should be, 'a community of communities' (Cameron 2005). Conservative Englishness may celebrate the 'cultural continuum' of nationhood but it needed to deal with a more complex world and here one may suggest that these reflections on nationhood do not necessarily intimate a return to homogeneity but are a reminder of the need for commonality. As Matthew D'Ancona suggested, the political question for the country is 'whether we have the courage to decide what we should agree upon' and not how do we make England more or less English (2002: 12). There is a moral fuzziness to Englishness based on the recoil from fundamentalism and the 'treasured belief in doubt, reason and compromise'. If this has led the English pragmatically to accept multiculturalism as an historical fate there are points of 'non-negotiable conformity' that even that fuzziness requires (D'Ancona 2005). That is a valid point and it is one that non-conservatives can also accept (see Lloyd 2002; Colls 2002: 380). Moreover, both the left and the right were adjusting their arguments according to the changing 'location' of English politics because this 'location' of England had been modified as a consequence of devolutionary changes within the United Kingdom and also of changes within the European Union. These modifications set the context for the contemporary conversation about national identity, how best it could be promoted or defended, and these are matters considered in the final section of this book.

Part III

Locations of Englishness

8

Region: resources of identity

During the debates of the 1970s Enoch Powell argued that at the heart of the devolution question was neither Scotland nor Wales and certainly not Northern Ireland but the question of England (Heffer 1998: 746) and it has been a point made subsequently by all serious commentators on constitutional change in the United Kingdom. Vernon Bogdanor, for example, observed that England was hardly mentioned in Labour's devolution legislation though it was probably the key to success of the enterprise (1999: 264). *Why* England was the key was 'for simple demographic and therefore democratic reasons' (Taylor 1997: 769) and it remained, according to Robert Hazell, 'the gaping hole in the devolution settlement' because there was no party consensus about the options for its governance (2000a: 278). Hazell, the academic most sensitive to the nuances of the 'English Question', thought that this was a problem not easily answered and in idiomatic English style, he proposed that it was a question not susceptible to purely intellectual or logical terminology but was instead a political question and the answer would come ultimately from the people, not from intellectuals. 'Academics can highlight the inconsistencies and instability inherent in an incomplete process of devolution and lay out the range of possible solutions, but ultimately only the English people can say for how long they are willing to tolerate the anomalies thrown up by devolution and whether they are ready to vote for change' (2006a: 220). For Hazell, the institutional versions of the English Question related, firstly, to England's place within the United Kingdom and, secondly, to the appropriate administrative arrangements for England (2006b: 3). It can be argued further that the question also incorporates an emotional element and concerns the political structures most appropriate to the accommodation of local affections and national identity. The imaginative aspect of this relationship between the local and the national is far from straightforward and it was the difficulty at the core of the regional agenda of the Labour

Government after 1997. The problem with the institutional project for English regionalism was that it did not map onto the imaginative resources of regional affections and did not satisfy concerns about England's place within the United Kingdom.

That problem is not the absence of English identification with the local or the regional – that would certainly make the English exceptional – but with the sort of regional governance that has been proposed. One study of the Cotswolds, for instance, revealed how that area's idea of itself has been affected by the idea of Englishness and vice versa because 'regional identities construct and are constructed by national identity' (Brace 1999: 503). The dream of England captured in the rural landscape of places like the Cotswolds and the reality of England displayed in its predominantly urban life could represent two worlds that either contest and exclude or that complement and reconcile. The most influential cultural readings of Englishness have argued the former case and used this as a metaphor for England's social, political and economic backwardness (see Nairn 1977; Wiener 1981; Wright 1985). This too is a misreading of a more complex relationship because in the popular imagination the particular can substitute for the whole or the whole can be found in the particular and together form a stable sense of nationhood. During the Second World War, for example, Peter Scott's encounter with all classes of soldier convinced him that England means something different to everyone and for him it was the Devon countryside that made England worth fighting for (quoted in Wright 1985: 83–4). England, in this play of sensibility, was not a thing that could be touched or felt in the same way as one's native locality, rural or urban, but it was rather 'a collection of subjective experiences, conflicting and overlapping discourses, which can never be experienced in their totality by anyone' (Smith 1986: 12). Yet that does not mean that one cannot sense in the local, as Eliot sensed in the chapel in Little Gidding, that history is now and England. This, as one insightful German critic put it, may be a consequence of the English craving for the picturesque and their suspicion of the sublime. Politically this meant that, whereas the German looked to metaphysical union in the state, the Englishman 'loves his country, is proud of his nation, but distrusts the state'. The notion of the state as an object of veneration is especially difficult to accept by the sceptical English temper (Gelfert 1992: 41). Though this may overstate the distinction, the element of truth in this case – the ability to think of the whole (the state) in terms of the particular (locality) – was not the weakness of Englishness but was once thought to be its strength because it kept politics in proportion and the state in its place. For some, in Cornwall certainly (where spray-painted graffiti can proclaim 'You are not in England') and in the North-East possibly, the immediacy of the local affection or identity may displace Englishness entirely but most find in their particular location 'something of the nation' and so also much of themselves (Hale 2001: 190). And if, as it has been claimed, 'we are all tourists now' there could be no English nationality or even local pride if, by tourist, it is meant that people experienced 'home' as they would 'abroad' (Ousby 1990: 4; Taylor 1994). Rather, in the tradition of writings like H. V. Morton's *In Search of England* (1927) or J. B. Priestley's *English Journey* (1934), 'tourist' here must mean a journey of self-understanding through sensitivity to, and affection for, place and that is generally how most people, apart from the irredeemably alienated, do think of England. When, in 1991, Richard Parry found that the political identification 'English' had 'little political salience', obscuring 'regional identities within England, which in some places like the Northeast and Southwest are strong' this did not mean that national patriotism was absent (1991: 147–8). What it did suggest was that national patriotism is often experienced through local distinctiveness, an idea at least as old as Burke's homage to 'the little platoons'. The local, in other words, can be and usually is a 'resource of identity' for the nation (Bond and McCrone 2004). This seems to be the case even for those who think of their own place – in this case, the North-East – as forming England's 'internal national Other' for it has become a resource of identity for an alternative England and if this is described as a 'perverse Englishness' or a 'reverse nationalism' it *is* English and national nonetheless (Taylor 2001: 135). Indeed, one could argue that this alternative England can be felt all the more intensely because it is experienced as intimate and opposed to a remote, official England (of whatever momentary political colour).

Hard distinctions between town and country and regional and national need to be reviewed in order to capture for most people the mental location of England. A summary look at any current book catalogue would reveal clear evidence of interest in what is normally labelled the 'geography, history and places of interest' of English locality. This is not only the exclusive preserve of 'green and pleasant land' nostalgia as critics often suggest but also of 'dark satanic mills' nostalgia, where celebration of Gateshead or Hull is as vibrant (and rightly so) as that of the Lake District or the Sussex Downs. When John Betjeman tried to describe what England meant to him he resorted to the evocation of place names like Huish Champflower and Kingston Bagpuise, a tradition followed by Flanders and Swann in their post-Beeching lament for the railway stations at Midsummer Norton and

Mumby Row. For critics of 'deep England' this would be evidence to confirm the grip of the conservative (rural) imagination that has corrupted the country's culture and displaced the modern. That judgement would be cock-eyed and partial. Like Flanders and Swann – who also mention Selby and Goole – Betjeman admitted (as did Scott) that for others England 'may stand for something else, equally eccentric to me as I may appear to you, something to do with Wolverhampton or dear old Swindon or wherever you happen to live' (1943: 296). Here was recognition that the accents of place may be very different for different sorts of people but that such difference constituted one important element in identification with the nation – so long, that is, as one is prepared to look upon the local as *home*. When asked by researchers, English people can associate with abstractions like common values but they do identify more readily with 'common orientations towards, or rootedness in, place – be it the homeland as a whole, the rural idyll of the British countryside, or another of the multiplicity of geographical referents of the nation' (Wallwork and Dixon 2004: 35). That is why Stanley Baldwin's evocation of England as a place and a home is likely to continue to find a popular response in the future while Gordon Brown's praise of 'British values' will probably not. As Blake Morrison claimed, 'placism' of this sort can often be excluding but it can also serve as an antidote to 'racism', especially in a country as rapidly changing as England (Morrison 2002). However intense these feelings may be there is no necessary connection between attachment to place and the recent political project of English regional*ism*. A sense of regionality may obtain in parts of England but attempts to impose administrative clarity or political purpose upon them encounter longstanding problems (Black 1998: 8) One could suggest that rather like the medieval ideal of self-government at the King's command, English identity has been at once locally focused, regionally proud but institutionalised nationally, and remains so today.

For example, writing shortly after the end of the Second World War and anticipating contemporary debates, G. M. Young felt that if there was currently no demand for Home Rule in Northumbria or the East Midlands he could envisage a claim for regional rights in which the powers of the sovereign parliament would be delimited and possibly regional assemblies established. The result, he thought, could be an infusion of a form of federalism into the constitution. Young believed that the ancient powers of the counties and boroughs provided some scope for regional concentration, a concentration which would encourage a particular patriotism nesting within the larger security of

Englishness. In large measure, that has been the vision that informed the project of modern English regionalism (see Tomaney 2006: 167). However, Young was also conscious of the impact which the two world wars had had on the scope of modern government. To the older tradition of local government had been added the administrative rationalism of central government because that was what social democratic equity required (1947: 111). As a result, the merits of regionalism were discounted not because of a lack of local sentiment but because of a new popular concern with equality of public provision and for those in the poorer parts of the country, limited regional governance looked like a poor exchange for any potential qualification of national equity (Travers 1998: xii–xiii). The difficulty with English regionalism, then, as Young identified it, has been its intermediate and indeterminate position between traditions of local government and traditions of administrative centralism. On the one hand, local government has understood the prospect of regional government as a threat and an unnecessary layer of interference between itself and Westminster. Indeed, when regional assemblies were mooted by the Labour Government in 1976, the Association of County Councils opposed it on the basis that it would be at the expense of local government and its administration of public services (Bogdanor 1977: 172). On the other hand, if an institutional response to devolution for Scotland and Wales was required then surely the nation was the appropriate unit rather than the region, in which case the answer should not be regional assemblies but an English Parliament (see Chapter 10). Though English regionalism might be a convenient compromise for a government seeking to cater for nationalism in Scotland and Wales but without destabilising the United Kingdom – Hazell's notion of 'rebalancing' – this might be neither popular nor even efficient and this has been a criticism of long standing (see Smith 1977: 20). Indeed, for all the recent anxiety about an identity crisis, England's sense of nationhood remains deeply ingrained. Local allegiance is also deeply ingrained but in a manner which rarely means identification with an administrative region – however it may be defined. Despite the claims in the 1980s that England in particular, as well as Britain as a whole, was a nation dividing, despite the historical and cultural evidence of a north–south divide and despite hostility to the prevailing power of the Home Counties shown by other parts of the country (Johnston and Pattie 1989), there has been little evidence of any of this impacting significantly on English public opinion. Moreover, the degree of English 'regional' alienation may have been exaggerated since others have looked upon these differences more positively and noted that while the north–south divide is 'as old as the hills' it can be appreciated as 'an aspect of that individualism and eccentricity which the English used to be proud to stand up for in themselves and to tolerate in others, and which they stand at risk of losing if they choose to conform to standardizations and stereotypes imposed to suit bureaucracy' (Jewell 1994: 7). The problem for advocates of English regionalism continued to be that of mobilising the support *of* the English, whatever their local affections, for the policy of regionalism *in* England, whatever its strategic shape (Taylor 1993: 152). The difficulty with English regionalism, then, can be summed up succinctly: its intermediate status means that it can seem neither local nor national and therefore irrelevant to a public with little understanding of or identification with political institutions that are 'in between' (regional assembly) or that are 'beyond' (the European Union). If there is a prior question to this very distinctive English affair it is this: 'What is regionalism for?' Again, this is not a novel question.

In 1942 at a meeting of the Royal Geographical Society, G. D. H. Cole asked this of colleagues intent on rationalising the regional administration of England: 'But the question, when you start to draw up a map of that sort, is what are you drawing it for?' He could envisage drawing any number of regional boundaries within England and they would differ according to the purpose that was intended. Cole went on to argue that regionalism could be for either decentralisation from Westminster, what in the 1960s became known as de-concentration, or it could be for an extension of democratic control, but he was adamant that these two things should not be confused (cited in Garside and Hebbert 1989: 4–5). This was something that later commentators have also noted. For instance, Stephen Tindale's study for the Institute for Public Policy Research (IPPR) observed that since there are no 'natural' regions in England 'any division will be fairly arbitrary' (1996: 63; see also O'Neill 2000: 90). Unfortunately, though perhaps understandably, these two different senses of the regional, administrative and democratic, *have* been often used interchangeably by supporters of regional government. This is unfortunate, because it compounds the ambiguity of regional governance and so makes it easy for opponents to attack its incoherence but it is also understandable, because the *ad hoc* history of English administrative changes have made this ambiguity and incoherence integral to the debate. To point to these problems does not mean that there is nothing distinctive about provincial England, that those who propose regional government do not feel the urgency of the matter in post-devolutionary Britain or that the frustration which has attended its advocacy is not sincerely felt (Mawson 1998: 158–75). It is simply to say that many of 'the critical questions about the balance of power, the representation of interests and the direction of policy' can be hidden (as Cole believed they should not be) in the framing of the argument (Keating 2006: 157).

Regional resources

When the Labour Government came into office in 1997 it inherited a framework of Government Offices for the Regions established by the Conservatives in 1994. These GOs represented an acknowledgement by anti-devolutionists that it was appropriate to have some sort of institutional focus for central initiatives as well as a convenient point of contact for regional interests. This was especially the case for business which was increasingly supportive of regional policy for the purpose of economic development (Keating 2006: 153). Though reformers have often felt that the significance of English regionalism had been marginalised in the debate about territorial politics in the United Kingdom, two academics were sufficiently confident to identify what they took to be *the* renaissance of English regionalism in the 1990s. Despite all indicators that pointed to the contrary, they thought that beneath the surface 'the political dimension of English regionalism is stronger than might at first sight appear' (John and Whitehead 1997: 10). Another academic wrote of the 'quiet revolution of regionalization' which was slowly transforming the character of English administration (Tomaney 2002: 730–1). England, it was further argued, had been hitherto the exception to the general European trend of 'new regionalism' which was now an important aspect of the transformation of the traditional state (on this see Keating 2006: 144–53; for a Spanish comparison see Giordano and Roller 2004). It was generally the case that the weakest regions economically had also the weakest capacity institutionally and England needed to 'catch up with these trends if its regions are to be given a chance to compete effectively' (Bailey 2001: 12). This 'lack' too was now to be addressed, especially after 1997 with the election of the Labour Government and European experience suggested that 'at some point regionalism gains an unstoppable political logic which allows regionally based institutional structures and forms of political participation to become embedded in a nation state's political processes'. This was the one side of Young's post-war intimation of the future of English governance. The other, resistant, side was the admission that 'the political demand for regionalism could retreat as rapidly as it emerges' (John and

Whitehead 1997: 16). This would be a curious sort of renaissance if the élan was so lacking and if the impetus for it was so obviously fickle or so clearly dependent on external stimulus. It suggested a disconnection between an idea whose time had apparently come and the will, popular or governmental, to make it reality. It suggests, in other words, a misreading of English circumstances. However, the formulation of John and Whitehead did convey that subterranean existence of English regionalism which has been both the hope but also the frustration of those who have campaigned for English constitutional reform. On the one hand, and despite Cole's warnings, the hope has lain in the expectation that existing administrative structures mapped on a regional basis, though directly controlled by Whitehall, could be made democratically accountable to an elected regional assembly. On the other hand, the frustration has lain in the experience that such regional democratic accountability may be neither the real object of government policy, however officially well-disposed, nor (and this is much worse) any great concern of the electorate. Whatever the hopes and frustrations, the true articles of English regionalist faith, as Colls understood them, were these: 'First, devolution should be done in the interest of the regions, not the central state. Second, it should transfer sufficient power to bring national politics into balance. Third, it should work with regional identities as a way of re-inventing democracy and fostering social solidarity at ground level. Fourth, it must trust the people' (2000: 467). The two inter-related propositions are that regional restructuring in England is only worth doing if it is done in the interests of the region and not in the interests of the centre and if it is done to foster an engaged civic culture rather than to assist the administrative convenience of central government. In the history of the English regional debate these propositions were, at one and the same time, reasonable requests and large demands.

The first major argument for democratic regionalisation is that the majority of citizens in the United Kingdom remain subject to one of the most centralised modern states (Adams, Lee and Tomaney 2002: 212). But whereas Scotland, Wales and Northern Ireland have been given control over significant areas of policy, it is now England alone that suffers from excessive centralisation and from the supposedly consequent atrophy of civic initiative. The government of England continues to function under the inhibiting tradition of the old order which substituted for constitutional reflection 'a belief in the virtues of institutional change', preferring to ask questions congenial to the bureaucrat 'rather than inquire into the terms and conditions upon which we are governed' (Bogdanor 1979: 45). This is a double disadvantage because the system resists the diminution of central authority while providing almost unlimited scope for administrative interference with local government (Keating 1989: 158). Lurking in this English tradition is a culture of profound disdain for, even suspicion of, anything outside the sphere of central government and this culture has been peculiarly open to an incremental process of centralisation because there has been no necessity to struggle, as many Europeans have had to do, against authoritarian or totalitarian regimes. Because of the stability of popular identification with national political institutions the resistance to centralisation has been difficult to sustain. It had become one of those 'tacit understandings' which Sidney Low once observed to be at the core of British political practice and according to Bogdanor, this centralist philosophy has constituted one of strongest of 'tacit understandings', legitimising 'the possession of an overwhelming degree of power and patronage by the government of the day' (1977: 165). Moreover, this weakness of constitutional reflection on English governance has been compounded by possibly an even greater distortion, namely the centripetal force of London's cultural dominance of the nation. Here is a 'power structure and value system centred on the City of London, the Treasury and Whitehall, and the metropolitan culture (incorporating the elites of the political parties) which surrounds it' (Tomaney 2000: 687). Like the court of Louis XIV, the radiance of this power centre casts into darkness England's provincial cultures and the further north one goes the darker things can seem. In a passionate response to what he took to be the patronising ignorance of the metropolitan attitude to that which fell outside its ken – what he called the disposition of the 'Progressive Metropolitans' – Colls denounced the view that everything should be based in London and take its measure from there: 'It's hard to believe that anywhere else counts except as a reaction to the capital – including, one may add, regionalism itself' (2000: 466). This 'metropolitan curse', according to the editors of *Political Quarterly*, had afflicted England for too long and needed to be changed, and there could be little prospect for the flowering of English provincial life, they thought, without the promotion of regional political structures (1998).

The second major argument for regionalisation is that it will indeed promote a flowering of democratic engagement and encourage a 'vibrant civil society', the vogue phrase of constitutional reformers. The three key benefits of 'democratic devolution', as Kevin Morgan outlined them, are that that it can empower 'local knowledge', it can permit the development of policy that accords with local rather than central needs and that it can create the conditions for decision-making that is responsive and accountable to local opinion (Morgan 2001: 347). In the case of the English regions this was to be an aspiration rather than a confirmation since compared 'to Scotland and Wales, the English regions lack civic arenas in which key issues can be raised and debated, and actors within them are often poorly placed to grasp the scale of the challenges that confront them in this new era' (Tomaney and Ward 2000: 471). Indeed, one view from Scotland held that England did not enjoy a 'lengthy pedigree of public and private organisations' operating on a regional basis nor was there any 'necessary coincidence between boundaries associated with cultural or identity-based factors and those imposed for functional or operational reasons in various policy areas'. The conclusion was that the most important justification for devolution within England was the expectation that it *could,* not *would,* 'promote the social, cultural and civic development of the English regions' (Bond and McCrone 2004: 2–4). Unlike Scotland, therefore, in which the devolved institutions reflected a distinctive national identity, the prospect for England was the reverse: that democratically-based regional institutions would help to forge complementary social, cultural and civic identities. This was all the more necessary because central government policy over the years had generated 'an enfeebled conception of citizenship and a debilitated public realm – not only in the regions, but also in the country as a whole'. The object of policy should be a 'vibrant civic culture' and democratic regionalism provided the space in which it could flourish and grow (Marquand and Tomaney 2000: 10). Together both of these arguments could make a persuasive case for the re-balancing of the Union since English regionalism 'being a more civic-minded political phenomenon, is far more compatible with the spirit of a devolved and pluralist British polity than an English parliament sporting the banner of St George' (Morgan 2002: 806). Unfortunately for regionalists, this did not necessarily mean the regions already centrally designated and the clearest but most exaggerated example of dissent from official regionalism was Cornwall where local activists in Mebyon Kernow (2004) struck a wider chord when they denounced the 'network of bogus unelected and unaccountable bodies such as the South West Regional Assembly and the South West Development Agency' which, it argued, had taken control further away from local communities. One of the biggest complaints it sought to exploit was that institutions responsible for strategic policy were located in Plymouth, Exeter and Bristol and not in Cornwall itself (Biscoe 2002). However, the Cornish case was a distinctive one since Mebyon Kernow was not opposed to English regionalism but only opposed to Cornwall's inclusion within the South-West region. This opposition highlighted the general point that it would have been a miraculous conception that made the Government's bureaucratic regions correspond entirely with local patriotism. Mebyon Kernow preferred the Government to proceed 'with Cornish devolution and English regionalism separately and independently from each other without the one interfering with the other' (Mebyon Kernow 2004). Of course, Cornish nationalism remained a minority taste, the party was institutionally marginal but, if one took the argument according to regional identity seriously, the case it made was critical.

Each of the claims made by those campaigning for English regional devolution, therefore, was open to serious challenge. The idea that there was some inevitable 'tide of change' in favour of regionalism, especially a tide flowing from European experience, was especially contested. There was no 'Europe of the Regions', according to Gerry Stoker, on which the English were missing out. There were only 'diverse developments in different countries reflecting their distinct histories and circumstances' and this diversity did not imply that regional government was necessary in England (Stoker 2000: 66). Equally, the comparison with Scotland and Wales was not particularly helpful and perhaps misconceived. To argue that a 'vibrant' civic culture was lacking in a region like the South-East was as much a problem of the regional designation as the absence of a civic culture or cultures. Once again, civic linkages tend to be local and national rather than local and regional – just as they are elsewhere in the United Kingdom – but this does not mean a lack of civic culture, only a distinctive configuration of it (for a comparative measure of the 'political dynamics' of regionalism see Bradbury 2003). The argument is another illustration of the theory of 'lack' – in this case, a lack of regional civic energy – but a moment's reflection would cast doubt on that thesis for England has a rich culture of citizen participation. Even the Power Report challenged the accepted wisdom that the public was apathetic or disengaged or had little interest in its communities (Power 2006 41–56). Moreover, civic diversity *within* the officially designated English regions is as great as it is *between* them and this is as true of Manchester and Liverpool as it is of Truro and Bristol (for a criticism of the inherited 'spatial grammar of politics' in English regional discourse see Jones and MacLeod 2004). Furthermore, the confidence of regional advocates that the devolution of responsibilities would replenish civic involvement has also been questioned and it was just as likely that the reverse might happen. Since measures of 'social capital' – networks of association and bonds of trust – tend to be lower in the

North of England, regional government might compound the existing deficit of low levels of citizen trust in the efficacy of government since regional devolution could prove to be yet another disappointment of public expectations: 'Thus might be set in train a vicious cycle of declining democratic involvement and support, eroding social capital and producing increasingly ineffective regional governance.' Rather than leading to a renaissance in democratic institutions, then, devolution might 'actually serve to undermine' existing ones (Casey 2002: 73–4). This was perhaps an exaggerated concern but it was no more exaggerated in its pessimism than its alternative has been in its optimism. The approach of the Labour Government after 1997 often traced a path between these poles of optimism and pessimism, optimistic in its public commitment and its faith in the values of regional devolution but privately pessimistic in its assessment about the level of public support and about the wisdom of the enterprise.

In its first term, the Labour Government legislated for centrally appointed Regional Development Agencies (RDAs) in the North-West, North-East, Yorkshire and the Humber, West Midlands, East Midlands, East of England, South-West and South-East, and these came into operation in 1999. Non-elected Regional Chambers or Assemblies were also established in each region to scrutinise the work of the RDAs. For some, the development of English regions as 'functional spaces' had been consolidated by these new concentrations of institutions and elites and they now intimated a process of 'reconfiguring and rescaling' regional economic governance. However, what remained lacking was the democratic engagement of citizens, since the regions had yet to develop properly their potential as 'political spaces' (Jones and MacLeod 1999: 295; Hazell et al. 2000: 251). For others this incremental approach was rather timid given the opportunities which an incoming government with a large majority possessed for radical modification of the status quo – a missed opportunity in other words (Mawson 1998: 171–4). RDAs had become, according to one survey, 'simply sounding boards' for local government councillors and business interests rather than effective scrutinising bodies (Hazell et al. 2000: 251). For regional campaigners, however, the policy of Labour in its first term was not so much a missed opportunity as an opportunity frustrated. The indefatigable campaigner John Tomaney thought that Labour's approach to English devolution lacked coherence, was piecemeal and lacked an overarching framework because the Government lacked confidence in its vision. This was mainly because Cabinet Ministers were less than convinced of the merits of English regionalism and suspicious of the abilities of local politicians.

Tomaney thought that there was a very obvious Catch-22 in the government's proposals. It was implied that an indirectly elected regional chamber could forge the requisite popular legitimacy to move on to a further stage, a directly elected regional assembly. To build that popular legitimacy a regional chamber *required* some significant responsibility and authority but in order to acquire responsibility and authority it had to show a capacity to *acquire* popular legitimacy. This was to ask the impossible but the confusion of Ministers also reflected the confusion of regional ambitions as well – as G. D. H. Cole had famously noted (Tomaney 1999: 78; this was also a point made by two other researchers seven years later: see Pearce and Ayres 2006: 21). The exception to the rule of timidity in the first administration had been the establishment in 2000 of a directly elected Mayor of London and a 25-member Greater London Authority (GLA). This had been approved in a referendum in 1998 by 74 per cent of those Londoners who voted (34 per cent of eligible voters) and this approval confirmed a general acceptance that there was a need to provide some strategic planning authority for the capital city, one region which *does* have a distinctive identity within the United Kingdom and throughout the world (see Travers and Kleinman 2003). The considered strategy for the rest of England was one of 'wait and see' and this was a useful process of procrastination to cover up serious divisions of interest within central Government between those, especially in the Treasury, who saw regional policy as a method for improving the economic performance of lagging regions and those, especially in the Office of the Deputy Prime Minister, who were keen to promote regional government as an end in itself (Ayres and Pearce 2004: 67). If hope there was for regionalists, it was the hope that in its second term Labour would move more enthusiastically to permit directly elected assemblies in those regions which showed popular demand for them (Healey 2000: 39–44; Mather 2000: 28). Because pressure for regional government was less intense in England, this provided the Government 'with considerable leeway to determine the pace and scope of reform' (Ayres and Pearce 2004: 276). English devolution had become, according to one influential Labour insider, an essential requisite to achieve not only the modernisation of politics in the twenty-first century but also Labour's 'second term economic and social goals', thereby matching economic growth with the fabric of democratic regeneration (Mandelson 2001). That was to pitch very high the case for regionalism and to make the project a hostage to public fortune.

In May 2002, the Government published the White Paper *Your Region, Your Choice: Revitalising the English Regions* which set out its preference for elected regional assemblies of 25–35 members serving for a 4-year term. These assemblies were to have limited responsibilities for strategic planning, especially the use of European structural funds, could raise money through a rate on the council tax and would have their own borrowing powers. Their key political task was to oversee the operations of the RDAs for which the assemblies would set budgets and appoint the boards. The establishment of any assembly was dependent upon both popular support in a regional referendum and a reorganisation of local government into a single tier (Cabinet Office/DTLR 2002). While this approach was consistent with the minimalist strategy that critics associated with the Government, some commentators were more positive, arguing that if the process remained slow it was 'likely to be successful in producing a domino effect creating regional government across England'. This, it was thought, represented evidence of 'enhanced seriousness' by the Government with the 'unfinished business' of English devolution (Bradbury and McGarvey 2003: 235). 'Quietly and unobtrusively', as the Constitution Unit Report accurately described it, 'the Regional Assemblies (Preparations) Bill became law on May 8th 2003' and if supporters of regionalism were delighted, Ministers were more cautious (Tomaney, Hetherington and Pinkney 2003: 1–3). The Prime Minister, Tony Blair, spelt it out in a speech that same month in Cardiff stating that this was 'something that cannot be forced on people. People have got to want it. You have to be sure that this is what I call a people's desire and not a desire of the political class' (Parker 2003). If this was the case, and the people's desire was paramount, then the omens were not very promising. The legislation permitting regional referenda had passed through Parliament with little interest from either the people or from the political class: 'Imagine any other country, province or conurbation,' asked one commentator, 'where such a potentially far-reaching issue could be passed with so little public debate.' The danger, he thought, was that England could sleep walk into a constitutional mess in another fit of absence of mind and that 'England deserves better' (Hetherington 2003). But would the country accept regional devolution on the prospectus that was on offer? The test was set originally for the three northern regions: the North-East, the North-West and Yorkshire and the Humber, but Government concern that its proposals lacked support in the latter two regions led to the announcement in July 2004 that only the North-East would move to a referendum. The widely held view was that the prospects of victory in the North-East were high because of the solidity of Labour support and because it was assumed that the North-East did have sufficient resources of identity to support a directly elected assembly. Here was the opportunity, about which Young had speculated 60 years before, for Northumbria to have a modicum of home rule. The opportunity was refused.

Survey evidence provided by the Devolution and Constitutional Change research programme confirmed but also deflated the major claims of the campaigners for a yes vote. First, there was a strong sense of a north–south distinction and a vigorous localised, rather than regionalised, patriotism, but these attitudes were not strongly reflected in relation to political matters, especially regional government. Second, it was clear that there did exist a broad popular consensus in the North-East that central government was remote. Culturally, as well as politically, distrust of London was widespread but this did not translate into a further consensus that regional devolution would make any material difference and there was little confidence that a regional assembly would be any less remote from local concerns than Parliament at Westminster. Third, on the existing administration of the regions, there was popular concern about the lack of democratic accountability and absence of transparency in the operation of RDAs (insofar as people were aware of their existence) but there was little faith either in the calibre of politicians who might be elected to the proposed assembly. Moreover, the policy issues that most thought significant in their lives, like health and education, would not be the responsibility of the assembly anyway. The conclusion of the survey was that respondents were not convinced that a regional assembly would be either effective or deliver value for money and were concerned that it would tax them too much (Devolution and Constitutional Change 2005a). Those campaigning for a yes vote characterised their opponents according to the stereotype of the north–south divide, stressed the cultural and emotional remoteness of London and tried to play to the question of regional identity. The acronym RATS was coined to describe those campaigning against the assembly as 'Rather Arrogant Toff Southerners': RATS who would, of course, leave the sinking ship of the region when it was all over. Those campaigning for a no vote used a white elephant to symbolise the expense, wastefulness and uselessness of the proposed assembly. They played to the unease that an elected regional assembly would mean more politicians (of dubious quality), higher taxation (for little value), more complicated decision-making (another layer of bureaucracy) and actually weaker public accountability (powers would be removed from local government). The white elephant captured the mood better than RATS. In an all-postal ballot which closed on 4 November 2004, the turn-out was 47 per cent. The result was a resounding rejection of the assembly proposal with 78 per cent voting against and only 22 per cent voting in favour. The pattern of rejection was consistent across the region and each of the 23 council areas voted no by a margin of more than two to one (Devolution and Constitutional Change 2005b). As a consequence of the North-East result, plans for regional referenda elsewhere in England were abandoned. It was once argued that the English regions had never barked (Harvie 1991) but now that the most likely of these regions *had* barked, the message was clearly that devolution – at least in the shape proposed in 2004 – was not what it wanted and the expectation of the North-East setting in motion a domino effect that would move even the resistant South-East certainly did look, in retrospect, 'Panglossian' (John, Musson and Tickell 2002: 740). The day after the referendum result the leader column in the *Daily Telegraph* proclaimed it as a victory for 'England united'. In the fine old Tory style of patrician populism, it praised the electorate of the North-East who had proved that there was something 'intrinsically conservative' about the instincts of the English in their rejection of 'bureaucratic schemes' and in their preference 'for the organic and traditional over the synthetic and rationalist' (*Daily Telegraph* 2004). The defeat was accepted by the Deputy Prime Minister as 'emphatic' and the result left his regional strategy in disarray (Johnston 2004). On the other hand, it encouraged those who believed that the organic and traditional solution to the English Question could be found in an even more local answer than the regional option, one which would depend on revitalising the tradition of local government.

The new localism?

As one perceptive study showed, political conflict was as likely to be found along a local–regional axis as it was along the more familiar local–central axis. Though there had been a convergence of thinking that stronger sub-national governance was desirable there 'was much less agreement about the geographical scale at which this should be organised' and this lack of agreement had always been at the heart of the regional debate (Deas and Ward 2000: 287). There was a respectable intellectual case to be made for the proposition that a constructive regionalism did not require the establishment of regional government at all but an 'incremental and organic' approach (if not necessarily one along the lines envisaged by the *Daily Telegraph*). This attitude to regional policy claimed to be more sensitive to the fluid, multi-dimensional reality of local experience and to be alert to the fallacy of ascribing to the impact of political institutions values that derived from elsewhere. Indeed, when public institutions were seen as important to economic change 'commentators tend to mention local governments and special development agencies more than regional government'. Rather than pursuing 'constitutional and institutional reforms which might promise more than they can deliver', organic solutions 'based on networking and forging of relations between institutions' which did not threaten the 'turf' of local government could offer an alternative (Evans and Harding 1997: 28–9). In this perspective, local governments acting in partnership with regional agencies and private businesses could be better placed to deliver social and economic progress. And one of the reasons for the failure of the regional government option, as G. M. Young had predicted, was the general lack of enthusiasm and often specific opposition to the project by local councillors and their officials. Since the North-East was supposed to be the exception to this rule – and even here the public had rejected the option so overwhelmingly – it only served to reveal the depth of the problem with English regionalism.

Here was confirmation of that respectable academic thesis that there continues to exist a 'national world of local government' that is peculiarly resistant – in a very English way – to the claims of regional government, that there continues to be a preference for 'direct local relationships' with the centre and its decentralised agents like the Government Offices. In short, there remained 'an antipathy to regional-level working and a greater degree of comfort in working within Whitehall-led frameworks' the only prominent exception being the GLA. As a consequence, 'English local government's English-national frame of reference' serves 'to sustain centralised government in the biggest part of the United Kingdom at a time when in Scotland and Wales local government has helped to embed and legitimise devolution' (Jeffery 2006: 68–70). This judgement is accurate insofar as one assumes that Scottish and Welsh devolution can be considered on a par with regional devolution in England but neither the Scots and the Welsh nor the English *do* assume that to be the case – the Scots and the Welsh because they think Edinburgh and Cardiff provide their respective local governments with something of a national frame of reference, the English because they do not think that a regional assembly could ever provide such an appropriate framework. And because they do not, the argument for an English Parliament or for some the acknowledgement of English distinctiveness at Westminster, continued to make a strong claim to fairness and justice (see Chapter 10).

The condition of English local government, however, would seem an unlikely partner in any scheme of democratic devolution. According to a recent study, it appeared that much of the purpose and strength of local government had been lost. 'Local government has its hands tied; it cannot respond to local needs, it cannot raise its own local income, it has little scope for targeting and working in partnership with efficient service providers in the private and non-profit sector, and local people have no one to call to account' (Travers and Esposito 2003: 15). This had been caused by a financial system dedicated to achieving uniform personal and social services, a system that in this case better represented English public concern for national equity rather than for local difference, often known journalistically as the postcode lottery. 'We are relaxed only about matters of branding, "local pride", and control of the quaint or quirky as opposed to the useful functions of public administration,' suggested Matthew Parris, 'because localism in the latter case is taken to mean territorial discrimination' (2006). This dogged fact did not discourage an interest in localism across the political spectrum and in all political parties. On the one hand, it appealed to a younger set of Conservatives in the group Direct Democracy where the 'new localism' suggested a way to capitalise on what the North-East referendum confirmed, 'the electorate's disdain for politicians and functionaries'. The object was, where practical, 'decentralisation to towns and counties, and a proper link between taxation, representation and expenditure at local level' (Direct Democracy 2005a). The attraction of new localism also seemed to be the solution it provided to the larger constitutional question of re-balancing the Union since 'the powers that are currently exercised by the Scottish Parliament and the Welsh Assembly would, in England, be devolved to a much more local level or else removed from the orbit of the state'. At a stroke, MPs at Westminster would be put on an equal footing and there would be no need for radical constitutional modification of England's place in the Union (Direct Democracy 2005b). If this were just wishful thinking it did at least imply that the problem, whatever its solution, had been acknowledged.

A 'Tory agenda' such as that, argued Peter Hain (then Secretary of State for Wales), needed to be treated with 'extreme scepticism' even if it tapped a desire for personal choice and local control, because its real objective, he claimed, was 'the dismantling of public provision and privatisation'. The alternative, he claimed, was the programme which Labour had been developing since 1997, namely 'reform for our public services based on decentralisation with national standards, responsive to individual needs: universal services, personalised provision – delivered and managed locally' (Hain 2003). Localism would be permitted, as Parris thought it would be, only within very strict limits prescribed by the centre. Three years later and the Minister for Communities, David Miliband, was arguing for 'double devolution', a strategy that presented itself as a synthesis of both Hain's thesis and the Tory antithesis – the handing of power not only to local government but also to individuals and communities, 'a different form of accountability: direct to the citizen, rather than via the state' (D'Ancona 2006). One seasoned commentator was not convinced about the sincerity of either version of localism and thought that all of the parties 'were showing political cynicism of a high order'. While advocating a thorough programme of 'big bang localism' he was not a supporter of regional government in England since the upper tier of local government should remain the big city or the county. Below that tier 'personal services should be administered at the level of the urban community, municipality and parish. There need be no argument. That is what works' (Jenkins 2004: 17). This 'organic' solution meant working with the grain of local bodies, democratic and civic, to overcome the centralising prejudice, especially that traditionally sustained by the English curse of the 'national world' of local government (see Stoker 2004: 118; for a criticism see Walker 2002). If that was the appeal of the new localism, however it was defined and defended, it was obviously out of line with the experience of generations of public expectation. Localism, if it were to be popularly appealing, intimated a distinctive English approach that, in G. M. Young's terms, would confirm the tradition of local government within the larger tradition of central government priorities. It is also possible to rephrase it in the terms inherited from English medieval history with which this chapter began: self government at the King's command. However attractive the agenda for new localism might appear, nothing in its agenda, argued Hazell, was likely 'to reduce the centralism in the way England is governed'. Nor would it address the problem of coordination for which regional government was to be the solution, leaving the English Question up in the air (2006b: 10). The new consensus appeared to be that regional assemblies were, for the moment, dead but that the process of muddling through with administrative regionalisation would live on, for good or ill.

That was a process from which the Government's opponents sought to profit. Former Conservative Party leader William Hague, in a speech to the think-tank Policy Exchange, accused the Labour Government of pushing powers to the regional level against the popular mood 'which could see our county structure replaced with new abstract authorities' (Jones 2006). Moreover, the approach was denounced as not only contradictory but also as politically motivated. 'Having failed to nudge the country towards regionalism after its rebuff in the North-East', the Government was trying another route to achieve the same end and it was one which promised to deliver 'the twin benefits of breaking up England's historic shires while smashing the last vestiges of Tory power in England' (Johnston 2005). Regionalism had become, as one Conservative parish councillor in Yorkshire despaired, 'a many-headed beast, impossible to kill' mainly because it was such an attractive option to a Labour Government that wanted to offload potentially unpopular decisions that local authorities were loath to make. He also pointed out that there was a fatalistic potential in that trend which even opponents of regional government could not ignore. Its trajectory meant the incremental growth in power of regional bureaucracies and that 'one day we may find that we actually want to vote "yes" to elected regional assemblies – if only to call those bureaucracies to account' (Vander Weyer 2004). This was a conclusion that informed academic studies had reached as well.

The Constitution Unit's Devolution Monitor for England, for example, argued that despite Government reluctance to speak openly about it following the North-East referendum, the 'quiet regional revolution' was still on course. The standard regions of England 'are becoming used more and more commonly by departments seeking to reshape their sub-national functions within England'. What was driving this programme was not the question of identity, the 'democratic' element of the regionalism debate, but 'concerns for economies of scale and public-sector efficiency', the administrative element of the debate. Evidence of this were proposals to regionalise Health Authorities, ambulance trusts, police authorities, fire management boards and housing boards (Sandford 2006: 12). In this fluid situation, according to Hazell, 'the most likely outcome is the further development of regionalism in England' and the ironic reason for this appeared to be that the English 'seem not to mind centralisation in the government of England'. But if regional government is to become a reality it is likely to be a slow process of incremental awareness (Hazell 2006a: 237–9). One day English people may indeed find that they want to vote yes to devolved assemblies because, like many things in English political history, it has become a possibility that they cannot evade and so the requirement is to make a virtue of it, what Ernest Barker would have recognised as the condition of 'making do'. But as in G. M. Young's own day there are insufficient sources of *political* identity to make it a present virtue for enough English people outside London to choose it.

9

Europe: a necessary context

In his collection of cartoons *Round the Bend* (1948), the Canadian Russell Brockbank included in one of his drawings a newspaper placard with the headline 'Fog in Channel – Continent Isolated'. Of course, this was a joke but it would not have been funny if it had not struck a chord, confirming Alan Bennett's view that English humour is joking but not joking, serious but not serious. It was a 'chipper' attitude, recognisable, perhaps even considered indulgently, but also thought to be rather ridiculous if taken earnestly and it was an attitude brilliantly captured – also in jest – by Flanders and Swann. Their English (who were 'best', of course), when crossing that Channel, couldn't say much for the French, the Spanish, the Danish or Dutch, never mind those, like the Greeks and Italians, who ate garlic in bed. In 1963, the year that Britain's first application to join the European Common Market failed, their opinion of Europeans was, 'It's not that they're wicked or naturally bad/It's just that they're foreign that makes them so mad'. Again, the lyrics would not be funny if there was not a recognisable character (perhaps a part of every English person) to laugh at. The problem of interpreting Englishness may lie, like the dancer and the dance, in separating the joke and the non-joke, coming to believe either that the English are always best or that the foreigner is always mad. Either outlook *is* laughable but it is only matched by its companion, one that assumes the English are always worst and the foreigner always enlightened. The debate about 'Europe' can sometimes become a commentary on the fog in the channel, with Europhiles taking the joke all too seriously as a metaphor for the United Kingdom's, but especially England's, insularity, parochialism and even xenophobia, and Europhobes equally taking the joke all too seriously and condemning the madness of continental schemes to subvert national self-government.

It was Lord Denning who predicted that the Treaty of Accession to the European Community was like an incoming tide that 'flows into the estuaries and up the rivers. It cannot be held back,' and in so claiming he suggested an ironical reversal of the message in Brockbank's cartoon (cited in Mount 1993: 219). The very notion of the Continent being isolated because of fog in the English Channel, with all its evocation of Britain's splendid isolation, now became unimaginable. Far from the Channel being a barrier to European influences it had become a current for them. Today, the Channel Tunnel not only makes fog irrelevant but also symbolises the end of England's insular integrity (Darian-Smith 1999: xiii). The influence of the European stream would affect the normal flow of domestic matters cumulatively and significantly and such was the effect on policy-making that one academic proposed that studies of British history and politics that did not interpret them in a truly multilateral framework were now 'obsolete'. Not to do so was to isolate understanding in a fog of unknowing. What was required to know England was an awareness of European economics, European politics and, above all, facility in European languages. Without these basics, British academics 'should find themselves alternative and more limited topics, such as the regulation of sheep traffic on the Western Isles' (Kaiser 2002: 163). This was a joke but also one that was not joking because if the English academy did not look beyond London then the threat was that its research findings would not be worth tuppence. (However novel this may seem, Kipling had said something similar, and more pithily, a century earlier.) This view itself would be equally partial and incomplete if it suggested that the European Union remained the only comprehensive 'multilateral framework' that shaped identity. For national policy to be framed exclusively by this perspective would be as myopic as being unable to see beyond the White Cliffs of Dover. The question of Europe is one in which the usually balanced and measured tone of the English idiom has often been absent because what is really at stake are questions about contemporary English, rather than European, identity. According to Gisela Stuart MP (2003) the reality is that 'the issue of Europe has become tribal' and this is to revisit and to reconfigure in a European context the question of the civic and the patriotic – whether a common identity is a prerequisite for a stable Europe or whether the European Union, if it is to survive at all, must rely on the resources of identity only found within nation states. To simplify, it can be understood as a debate between those who think that the European enterprise involves a new collective solidarity and those who believe that it rests on mutual but limited and potentially revocable contract (Aughey 2001).

Is there something peculiarly English about this debate? Some have said yes. Anthony Barnett thought that opposition to Europe was more an English than a British disposition (1999: 299). If there is an element of truth in that, which there is, it is also possible to argue that support for Europe is *also* an English thing simply because the English constitute 85 per cent of the population of the United Kingdom. Certainly, it has been the claim of Scottish and Welsh nationalists that their respective peoples are more open to the project of European integration than the English, though survey evidence challenges the myth of 'Celtic' distinctiveness and reveals that the difference of opinion on European matters between, for example Scotland and England, is small and not particularly strong. On the other hand, there is evidence to suggest that in Scotland public attitudes have become slightly more pro-European while attitudes in England have become more sceptical. One scholar thought that this 'nuanced' divergence could be attributed to the 'different collective memories that the English and the Scots profess' (Ichijo 2003: 38). Or as Garton Ash neatly expressed it: 'for some, Britain can only be saved if we have more Europe; for others, England can only be saved if we have less Europe' (2001: 4). It is neat but, as Garton Ash would admit, insufficient, since it remains difficult, whatever the nuances, to separate 'English' from 'British' on the question of Europe. Nonetheless, it is possible to explore English contributions to the debate and relate them to notions of identity. They can be introduced by revisiting the idea of return only this time in the context of England's relationship with Europe.

Return to and from Europe

In *The English Nation: The Great Myth* (1998), Edwin Jones argued that the English nation was a state creation, one imposed at the time of the sixteenth-century Reformation by Henry VIII and Thomas Cromwell. English history was re-invented through a campaign of government propaganda in which the past was turned in 'upon itself and the popular myth developed that the English constituted an elect nation'. Here, in other words, was the origin of the idea of the exemplary exception, an idea which required the abandonment of the rich medieval heritage of European Christendom. This inwardness and Anglo-centricity dominated public life for the next four centuries, informed by 'the great myth that England has always been separate and independent from mainland Europe and has always had its own national institutions, born unaided out of the national wisdom and strength of character of the English'. Whatever its psychological satisfactions this myth is simply that, a myth, and it is one based on 'a false understanding of the past'. It ignores the fact that for the 'first millennium of its history' England was not only integrated into the culture of Europe but also belonged to the Universal Catholic Church. This is not only a matter of historical interest but also a matter of political effect. The reason for the lack of English enthusiasm for European integration lies not in rational calculations of political or economic self-interest but can only be found at 'the subconscious level of the "folk memory", incorporating the Great Myth'. This has been 'the main factor' in making the English 'adopt different attitudes from those of most other European countries' but it is now something that has to change if the country is to prosper in the new millennium. To meet the demands of the age, 'the English people need to recover the flexibility of mind which belonged to their pre-Reformation ancestors' and to re-think themselves as belonging to 'a wider concept than England itself'. This means returning to their real identity rather than the one 'taught relentlessly to so many generations by the official view of their past' (Jones 1998: 251–6). This 'official view' threw up that fog across the Channel but as it clears so too will the obstacles to England's return to the European fold.

In Jones's perspective, the myth lies in the decoupling of the English exception from the European exemplary since exceptionalism was a propaganda cult designed specifically to deny the historical example of England's European pedigree. The insidiousness of that propaganda cult continues to befog the English minds, all too frequently making English people take the wrong example from history. And the wrong example is to choose separateness rather the 'common identity among the peoples of Europe' (Jones 1998: 257). If this return means the recovery of what is real, not only in the sense of historically original but also in the sense of spiritually authentic, then for those who advocate European integration it justifies a whole process of revisionism and re-education because, happily, a more useful English past which serves that end just happens to be the accurate English past. England's history can legitimately be rewritten to foster an appropriate European identity since European history is really its true history (see for example Haseler 1996: 185).

To take one example, the Glorious Revolution of 1688, that great symbol of Whiggish history, can be brought into line with the requirements of a European vocation if one can understand the real purpose of 1688 to have been the attempt to establish a consensual legal framework for political life. Unfortunately, that other Whiggish institution, the political party, and its partisan transformation of parliamentary politics frustrated the original purpose. Greater legal activism, then, by the European Court of Justice would not challenge the principles of 1688, but would restore them to their original purpose (Loveland 1996: 535). If the old historical version proposed that the continuity of English experience defined national identity in opposition to continental Europe this revised version proposes that the true (but imaginatively concealed) continuity of English experience has been inextricably bound up with the fate of its neighbours across the Channel. England, the prodigal child of Europe, can now return home and what once was thought dead becomes alive again and what once was lost is now found. To the average taxpayer, membership of the European Union may not feel like the bringing of the fatted calf but the important thing is that the country should no longer sin against its identity. The Jones view, at least in the honest and forthright manner in which it is presented, is (to use an Irish expression) an advanced form of Europeanism. In particular, its identification of European values with Christian, specifically Catholic values, would not be to the taste of its secular supporters in Britain though that most consistent of advocates, the journalist Hugo Young, cited his Catholic childhood as a factor of sympathy with the idealism of Adenauer, Schuman and De Gasperi (Young 1998: 50). Though Jones is not representative of the pro-European case in England he does capture what is often distinctive about it and what is distinctive is impatience with English exceptionalism. At its best, the idea of return invites people to re-examine national prejudices in the light of changing political circumstances but at its worst, it expresses another sort of inverted Podsnappery in which 'the majority of modern commentators on the constitution appear to assume as a matter of course that foreigners generally do it better than we do, especially if they are our partners in the European Union' (Johnson 2000a: 127).

In English terms the Jones view may be more distinctive than representative but in European terms the reverse is true. As one brilliant study has argued, the 'grand narrative' of Europe-as-Christendom 'retains its potency, for better or worse, as the core of the idea, the culture and identity of Europe at the beginning of the twenty-first century' (Perkins 2004: 14). But how true, historically and politically, is that of England? For Perkins there are substantial historical reasons why English identity 'may be less firmly rooted than that of other nations in the narrative of Europe-as-Christendom', reasons which are not part of a politics of illusion. Whereas in England the common life of Christendom found expression in the cultivation of shared ethics and was closely connected to an ethos of patriotism, in continental Europe it 'retained a strong sense of historical, cultural and sociopolitical significance even in its secularized forms' (Perkins 2004: 6). England's relationship with European cultures was, in modern times, always equivocal and splendid isolation from them was never as radically complete, as Jones would imply. Of course, the Perkins thesis does not mean that the sort of positive European engagement that Jones derived from his historical understanding is necessarily ruled out. But it does not follow that the English need to return to the true European path – also with its implication of returning to the 'true faith' – or that the only options open to them are (self-deluding) isolation and (self-realising) inclusion. For any system of thought, like the inward English ideology that Jones criticises, to have survived for so long at least suggests that the misreading is more likely to be his rather than a generalised English myopia. It all depends on what you are comparing and if you compare England with the six original members of the Common Market, 'countries sharing a large body of Roman and Holy Roman – i.e. Carolingian – heritage', then its history does look exceptional, even exemplary. Things look different when put into the context of a possible Europe of thirty member states but only because 'exceptionalism is the norm' (Garton Ash 2001: 7). Unfortunately for advocates of European integration, that admission opens the way for the opposite sort of political return to that which Jones proposes, a return that challenges rather than embraces England's European 'vocation'.

From this point of view, the call to embrace fully European citizenship is a call to abandon English patriotic consciousness. In an attempt to explain why the European adventure has proved to be so attractive to the liberal elite (if not to the British public) Kenneth Minogue thought that the appeal was bound up in 'the charm of potentiality' (1992: 27). Its charm lay in permitting the intelligentsia, guilty about Empire and alienated from English traditions, to substitute moralism for the national interest. That disposition towards moralism has been a characteristic of English liberal thought and the European ideal provides a perfect context for its flourishing. The Commonwealth only became attractive to left-liberals when they came to think of it as a philanthropic enterprise and Europe has now inherited that philanthropic spirit. It has fostered a very distinctive mix of English self-righteousness and self-loathing, a combination which has also fostered self-deception. Interestingly, Minogue defined England's European problem to be the decoupling of the exception, in this case a conception of national interest, from the exemplary, in this case a conception of the good. In short, the general problem lies in the idea 'that Britain must become a moral exemplar to the nations' and that while other countries 'sordidly follow their national interest' the British, by contrast, 'have the higher calling of becoming the model for the new order of things'. When this distinctive English disposition engages with the European ideal, the selfless abstraction of 'Europe' becomes an ethical imperative against which the national interest does indeed appear sordid and invites the divesting of moral impurity. As one influential textbook put it, using a peculiarly English social discomfort to describe a very different political relationship, defending one's national interest has made Britain the 'awkward partner' in the European Union (George 1998). Or, as Minogue put it, that Europe is often described as a 'club' and its members as 'partners' makes the English rather uncomfortable about not being 'good chaps', pricking the conscience about not exhibiting the 'exemplary virtue' of playing up and playing the game – even if it meant losing every time. The attraction of exemplary moralism decoupled from national self-interest is attributed to 'the evident loss of British hegemony' in the aftermath of Empire and has become a 'power-substitute'. However, within the European Union this power-substitute has substituted national disinterest for national interest – 'volunteering for impotence, one might say' (Minogue 2004a). As a consequence, the country has been exploited by grasping, self-interested foreigners (and the English, of course, could never be grasping and self-interested in that way).

As a Labour MP once argued, there is a triple abnegation in the history of relations with the European Union. 'Nations can fail. They can abdicate and give up. They can be confused and divided. None before Britain has ever opted for all three at once' (Mitchell 1992: 141). It is a view that Minogue suspects is at the heart of the moralising style, a style that requires people to think no longer in terms of nationhood but in terms of Europe: 'The logic of this move is that certain components of the national interest – those concerned with our specific national advantage, for example, and those arising from historic association – must in the name of a higher cause be subordinated to whatever may emerge as the new European interest' (Minogue 2004b). That prospect is dangerous since it proposes to return to a Europe without the substance of popular loyalty and identity. The danger, in other words, is the danger of a vacuous internationalism and it is a condition that is far from exemplary. Roger Scruton distinguished cosmopolitanism, an appreciation of other European cultures because of deeply held national affections, from internationalism, the project of the European Union which he described in Faustian terms: 'People will be set in hectic motion, moving constantly from place to place, only to discover that all places

are alike – and losing, in the process, the local attachments that made
their lives worth living' (Scruton 2005: 35). The association of the
English intelligentsia with the European idea, he thought, is indeed a
Faustian pact and reminiscent of past failures of judgement (the echo
of Orwell's criticism is unmistakable). According to a critic who had
inside knowledge of the working of the European Commission, the
idea is seductive because of the supposed virtue of its ethos (cooperation) and its telos (peaceful union). The reality is very different since –
in a phrase to evoke rooted English antipathy – the 'ethos and telos are
precisely those of the Jacobins' and that ethos is totalitarian and its
telos, imperial (Connolly 2004).

That sort of language confirms the view that the European question
disorders the perspective of normally prosaic English political
discourse (for those attuned to the constitutional debate in Northern
Ireland, however, the tone is rather familiar). As Denis MacShane
suggested, opposition to 'Europe' had become the new populism and
for those who support the European project – especially on the left –
combating this populism should be the touchstone of progressive politics (2004). 'Euroscepticism,' he claimed, 'is a misnomer' because it
was really a form of xenophobia: 'What we are actually talking about
is hatred of Europe and a sense of superiority which has always been
the Achilles heel of Britain through the ages' and these remarks were
addressed as much to those within the Labour Party as to those outside
it (cited in Sylvester 2004). In similar vein, a leader in *The Guardian*
argued that this represented the peculiar English 'island of the mind',
to be explained only 'by the dislike of abroad and contempt for
foreigners that riddles the national psyche' (2004). Though that sort
of argument unfairly defines as an act of extremism almost any criticism of the European Union, it has served a convenient function in
which the exceptionalist understanding of European relations is
befogged with anachronistic notions of sovereignty and nostalgic
notions of England's significance. Only those who are mired in the
fallacies of nationalism could think according to the zero-sum game of
'losing sovereignty' in Europe and speak, as Lord Tebbit did, in terms
of 'them' and 'us', arguing that 'we have either got to surrender to
their will or persuade them to change the nature of the community
entirely or to face the fact that there is not really a place in their kind
of Europe for us' (Tebbit 2004). Only those obsessed with the idea of
England's 'leadership role' could be so ignorant of the realities of
power (Barder 2001: 369) and for all the emphasis upon national
interest and political realism the case made by those opposed to
European integration remains itself highly abstract, nostalgic and

idealist. It led Lord Gilmour to condemn Conservative Eurosceptics as aspirant 'Little Mercians' or 'boundary folk', who wanted to cower 'behind Offa's Dyke, in the form of the English Channel' keeping Europeans at bay and making sure only that the country remained 'a satellite of the United States' (2001).

These two understandings, the first arguing that the cult of the exception, decoupled from the example of Europe, is a misreading of England's identity, the second arguing that the European exemplary, decoupled from the exception of English experience, is a misreading of the national interest, may be taken to represent the limits within which discussion of the European enterprise is confined. They are, however, very broad and flexible limits, permitting within them a large and diverse range of viewpoints. It has been suggested that there are three 'conceptual lenses' through which the relationship between Britain and Europe can be framed. These are the political, economic and cultural-historical (Statham and Gray 2005: 74). While frequently couched in political and economic terms, the debate in England gener-ally reflects an 'identity-driven approach to European integration' in which the political and the economic questions, for example whether or not to join the Euro or whether or not to accept the European Constitution, are unavoidably symbolic dimensions in the 'construc-tion' of Englishness or indeed, Europeanness (Risse et al. 1999: 162–3). After 1997, there has been an attempt especially, but not exclusively, on the left to shift the positive arguments for European integration more squarely onto the ground of culture, a cultural 'turn' which is in part connected with the postmodern 'turn' of critical thought and this suggests that the political and economic arguments for European integration may have become less compelling.

Loyalty and identity

Promoting the positive case for a European identity, advocates are confronted initially by a paradox. If European integration is self-evidently beneficial, if its history has been self-evidently successful and if its values are self-evidently progressive then why has it not devel-oped deeper emotional attachments amongst its various peoples? This was the starting point of Mark Leonard's reflections in *Rediscovering Europe* (1998a) and Leonard, who has been prominent in pushing a 're-thinking' of Britishness and Europeanness in Labour politics, thought he had the solution. A significant part of it was to re-connect popular cultural patterns with the business of institutional integration – 'As a result of greater mobility and convergence of consumption, people have a growing sense of Europe as a continent and an emerging "European" identity' – but unfortunately, what was meant by 'Europe' did not correspond to the political structures of the European Union. Whereas Jones had a very European idea of integration that meant an English spiritual re-connection, Leonard has a very English idea of integration that meant confirmation of consumer culture and lifestyle choice. 'The fragments of this emerging European cultural identity and lifestyle,' he claimed, 'are stored away in holiday snapshots and memories of art, literature, music, buildings and landscape.' This is 'everyday Europeanism' based on cheap flights, cheap holidays, the Eurovision Song Contest, eating European foods and watching European footballers playing for English clubs. The nation of shopkeepers knows a bargain, can calculate its consuming pleasures and *this* Europe is often a bargain and always a pleasure. The *other* Europe, made in Brussels, is expensive, exclusive – it is 'club-class' not tourist-class Europe – and a bore – 'bureaucracy, red tape and grey officials' (1998a: 10–12, 52).

Nor is citizenship alone enough because the citizenship rights guaranteed by the European Union mainly affect only a very small proportion of people. As a rule, these rights are not new anyway but simply a repackaging of national rights 'with a European gloss' (1998a: 26). Though this was apparently at odds with other theorists who believed that the universalistic notion of citizenship could be realised at the supra-national level in Europe, all shared a common assumption: the emergence of a 'new cultural politics' (see Delanty 1996). Lacking, thought Leonard, was 'an over-arching narrative' linking symbols to integration and identity to content. In accomplished Blairite style, the recommendation to European leaders was that 'presentation and content have to be integrated' (Leonard 1998a: 60). The Europe of the institutions must become part of the Europe of the good life – 'sun, sea, olive oil, wine, chocolates, beer, and holidays' – and this required political action on 'quality of life' issues like sustaining a 'common space' for cultural diversity rather than the popular image of Brussels as a homogenising force. This is where the new conditions of legitimacy can be discovered. Whereas the nation state derived its identity in war and struggle it is only from the 'patchwork of sounds, smells, pleasures and fears that make up our lifestyles that a workable identity for an integrated and democratic Europe can emerge' (1998b: 142). Leonard's perspective has become widely shared. Former Commissioner Chris Patten, for example, thought that a healthy European democracy would only emerge when there was a popular and emotional commitment to European identity, something he detected in support for the multi-national Ryder Cup golf team (2002). And in 2005 the Minister of State for Europe aspired to a Union in which, whatever the member state they happened to be in, all Europeans could 'feel in some way at home' (Alexander 2005: 39; for a similar vision of a Europe where 'we are at home even when we are abroad' see Garton Ash 2005). That there is an element of Leonard's vision that makes it more than just wishful thinking has been confirmed by other research into English attitudes (see, e.g., Bruter 2004) but there are equally persuasive counter-indications.

This cultural vision of Europe is linked to the radical idea that the European Union is a completely new style of political formation, one that cannot be grasped by the fixed categories of power and statehood in which its opponents remained trapped. The idealism of imagination involved here presents the European enterprise as both an exception – it has been formed in a culture of peace not war – and as an exemplar – its exceptional social well-being and prosperity inspires political reformers well beyond its borders. The old Whig idea of constitutional liberty and the old liberal idea of civilising mission have been translated from the insular to the continental scale. Here is a specifically English, secular, materialistic rendition of Europe-as-Christendom and its clearest expression can also be found in Leonard's short book *Why Europe Will Run the 21st Century* (2005a). This book makes a virtue of Robert Kagan's criticism in *Paradise and Power: America and Europe in the New World Order* (2003) that contemporary Europeans have lived too long under the illusion that Hobbesian state power is no longer important. For Leonard, the European Union has devised a new way of exercising power that is changing the way in which global politics works. Old-style military force continues to allow the United States to impose its will but it is beginning to have diminishing effect. By contrast, the European way of power is 'transformative' which effects change within member states by forging shared values through continuous negotiation. Its culture is law-based not force-based and it has worked by the power of attraction. The example of the European model is reshaping the globe as other parts of the world attempt to emulate its successful construction of regional stability. This European reach is not imperial but 'post' imperial and its influence is exerted not through the imposition of alien rule but through the invisible force field of trade. Its character is not that of a superstate but that of a superpower and Leonard here was putting intellectual flesh on the bones of Tony Blair's speech in Warsaw which called for a European 'superpower but not a superstate' (Blair 2000: 18). And in turn, both echoed the claim of Robert Cooper – 'We are post-modern states living on a post-modern continent' – and his guidance for the postmodern state was: 'never forget that security can be achieved more by cooperation than by competition' (2000: 33–5). Or as Leonard put it, whereas America's growing power provokes resistance, Europe's exemplary 'network of centres of power' invites collaboration. Indeed, 'no one wants to counter balance it – they want to join it' (2005b: 23). This novel form of power is one the English need to embrace wholeheartedly since its flourishing is not only compatible with, but necessary for, their security and well-being. Because it is really a 'transnational' rather than 'supranational' system – 'transparency through interdependence' – there is nothing to fear about loss of sovereignty (Cooper 2000: 24). This is the future, it works and it is inevitable, not because the European Union 'will run the world, but because the European way of doing things will become the world's' (Leonard 2005c). It has not been the abstract ideal of unity which has promoted the European enterprise and its exemplary achievements but the uncertainty of the nation state in its quest for security and prosperity (Milward 1999: 435). Such an enticing image of the progress of the European Union Cooper described as 'a collective owned by the members, enhancing their powers rather than appropriating them' (2005).

Though there is acknowledgement by subtle advocates of European Union that a distinction exists between 'political' and 'popular' Europe, though one that could and should be reconciled, those critical of European Union believe that they could not and should not. 'The case against "Europe" is not the same as a case against Europe', argued Noel Malcolm: 'Those who are in favour of Europe – that is, those who favour increasing the freedom and prosperity of all who live on the European continent – should view the creation of this hugely artificial political entity with a mixture of alarm and dismay' (1995: 52). Or, as Mark Steyn joked (but didn't joke) in the tradition of Flanders and Swann, if embracing Europe meant indulging in the best of wine, food and culture who could object? – 'Unfortunately, embracing Europe means embracing German corporatism, French public-service ethics, Belgian foreign policy, Swedish tax rates and Greek state pension liabilities' (2004b). The problem lies not with the limited thinking of English constitutionalists obsessed with the question of sovereignty since sovereignty really means constitutional independence and it distinguishes a relatively autonomous region within a state from the state itself. The English, then, do not have a unique problem with sovereignty because of their parliamentary traditions; though states differ in how they are constituted this has nothing to do with the question of sovereignty. The real problem is to be found in the 'biased finality' of the promoters of 'Europe' who assume that there can be only one destination (Helmer 2001). 'The possibility that people might argue in favour of rival positive goals for Europe was thus eliminated from the consciousness of European politicians' (Malcolm 1995: 53). As a consequence 'Europe' has become immune to political realism, is subject to political illusions and one of these illusions is the quest to forge a citizens' Europe to sustain, as Leonard hoped, the legitimacy of European Union institutions. Since the mid-1980s, criticism of this project is usually associated with conservative politics but it is not confined there and one challenging evaluation of its prospects from a non-conservative can be found in the work of Cris Shore.

Shore's analysis challenged the European idea from a number of angles. First, he questioned (as did Leonard) the expectation that European citizenship could detach 'rights' from 'identity' and establish thereby a new form of 'supranational' belonging, one based exclusively on civic rather than patriotic attachments. In Shore's view this was not only undesirable but also impossible since citizenship without some emotional grounding was a merely abstract conception (2004). His assessment of the European debate matches Stapleton's judgement of the earlier English debate about the civic and the patriotic. Secondly, Shore's anthropological study *Building Europe: The Cultural Politics of European Integration* (2000) revealed that the extent to which the 'European consciousness' of the Brussels bureaucracy does exist it is often self-serving and sometimes corrupt. That bureaucracy had become cut off from popular loyalties in the very process of attempting (but failing) to detach citizenship from national identities (Shore 2001: 20). Thirdly, when this technocratic Europe does try to forge a people's Europe the result is expensively flashy, banal and superficial (rather like Leonard's own example of the Eurovision Song Contest). Its assumption that all national identities have been constructed and state-promoted – they are state-nations and not nation-states –is a profound misreading of nationality. Unfortunately, argued Shore, 'the problem is that those cultural elements which give shape and form to existing national identities (including language, history, religion, myth, memory, folklore and tradition – in a word, "culture") are precisely those factors that most divide Europeans'. He did not deny the undeniable, the novel prominence of Europe (Malcolm's second sense of the term) in English life from second homes abroad – popular TV programmes about relocation suggest that everyone in England wants to leave for the South of France – to Italian pasta and Greek olives. However, Leonard's happy shopper view of European culture only confused 'patterns of consumption with processes of identity-formation'. All the evidence suggested that for the British it is the Anglosphere (the United States and Old Commonwealth) rather than the Eurosphere with which they most intimately identify and this appears to confirm the argument that 'the key elements of identity-construction are language, a sense of shared history and memory, and kinship' (Shore 1998: 151–4).

This may explain why most Eurosceptics continue to speak warmly of the American special relationship and have recently revived an interest in the Commonwealth. Here is a yet another return, a return to the neglected third circle of Churchill's imagination and, like Churchill, with the European Union as perhaps the least significant of those circles. This is a Commonwealth with six of the fastest growing economies in the world and 'potentially a global network of power, ideally suited for the 21st century', one that provides the United Kingdom with new opportunities for political influence (Howell 2006: 1; Lea 2006). These alternative arenas are important since, *pace* Leonard, the conviction remains that the European Union does not represent some new and unthreatening form of political association but one committed to the dissolution of nation states. It requires the creation of a United States of Europe and for the United Kingdom to be engaged in that venture is ultimately misguided. The quest to be 'at the heart of Europe' represents not only a failure of political judgement but also involves substantial self-deception. The European Union sees itself as the successor to nation states and what the deliberations about the European Constitution revealed was the ambition to establish a set of institutions 'exercising power in the name of the European people, and overriding national laws and parliaments within the areas of sovereignty ceded to them'. This was not a new objective but the reason why 'the common market was first created' (Blackwell 2003a: 2).

Two faces of inevitability

Constructing and deconstructing the cultural characteristics of what J. G. A. Pocock (2000: 49) once dismissed as the 'Euromorph' is an interesting occupation but it needs to be placed within an English pre-occupation of longer standing. In one of the most concise and elegant expositions of the constitutional relationship, Nevil Johnson wondered whether one could ever reconcile the European idea of 'ever closer union' with the English political value of 'self-government'. The relationship with Europe was so awkward, uncomfortable and intractable not because the problems were economic but because they were political. For Johnson, the nation-state provided 'the only endur- ing framework within which democratic self-government has been possible' and it retained the capacity to nurture the loyalty of its citi- zens. Despite the reassuring words of political leaders, like Blair at Warsaw, about the continued vitality of nation-states within the European Union 'experience teaches us that those who drive the project along – and they are tiny and privileged minorities – do see *finalité* as supplanting nation states and replacing them with some kind of pan-European government' (2000b: 57). Johnson thought that there were three options for the United Kingdom: committing to *final- ité* (the loss of self-government and, implicitly, the political character of Englishness), leading a strategy of reform (reconciling self-govern- ment with European co-operation in a less awkward arrangement) or withdrawal (the return to complete self-government).

The first of these options has little public support in England and neither does the last. There is no widespread enthusiasm for the European Union and there is little support for further measures of integration – neither membership of the single European currency (Euro) nor the proposed European Constitution have been popular options. There is little evidence in the shires and the cities of England of 'a successful re-articulation of the European project in ways that are popular *and* idealistic' nor any imminent sense that such a discourse is likely to supplant the 'still nationalistic discourses that dominate discussion of Europe' (Painter 2000: 235). However, this unfavourable disposition does not translate into a serious contem- plation of withdrawal – the United Kingdom Independence Party (UKIP), which has campaigned on that issue since 1993, remains on the fringe of British politics. Elegant arguments proposing that the English are really European but don't know it remain unpersuasive, as do elegant arguments that the European Union is eradicating what it means to be English. What experience obliges politicians to believe is that European issues may have a profound significance for political activists but little meaning for voters. Pro-Europeans have been frustrated by the reluctance of the Labour Government to promote the virtues of integration but the lesson learnt by the Conservative Party seemed to be that 'Euroscepticism could be as embarrassing as a striped polyester bow-tie at a Notting Hill Party' (Rees-Mogg 2006).

Despite their very different objectives, however, both pro-European and anti-European arguments have shared a common thesis of inevitability. The strength of the pro-European position has relied more on a sense of inevitability than on public support. European Union is 'the future we cannot avoid' and size certainly does matter for exerting influence on issues like security, crime, climate change and migration. Alone, it claims, the United Kingdom would not be given a hearing in world counsels but by contrast, the European Union 'is listened to attentively', especially in trade negotiations (Stephens 2005: 19). The lesson is obvious and the political logic self-evident. For example, Stephen Haseler in his book *Super-State: The New Europe and its Challenge to America* (2004) viewed the enlarged European Union not only as a superpower but also as a 'super-state' in the making. Though this was an assessment prior to the rejection in 2005 by the electorates of France and the Netherlands of the proposed European Constitution, the dynamic of inevitability was so strong that the logic of assimilation would simply reassert itself. Haseler's 'core Europe' – similar to Garton Ash's 'Carolingian' Europe – would continue to act as an integrating force pulling other, even reluctant, states like the United Kingdom into its orbit. This European superstate would rival the United States, acting as a countervailing power in global politics and, as Roy Hattersley also thought, this 'superstate – which does not require Brussels to dictate the shape of bananas in British shops – is historically inevitable' (2004). It was not only inevitable but also desirable. This inevitability, not of fate but of will, has been what Eurosceptics fear and their arguments are designed in part to confront its mood of predestination.

One article of Eurosceptic faith has been that the 'turn' towards Europe can be attributed to the political elite's lack of confidence in the British political system. As a consequence of political weakness rather than a deliberate intention to betray, all sorts of pious humbug about British values has been married to fatalism about the future of sovereignty. The imposition of European rules has also appealed to government as a way of imposing necessary economic disciplines by avoiding domestic political constraints (Kettell 2004: 55–8). This elite attitude demonstrated an absorption of the pro-European thesis of inevitability and served to demoralise public opinion which also thought – whether it approved or not – that there is indeed an inexorable trend to the process of European integration. Even the failure to ratify the European Constitution would prove only a temporary setback in this process. According to the Conservative MEP Daniel Hannan, that failure made the situation even more dangerous since it confirmed an English desire to be left alone, to ignore what is going on until too late, 'fantasising about the kind of EU we might ideally like to have, rather than dealing with the one that is in fact taking shape on our doorstep' (Hannan 2006). There is never any room for complacency even though complacency was an English political sin. The anti-European sense of inevitability derives from the *anti*-fantasy – the identification of the 'real' inner logic of European integration which is unchanging and unchangeable. The 'telos' is clear, only the wilfully ignorant or devious refuse to accept it and the objective is precisely as those like Haseler and Hattersley have pronounced it. The fantasy is to assume or hope that the European Union can be reformed to make it more compatible with British objectives and there is nothing more devious than the politician's line that 'things in Europe are going our way'. If that understanding of inevitability, not of gain but of permanent loss, is correct, the question that needs to be asked is would it be right for Britain to pin its future 'on becoming a component part of a more integrated European state?' The answer is implied in the question: 'there can and should be real doubt as to whether the loss of Britain's distinctive constitutional freedoms, legal system, economic approach and freedom to pursue its own global alliances is a price worth paying' (Blackwell 2003b: 17–18).

These two faces of inevitability, however logical and persuasive, are not ones with which the public feels comfortable and in their logic and finality they both appear to be rather un-English. On the one hand, the certainties of pro-European inevitability can appear unpatriotic and the tone in which they are sometimes conveyed either patronising or hectoring. One critic argued that the way pro-Europeans respond to challenge is rather like an envoy of Philip II reporting on Protestant heretics: 'They may have reason on their side but they must recant or be burnt at the stake. The answer to European reformation is not humility but counter-reformation.' It is a criticism that evokes centuries of English tradition and puts Jones's thesis into a contemporary frame (Jenkins 2005a). In the new millennium, however, there has been the unmistakable sense of a spell being broken and Gisela Stuart's experience on the Convention on the Future of Europe may be indicative. Not once, she wrote, did anyone on the Convention question whether deeper political integration is 'what the people of Europe want, whether it serves their best interests or whether it provides the best basis for a sustainable structure for an expanding Union'. More specifically she was told on numerous occasions: 'You and the British may not accept this yet, but you will in a few years' time' (Stuart 2003: 2). Reading of Stuart's experiences, a conservative pro-European admitted that 'emotional faith in the concept of Europe can no longer blind us to the rational objections to the European constitution' (Hastings 2003). On the other hand, the certainties of anti-European inevitability can appear too doom-laden and the tone in which they are sometimes conveyed either alarmist or insular. Though it is a message that strikes a chord with English opinion it is difficult to convince the public that the European Union is the major source of present ills. For example, Richard Body's nationalistic refrain may be magnificent but few think it is practical politics: 'Remaining in the European Union, and made into one of its dependent regions,' he wrote, 'the English will be of no more account than the Walloons or Bavarians.' How, then, 'can the values and beliefs of England be exported around the world to those who would wish to embrace them if England herself is but a province of somewhere else, and the English no longer a sovereign people governing themselves?' (Body 2001: 137). For critics, this fantasy appeals to those in an uneasy state of 'not belonging' and who 'are culturally resistant to the European idea', desiring it to be, as Body hoped, a mere interlude (Cohen 1995: 62). It is a sign that the fog in the Channel can still be thick (Barnard et al. 2003: 475).

The clarity of these alternative visions – and they have been the visions that have dominated the public debate in England – is their very insufficiency. The fixity of the European ideal as an exemplar and the fixity of the national ideal as an exception do not capture adequately the complex nature of public opinion. The tactical calculations by the Government for the aborted referendum on the European Constitution – in or out of Europe – would have equally misread the choice that most people think needs to be made. And the choice for most people, insofar as they do give it a thought, is not Yes or No but what kind of Europe? A substantial element in their attitude is the sense that whatever they *do* think has little impact at all and that the kind of Europe they will get is what is thought to be good for them. Pro-integrationists charge newspapers in England with responsibility for this because they misreport the workings of the European Union but this too is a misrepresentation of the mood. The complexity of that mood means that though there are 'caricature and distortions' in the media the failure of overtly Eurosceptic political parties 'might well be an indication that the public is aware of this fact'. It also means that Euroscepticism provides good copy 'because it resonates with long established British perceptions of Europe and the Europeans' (Spiering 2004: 146–7). The former represents English discounting of doom-mongering, a national insouciance of the sort captured by Keynes's remark that, anyway, 'in the long run we are all dead'. The latter represents a wariness of grandiose rhetoric that may conceal self-interested purposes, a fear that English moralism will be exploited by continental cynicism since it is always assumed, as Minogue assumed, that the English are *never* cynical. If that mood can be captured neatly the term would probably be 'pragmatic', unconvinced that life outside the European Union would be as rosy as those like Body have claimed and unconvinced that life inside requires uncritical support for 'ever closer Union' as those like Haseler demand.

Today the European Union appears not only undemocratic but also rather dated, not up to the challenge posed by the new economic powers of India and China and no longer so central to American concerns. A sign of the new times was Gordon Brown's Hugo Young Memorial Lecture (2005) where he argued that European economic integration had been superceded by global economic integration. For fifty years, argued Brown, the expectation had been that European companies, brands, capital and companies would come to replace the national: 'But now we find ourselves in a world where national and European flows of capital are superceded by global flows, European sourcing by global sourcing, European companies and brands by global companies and brands' (Brown 2005). Though Brown did not spell it out, the implication was that the debate about European integration had moved on. The really serious debate was now between those who propose to meet the challenges and to address public discontent. The argument of the first group is that it is necessary to have less Europe, 'to swap the pretensions of a United States of Europe for more national democracy, to decentralise rather than harmonise, to enjoy a flexible diversity of countries experimenting with policies to find what works rather than entrenching worst practice' (Browne 2005b: 13). In short, the Anglo-market model will be the salvation of Europe and not the Franco-German (Carolingian?) social-market model (see also Scott 2005; Boyfield and Ambler 2006). The argument of the second group is that these objectives can best be promoted by enhancing rather than diluting the political and economic structures of the European Union, that it is illogical to condemn Europe for a lack of democracy and responsibility while at the same time opposing the constitutional changes necessary to achieve them. Anyway, Britain and the European Union 'are on congruent rather than divergent paths' and there is a developing consensus that 'advancing skills, building up science expenditure, promoting labour-market flexibility and competition while sustaining a more responsive welfare state' is the way forward (Hutton 2005). More Europe is better. The strength of the first argument is that it fits better with public opinion but the strength of the second is that the public accepts the European Union as a (if not *the*) 'necessary context' for national policy (the phrase comes from Condren 1999: 20).

Perhaps the most insightful and judicious remarks are Jeremy Black's. One aspect of English divergence in Europe, he noted, is this: while it 'has bought membership it has not bought the myth'. If scepticism about the membership of the European Union is widespread, 'this is but a pale echo of the indifference or hostility that greets the European myth'. In other words, the historical recovery that Jones wishes for is extremely unlikely to move the English people and Black's sense that the global future can be understood as one of larger economic blocs with the United Kingdom 'obviously part of the European one' does not 'imply that any given strategy for Europe can claim necessity'. His conclusion captures as well as any the centre of gravity of public opinion in England. The European Union is of value but only so long as its pretensions are kept in check, only so long as it ditches the unwarranted presumption to tell people that they are European and that they must act in a prescribed manner. In defending the configuration of national character, 'politicians are fighting not for selfish national interests but for the sense of the living past that is such a vital component of a people's understanding, acceptance and appreciation of their own society and identity' (Black 1994: 267–70). That is Europe in the English idiom, it is a *popular* idiomatic balance, one that can be misrepresented by the larger claims and counter claims of the familiar European debate. It is also the sort of idiom in which Garton Ash has tried to evoke the character of English/British Europeanness. It is unlikely that *a* European identity can ever be '*the* identity' as some, like Jones, would desire but there is sufficient common experience for it to become part of the 'necessary context' of national self-understanding. 'The answer to the question "Is Britain European?" has to be "yes, but not only". Britain's European identity can only ever be a partial identity,' continued Garton Ash, 'for Britain has always been and will remain – so long as there is a Britain – a country of multiple overlapping identities' (2001: 13). As for Britain, so also for England, the identity of the two having been bound together for so long and it is to this question of England in Britain and Britain in England that the next chapter returns.

10

England: a British relationship

In September 2002 the then Home Secretary David Blunkett appointed Professor Sir Bernard Crick to a post which the BBC, in tabloid style, referred to as 'Britishness chief'. Crick had actually been selected to chair a committee to advise the Home Secretary on the design of a citizenship syllabus for those seeking full British citizenship. This involved the provision of language skills and practical information about Britain such as the National Health Service, schooling, political institutions and the values that inform them. When called upon to comment on the character of Britishness, Crick's initial response implied a strictly formal understanding. 'My own view,' he observed, 'is that Britishness is a series of legal and political agreements between different nations' (BBC 2002). If that were so, then Britishness would be an arrangement not an identity, no more and no less substantial than the Europeanness discussed in Chapter 9. If it were *only* a series of agreements between nations then technical or legal knowledge of what things are would be sufficient, since the relationship would be simply one of contract and convenience – and that is indeed how some do understand it. This is the 'four nations and a state' view of the United Kingdom, the recent lineage of which can be traced to Linda Colley's influential *Britons* (1992). There are those, of course, like Nairn, who desire it to become four nations and a British funeral, who find popular authenticity exclusively in national identity. Crick was too subtle a thinker to be satisfied with a partial abstraction and, in an Oakeshottian aside, added that instruction in Britishness was really something that consisted of living in Britain itself, one that involved practical knowledge (*how* things are) rather than technical knowledge (*what* things are), a view he shared with another prominent conservative philosopher (Scruton 2006). This notion of Britishness as a way of life, as not so much a set of rules as the spirit of those rules – to allude to Lord Tebbit's own famous 'test', how the rules of the game of cricket assume sympathy with the spirit of the game of cricket –

implied sentiments of loyalty much deeper than legalistic arrangements. Here again we find that conversational tension between citizenship and patriotism as one of the dominant themes of British public
discourse. This is a real tension because these ideas are not logical
alternatives but abstractions from a complex and ambivalent reality in
which the United Kingdom is both a series of legal and political agreements and for the vast majority of its citizens, albeit to varying
degrees, also involves a deeper sense of loyalty. The German sociologist Karl Mannheim thought that the idiom of English politics revealed
'a peculiar genius for working out in practice the correlation of principles which seem to be logically opposed to one another' since good
government was thought to be less about logic and more about practicality (cited in Kent 1998). It is all too easy to try to resolve complexity by settling for one or other of these abstractions: either claiming
that the nations are real and everything else is a (British) superimposition or that the nations are mere 'constructs' to be de-constructed and
re-constructed according to need. In this view, the specific English
problem presented itself as a potential double disability. Removing the
legalistic, constitutional superimposition of Britain threatened to
remove a vital institutional element of English identity while
Englishness itself may have been already deconstructed beyond
redemption. The connection between these positions was illustrated in
both parts of Ian Ward's thesis that 'the fate of England is inexorably
linked to that of its constitution' and that 'Englishness is an impression', one rooted in the very 'fictions' of that constitution (2000: 236).
That thesis is insightful when it confirms that institutions are also
ideas, albeit ideas which are not fixed and final, but it is a misreading
when it exaggerates the fateful distance between institutions and ideas.

Consider, for example, another of Crick's observations a decade
earlier. It has been well said, he remarked, that Englishness is 'a relationship quite as much as a clear thing in itself'. The insight here is not
that Englishness is just a relationship defined by some 'other' or
'others' (and so without identity), nor that Englishness has a fixed
meaning (an eternal identity), but that the Englishness of Britain and
the Britishness of England are bound up intimately together in a way
that, for example, England is not bound up with Europe. If
'Englishness predominates in Britishness' then Englishness 'was influenced by, as well as influencing, the other nations' (1995: 174). Or, as
one scholar has suggested, 'Englishness is *both* a relationship *and* a
category', an identity consisting of 'bundles of values' that are thought
to be intrinsic but ones which are measured against external and internal 'others' (Langlands 1999: 57). And not just measured, as Crick

might add, but also made. The English may have thought of themselves, as Spenser once thought, an 'Inclosure of the best people' but
that inclosure was never hermetically sealed and the character of the
best people was fashioned by those who came in from the Britain
beyond and from beyond Britain itself (Daniels 1993: 6–7; for an
excellent summary see Dodd 1995: 25–30). To claim, for example,
that a 'Bavarian' self-description means that you know immediately
something about the political opinion of the German who makes it,
but that a self-description of English may mean 'anything at all', is
both true but unexceptional and as a lament again misreads experience
when it suggests that Britain is less an expression and more a repression of Englishness (Hensher 2002). To read the relationship in this
way, however, is a growing, if not yet a politically significant, tendency
in England. Devolution to Scotland, Wales and Northern Ireland has
clearly modified the relationship between England and the other parts
of the United Kingdom as a legal and political agreement and as a
consequence the English question has become in large part England's
British question. The question, in short, is to what extent this constitutional modification has undermined English patriotic identification
with the United Kingdom. It was a question which agitated Keith
Robbins who believed it was wrong to argue that the British state was
the product of the coming together of four distinct historic nations but
that it was equally wrong to claim that the survival of the British state
required only forbearance of the minority nationalities. It also
required the acquiescence of the English majority whose interests were
modified by those of the Scots, the Welsh and the Irish: 'Whether the
English, whoever they are now thought to be, will continue to show
this forbearance is perhaps the most problematic of all current uncer-
tainties' (2003: 451). Robbins intimated the outline of a 'politics of
resentment' and if devolution was designed to restrain that style of
politics in Scotland and Wales it could also provoke it in England
(Wright 2000: 10). There is a good deal of self-pity in that politics of
resentment but it is worth paying attention to the self-pity since it
comes from many sources, both expected and unexpected, justified
and unjustified.

England's Gaberlunzies

In *After Britain* (2000), Tom Nairn used the term Gaberlunzie to
describe the political personality of a Scotland imprisoned within the
institutions of the United Kingdom ('half-life, national waif'), a term
he took from the poetry of Douglas Dunn. J. G. A. Pocock, however,

used the term to define the style of politics he believed Nairn's Scottish nationalism expressed, a culture of grievance, in equal measure one of self-righteousness and self-pity (Pocock 2000: 47). It was a style that Pocock now believed had become quite prevalent in England, though there was an added ingredient in the mix and it was 'the angry self-contempt of English Gaberlunzies' that struck him as rather distinctive. Sometimes there is a good deal of playfulness in this English self-contempt but sometimes not. Stephen Haseler's *The English Tribe* (1996), for one, is seriously disdainful of England's pernicious trinity of 'land, class and race' and for him Englishness was only permitted insofar as it abolished itself immediately. While Pocock was correct to detect a strain of self-loathing in this sort of argument what he did not detect was a very different culture of self-parody. Jim White, for example, thought that what defined English national identity could be summed up by the sort of advertisement that proclaimed 'perpetual Sofa Kingdom sales that "must end noon Friday"', an insight harmonising one side of the nation – consumers – with its other side – shopkeepers (2006). Intellectuals were more likely to suffer from self-loathing than self-parody and Pocock was certain, in England as in Scotland, that letting 'Gaberlunzie tell the whole story amounts to the claim to victimhood and nothing else' and this cult of victimhood would be a travesty not only of the past but also of the present (2000: 48). The Gaberlunzie factor in England, like its Scottish relative, exists in the national undergrowth but frequently reveals itself to full public view.

Writing in the *Daily Mail*, a newspaper that has been sensitive to the Gaberlunzie lament, the actress Joan Collins deplored the 'self-destruction of values' in England she now detected in public life. Though she was proud of the country of her birth, she felt that those who identified themselves as English suffered from a negative 'political correctness' that frowned upon their nationality: 'I believe that when a country loses so much respect for itself that it can no longer even be identified by its historically correct name, insecurity and lack of respect filter down to its inhabitants.' Her conclusion was that 'it's frightful how quickly a whole country of self-loathers can be bred' (Collins 2005). The problem lay not with the whole country, the patriotism of which remained as sound as her own, but with its intellectual elite who set the cultural tone. The temptation to dismiss that opinion as the mere prejudice of snobbish Middle England would need to be qualified by the remarks of a very different sort of cultural commentator. Writing in *The Guardian*, Mark Lawson observed in recent decades 'the grumpy assumption in the senior common rooms' that 'progressive politics and historical resentments' spoke against anything defined as English. It had become 'a nationality which has almost disappeared from the media in recent years'. If it was now 'bad form' not to stress the distinctiveness of the Welsh, the Scots and, of course, the Irish (of whatever sort) it was equally 'extreme bad manners to treat the English as a race apart'. For an artist to be associated with Englishness risked being classified as conservative, retrograde or worse, a Little Englander, someone who was by definition 'resistant to multiculturalism or pan-Europeanism and therefore a de facto racist'. Here was a 'perception of Englishness as an illness for which doctors would hopefully soon find a cure'. Lawson felt that there was awkwardness amongst liberal-left intellectuals about celebrating Englishness that was symptomatic of a deeper national malaise (for a similar criticism see Bragg 2004). However, the times were now changing and Englishness was becoming fashionable once again (M. Lawson 2005). What is interesting about the views of both Collins and Lawson is that they emanate from very different political milieus and yet share a similar resentment. Moreover, they are also more deeply rooted in English culture than their recent provenance would suggest, for they are reminiscent of the complaint by the novelist John Fowles that the English were often assumed to 'need less defining than redesigning' (1998: 80). And to the extent that the English are sometimes patronised as if they may behave only on licence and even then as a suitable case for treatment, these complaints are fully justified (for an example of this patronising attitude see Howe 2002). A prejudice is never made legitimate by being anti-English even when it does appeal to a tradition of national self-loathing. The Gaberlunzie factor merely gives that grumpiness a distinctively political edge and feeds those anxieties of the English examined in Chapter 4. Examples are common and there are often common features.

One of them is a feeling that there exists a conspiracy to remove the very consciousness of England as a separate country, replacing its territorial integrity, its history and cultural substance with administrative regions on the one hand and English 'icons' on the other. (Indeed, the Labour Government's search for icons of Englishness was an illustration of life imitating art, in this case Julian Barnes's novel *England, England*, in which the entrepreneur Sir Jack Pitman constructs a theme park England on the Isle of Wight based on the 'Fifty Quintessences of Englishness'.) What is even more sinister, this de-territorialisation and de-culturalisation is also thought to be part of a larger project to surrender sovereignty to Europe. If Lloyd George only solved the Irish Question by conjuring it out of existence the suspicion here is that there is a move to solve the English Question by conjuring the nation out of existence. Contemplating the European Union's map of England in which it had become ten regions 'with no care for topography', one *Daily Telegraph* journalist realised finally that 'England's gone. Wiped off the map completely, while Scotland's a nation once again. I suppose I kind of knew this long ago, but it's horrible to see right there in full colour' (Woods 2006). Another wrote of a distinctive English 'shame about our origins' and desire to apologise for the past. This led to a longing to be loved by other nations, a longing which always went unrequited because everyone else had a chip on their shoulder about England's historical success. The 'collective wish of most foreign countries is to humiliate us and make us grovel' which leads to the question: 'How can any race of people abjectly submit themselves to such a state of affairs?' And the answer is: only one 'which has lost all self-confidence and no longer believes that it has a future'. If Roger Scruton was gently elegiac about his country, here was a brutal Anglo-Saxon version of the same sentiment: 'England is f****d' and the most depressing illustration of this condition was the 'craven way' in which matters solely affecting England were decided by those who were not English (Fulford 2005). Here was the post-devolutionary politics of resentment about which Wright warned and which could be expressed in unabashed populist style, a style that linked high, middle and low-brow commentary about the 'obtrusive influence' of non-English MPs at Westminster (Sissons 2005).

A closely related theme has been that particular resentment given voice by Jeremy Paxman's remark that 'down here' – by which he meant England – 'we live under a sort of Scottish Raj'. Paxman was a very English Gaberlunzie in this case since he combined exaggeration with understatement, making a charge and drawing its sting. He exaggerated by characterising Scottish ministerial influence as pomp and imperialism while he understated his grievance by emphasising English tolerance: 'Do we complain about it? No we don't' (cited in Peterkin 2005). One intelligent Scot identified Paxman as the 'unofficial head prefect' of those well-connected English Gaberlunzies who for decades had been 'quietly moaning into their gin and tonics' about the political and cultural influence of those from north of the border. What had begun to shift the balance from tolerance to intolerance, from moaning quietly to moaning openly, was that the United Kingdom had become a 'two-class state: those with home rule (Scots and Welsh) and those without (the English)' (Neil 2005). Scottish influence in England and English influence in Scotland depended on what Richard Rose (1982b) once called 'unthinking unionism' but after devolution unionism could be unthinking no longer. Unfortunately, thinking in Gaberlunzie mode is often no more than irritable growling since to make the nationality of Scots (or the Welsh or the Irish) in prominent public positions the *only* significant factor in assessing their worth is an unwarranted form of reductionism (Seenan 2005). It just happens to be one consequence, though it is not necessarily the fatal consequence, of institutionalising identity politics within the United Kingdom. It also just happens to be a consequence of the new political idiom in which issues that decide elections are as likely to be 'cultural, even existential' as they are to be economic and institutional (Kruger 2006). If Scottish resentment at governance by the (Conservative) English informed the case for devolution, a case that was cultural and existential far more than it was economic and institutional, then it is not at all unusual that the English 'worm' would turn in that direction as well (see Linklater 2006). It could only be expected and in some cases, but certainly not all, it expressed the long tradition of what Jim Bulpitt once called the 'Sod Off' school of Anglo-Scottish relations (Bulpitt 1983). However, it is neither that expectation nor that tradition which really distinguishes the English Gaberlunzie but something else.

That 'something else' is an exaggeration of language which is at odds with the economic or institutional effect of devolution on England but is not at odds with a certain existential mood. It is an exaggeration of language that can slip into even the most sensible of discussions. One commentator wrote of the 'sense of constitutional oppression' swirling in the recesses of the English collective consciousness (Johnson 2004a) and another thought that the project of devolution had 'discriminated against' England, creating a situation resembling that of the American colonists in 1776 (Rees-Mogg 2005). Here is a trope very familiar in English cultural history and it conjures up that image of Orwell's gentle people, a people with a profound sense of justice and fairness but a people difficult to rouse and slow to criticise. When the time comes, however, it is a people stubbornly determined to do what is right and to re-claim its rights (see Heffer 2006b for an illustration of the style). That self-understanding conveys rather neatly the mix of self-righteousness – the English are exceptionally tolerant and fair – and self-pity – these exemplary English virtues have allowed others to take advantage of their good nature – which informs the national Gaberlunzie. It is an attitude that we have encountered in a certain disposition towards other nationalities in the European Union who are also assumed to take advantage of exceptional English good nature. There is a ridiculous element in this view since it would be quite bizarre, as well as self-diminishing, for a large nation like England to define itself exclusively in grievance against a small nation like Scotland or even Wales and to transform the constitutional anomalies of devolution into evidence of systematic victimisation. But there is also a serious element in that a sense of fairness is important to the English sensibility and though some may not think it to be an urgent problem, others that it is not a problem at all, the asymmetrical character of the devolutionary arrangements has raised it and it is a problem that is unlikely to go away. Wright thought that it was a problem that could only be avoided if English people did not know, or care, very much about it. He felt that if this was the case in the past (a people difficult to rouse) it was beginning to change (a people stubbornly determined to have justice). 'The fact that there is no easy answer to the English Question – or even that some answers may be more troublesome than the question – will not stop it being increasingly asked' (Wright 2006). From the perspective of an MP like Wright, the English Question very soon becomes the West Lothian Question. This *is* a genuine issue, a British and not exclusively an English problem, and one that the House of Commons Select Committee on Scottish Affairs thought could undermine the whole devolution settlement (see Helm 2006).

The West Lothian Question was the name given by Enoch Powell to the potential anomaly of devolution raised by Tam Dalyell, the MP for West Lothian, in his book *Devolution: The End of Britain* (1977). In particular, the West Lothian Question was a recognition that the establishment of a Parliament in Scotland would mean that Scots MPs at Westminster could speak and vote on English matters but could not speak and vote on devolved Scottish matters. Moreover, as complaints about the Scottish Raj reveal, those Scots MPs could also exercise departmental authority over English affairs, as indeed they have done since 1997. As a consequence of that particular, the West Lothian Question really stands for the England-in-Britain Question, not the Scotland-in-Britain Question, and how England seeks to resolve that Question, as the Select Committee on Scottish Affairs recognised, will determine the future stability of the United Kingdom. It should be noted that not everyone has understood recent constitutional change in such a dramatic fashion. One respected constitutional theorist argued that devolution had allowed the Government even greater freedom to administer the United Kingdom as if only England existed and that change was less significant than it appeared at first sight, a view which Tony Blair appeared to share when he once injudiciously likened the Scottish Parliament to a parish council (Johnson 2004).

The general reading of the consequences of devolution on England has been different from Johnson's interpretation, recognising what England lacked (again) rather what it had gained from constitutional modification. Hovering over the technicalities of the West Lothian Question has been the spirit of party politics, a spirit ancient as well as modern. Disraeli had once phrased the Tory complaint thus: 'The Whigs are only maintained in power by the votes of the Scotch members' (cited in Watson 2005: 17). If in the course of the last thirty years the Scots and the Welsh had come to think of the Conservatives as an English party, then there was a possibility of the Conservatives embracing that identity and denouncing Labour as a vehicle for imposing a Celtic mafia – or 'McMafia' – on England. After all, in his popular history of the Conservative Party, Lord Blake had wondered openly why (even at a time when Tory support was still well-established in Scotland) its leadership had not been more rather than less English-oriented (Blake 1970: 273). That temptation, especially in Opposition, has always been there but the barking of this dog has been muted and it explains much about the politics of nationhood in Britain. The Conservative Party has been aware of the pitfalls of a 'little England' strategy and they have been pointed out by its political opponents – potentially breaking up the United Kingdom and bringing about the very thing that the Party has warned against consistently (see Bunting 2006). However, there is some point to the argument that it is 'living in the past' to believe that the Government could go on legislating for England in exactly the same way it did before devolution (Hague 2006).

For those nationalists on the left and the right, of course, there can be no logical resolution of the English Question within the United Kingdom and the logic of that contradiction revealed the necessity of English separatism. If the cry of English regionalism had proved unappealing to the electorate it had actually been a 'good cry' for those promoting the case for England's independence. From this perspective, regionalism constituted a scheme to deny the legitimacy of the English nation, a manifestation of that 'obsessive desire by much of the political class to eradicate the notion of nationhood' in England (Heffer 1999: 105). If that view were taken as a predictably exaggerated conservative response it was a view equally shared by some on the left who argued that you 'cannot turn a nation into a collection of regions until you have first allowed it to become a nation again'. The only ones excited by the prospect of regionalism in England were the 'Celtic elite' and could English people trust that elite to 'care passionately about the democratic needs of the people of Essex' (Weight 1999: 26)?

The answer seemed self-evident. On that common ground stood Nairn at one end calling for the English just to get on with breaking up Britain and Heffer at the other calling for the English to realise how they had been 'conned' by devolution. Both of them thought that politics were now 'after Britain' and both shared the view that there now existed different *patriae* in these islands no longer united by a common British identity (Heffer 2004). This may very well *become* true (the rhetoric does not describe the situation, it attempts to call it into existence) but it failed to capture either the subtleties of the present condition or the subtleties of public opinion. Nevertheless, the practicalities of addressing the place of England in the devolved United Kingdom remain because how is it possible to institute this preference for the national while not dissolving the Union? Two possibilities suggested themselves: either a modification of procedure at Westminster to provide for English votes on English laws or the establishment of a separate English Parliament on the model of that in Scotland. The first would mean that the United Kingdom remained a sort of 'federacy' with a strong English core, Westminster acting as the institutional focus of English identity, and the second would turn the United Kingdom into an explicit federation (Gamble 2006: 24).

England first

Speaking to the Bow Group at the Conservative Party Conference following the electoral defeat in June 1997, Michael Ancram identified what he called the 'English dimension' of British politics. In a measured and cautious fashion, he thought that the issue of fairness was inextricably linked to the question of the stability of the United Kingdom's constitutional arrangements. The Conservative Party, argued Ancram, must never become the party of English nationalism but should remain the party of the Union. The best way to defend the Union, he thought, was to make sure that all its component nations were treated fairly which meant that 'we are entitled, if not obliged, as unionists to get a fair deal for England' (cited in Sear 2003: 20). It was a theme taken up later by party leader William Hague in a speech to the Centre for Policy Studies where he claimed that devolution had 'unbalanced' relationships within the United Kingdom. The patriotic task of Conservative policy should be that of re-balancing the Union – 'consistent with the Britishness of our existing constitution' – while dispelling the 'dark clouds of nationalism' that were gathering in England (Hague 1998: 12). This was a potential danger also identified by John Barnes in a study that provided intellectual rigour to the party debate about the response to constitutional change. Though Barnes advocated an 'advanced' position for a Conservative – a 'federal Britain' – the necessity for radical measures was based on those same dark clouds. While he thought that there was 'little *immediate* danger of a resurgence of English nationalism' it was England's response to devolution that would be crucial and his advice was that a 'prudent conservative will expect the worst' (1998: 10). In Conservative deliberations, fairness, re-balance and British consistency were subsumed under the cry of 'English votes on English laws' and this cry was intended to head off the 'worst' – a United Kingdom subverted by resentment. It was favoured by Hague in July 1999, was considered sympathetically by Lord Norton's Commission to Strengthen Parliament (Conservative Party 2000) and became part of the Party's Manifesto for the General Election of 2001 (Russell and Lodge 2006: 84). It was also a solution favoured by Michael Howard who succeeded Hague in 2003 and continued to be party policy in the election of 2005. Though it is tempting to argue that this policy had little impact on public opinion, it is difficult to abstract its persuasiveness or otherwise from the Conservative defeat. Polls consistently show that 55–56 per cent of the electorate sympathise with the proposition and this is also replicated in Scotland. As an editorial in *Scotland on Sunday* argued, a majority of English MPs supported devolution and it was now time for Scottish MPs 'to play fair by the English' (2006). A more blunt challenge to the prevailing arrangement was phrased thus: 'If it was iniquitous for English rule to be imposed on Scotland, isn't it all the more iniquitous for Scottish rule to be imposed on England?' (Wheatcroft 2006). Of course, this is a false question because (like the Conservative Party) the Labour Party is not a Scottish Party but a British one, the majority of its MPs being also English, but a false question can have interesting political consequences and in February 2006 the issue of English votes on English laws resurfaced in the House of Lords in the shape of Lord Baker's Parliament Bill.

Baker admitted that in the past the West Lothian Question had been really a synonym for opposition to devolution, formulated in a manner such that it could not be answered, but this position was no longer sustainable. It was no longer the case that the West Lothian Question was unanswerable or that, as the Labour Government would prefer, a question which should not be asked, and 'the case for English votes for English laws is unanswerable'. Baker dismissed the two major objections to the proposal – that you could not separate out parts of Bills that were exclusively English and that it would undermine the sovereign integrity of Parliament by creating different classes of MPs at

Westminster. It was possible, if the political will were there, to designate specific legislative proposals and the argument about the integrity of Parliamentary representation no longer applied since devolution had already created different classes of MPs (House of Lords 2006: cols 902–11). Baker's Bill would have given the Speaker of the House of Commons the power to decide the territorial scope of legislation, designate national categories of MPs and to rule who could vote accordingly. Only on non-devolved matters such as foreign affairs would all MPs be eligible to vote. Such a simple and apparently economical solution had large implications for the conduct of government and one immediate effect would be shrinking the pool of potential ministerial talent available to the Prime Minister. In the aftermath of the Government reshuffle in May 2006, Lord Baker wrote to the *Daily Telegraph* complaining that the appointment of John Reid, MP for Motherwell North, as Home Secretary and Douglas Alexander, MP for Paisley and Renfrewshire, as Transport Secretary was 'an affront to all English voters' because both of them would 'have to make controversial decisions in a country no part of which they represent' (Baker 2006). This was not an exclusively Conservative obsession since a Labour Peer also wrote that putting Reid in charge of 'English' law and order was 'a constitutional absurdity' (Hattersley 2006).

However, things are not quite as simple as they might at first appear. First, the responsibilities of the Home Office are not exclusive to England (and Wales) since immigration policy and national security are matters reserved to Westminster. It remains difficult to extract what is English from what is British and one estimate reckoned that more than two-thirds of all legislation at Westminster applied in some measure to the United Kingdom as a whole (Hazell 2000b: 18). The very weight of English influence in British politics also means that legislation which applies exclusively to England can have funding implications for the other territorial jurisdictions. There can be a distinction, in other words, between territorial application (England only) and territorial effect (United Kingdom-wide) (Russell and Lodge 2006: 86). If that is the British side of Westminster governance there is, secondly, an English side. Take, for example, the representation of English regional interests in the European Union. It has been felt that the English regions have been unfairly treated since devolution but one study suggested that the truth is more complex. English interests are both 'underrepresented and overrepresented in terms of access arrangement'. They are underrepresented because the devolved institutions do have a higher profile and agenda; they are overrepresented because ministries in London have overwhelmingly English responsibilities. In this sense, the English regions are 'insiders' in the policy process if only because support 'tends to be generated in central government' for English regional interests, and because policy is not explicit does not mean that it is not implicit (Bulmer et al. 2006: 87). If the first of these considerations can be used to justify the role and equality of all MPs, the second can be used to qualify the Gaberlunzie complaint that English concerns are neglected in the new order. There has been, argued one expert, 'a kind of rough justice at Westminster', one which in the past meant that non-English MPs – insofar as their nationality was more important to them than their political ideology – had more cause to feel the rough than the smooth. It is only when the arithmetic in the House of Commons is very close that English MPs 'are more likely to suffer rough justice' and that has been rarely the case (Hazell 2006a: 226). It may be, as Hazell has suggested, that the House of Commons is already beginning to transform itself into an English parliament within its Westminster shell. Perhaps it could develop in a quasi-federal fashion and acquire the conventions required to make it function as a predominantly English legislature. One such convention might be that a defeat for Government on English business would not be taken as a vote of confidence (Hazell 2000b: 17). If that indeed were possible, does not the case for an English Parliament become more acceptable? Others certainly think so.

In January 1998 Teresa Gorman MP introduced a Private Member's Bill in the House of Commons calling for the establishment of an English Parliament. Since the United Kingdom Parliament would have so much less to do after devolution, she proposed that the English Parliament should meet in the Commons Chamber two or three times per week. Hazell's shell, in other words, would be differentially constituted, being British on some days and English on others. The debate was a perfect illustration of the 'serious but not serious' approach – a seriously felt sense of political imbalance combined with an unserious commitment to the political objective and both delivered in a good-humoured fashion. Mrs Gorman was right about one thing – 'there is no demand for the regional assemblies' – though her assumption that the only half-way house between the *ancien regime* and the break up of the United Kingdom was an English Parliament, did not necessarily follow. Her stated intention was *not* to ride the 'coach and horses of nationalism' since Mrs Gorman's constituents were not wildly nationalistic, but they did 'feel English and, like the Scots and the Welsh, we want to retain our national identity' and only a Parliament, not regional talking shops, would do (House of Common 1998: col. 589).

That view reflected the sentiment of the non-party pressure group the Campaign for an English Parliament (CEP) formed in 1998 and which claimed in exaggerated fashion that England no longer existed because 'it is being denied any national political institution of any sort to make the statement that the people of England are a distinct nation' (CEP 1998a). Though the CEP has a legitimate case, it has been disposed to make that case in the overheated grievance rhetoric of the English Gaberlunzie, bemoaning the democratic enormity inflicted upon 'the over-taxed, under-funded and under-represented people of England' (CEP 2003). A separate Parliament, it argued, was required to recognise English national identity, since that identity had been deprived of its proper expression except in sport. In short, the interests of English people have been consistently ignored and there existed no specific mandate from the people of England for the current system of governance imposed upon them. They were not permitted a referendum on constitutional change and had been fobbed off with an unpopular policy of English regionalism (CEP 1998b). Here is an injustice that must be put right (Knowles 2005).

The CEP's idiom is jingoistic but only in a very precise sense. Its English nationalism is formally reluctant rather than overtly separatist. Originally, jingoism professed a reluctance to fight, but warned that if the English had to, then they had the ships, the men and the money, too. Similarly, the message of the CEP is that it does not want to break up the United Kingdom but wishes to see it continue in a different, federated form. But if the Union does break up, then England will be secure: it will have 85 per cent of the men and women and it can also keep its own money by ending subsidies to the other nations, in particular the Scots. The English Democrats Party, which shares the CEP's outlook and its particular form of jingoism, also argued that since 1997 England has been reduced to 'an enfeebled jelly'. According to one of its leading activists, Christine Constable, the Scots and the Welsh (politically) now 'eat in the finest restaurants' while poor old England is 'like a tramp living in the gutter and pressing its nose against the glass' (cited in Stenhouse 2003). The Labour Government had set in motion a process with the intention of 'destroying England as a nation state' (Constable 2006). England, of course, has never been a democratic nation state in the sense meant here but the urgency of the anxiety is not diminished by such considerations and that is because the wish is father to the fear. The wish is that England *should* become a nation state if and when the United Kingdom crashes and the fear is that the English will be lost in the constitutional wreckage if they don't (see englishdemocrats.

org.uk/general.php). Here is a perfect example of the anxiety of antic-ipation and with it all the ingredients for a nationalist platform: a sense of injustice, a feeling of powerlessness, the mood of exploitation and the occasion for righteous anger. For example Fergus Shanahan, deputy editor of *The Sun*, anticipated St George's Day by announcing that he was 'fed up with the way Scotland is allowed to run England'. The litany of complaint was familiar: the English paid most of the bills, non-English MPs decided key matters like tuition fees or founda-tion hospitals and the Government was 'stuffed with Scots'. Self-pity – the English are so hopeless to let this happen; and self-righteousness – the English are the real backbone of the country – together inform the conclusion: 'It's time England had a new Parliament – for the English' (Shanahan 2006). Such opinions need to be treated with a certain caution because they are often couched, as this one was, in the tone of music hall banter. Only the politically tone deaf could fail to hear it because there are equal measures of playfulness and seriousness and that is the discourse at which tabloid culture excels – it *is* a living icon of modern Englishness. Parading a prejudice, especially such a vener-able prejudice as getting one over on the Scots, is often a way of containing it and despite the uncompromising finale, no programme of action need follow. Irritable growl syndrome, after all, is a condition that cannot be cured but only mitigated and people not only learn to live with it but can even learn to enjoy it. This has also been a charac-teristic of English behaviour where 'mustn't grumble' is itself a sort of grumble. What would be the potential consequences of an English Parliament if the wish did become reality?

An English Parliament appears to be the obvious way to bring symmetry back into constitutional relationships. The only problem is that it probably would not, since the sheer weight of English business and the sheer size of its problems would probably unbalance any imag-inable federation. 'No federation,' according to Hazell, 'can operate successfully where one of the units is so dominant' (2006c: 42). The suspicion, then, is that to campaign for an English Parliament is tanta-mount to campaigning for English independence. This may not be what is intended but it could be the result, though that observation does not de-legitimise, only contextualise, the campaign for an English Parliament. It merely indicates that those who do support this objec-tive must accept with equanimity, as most appear to do, the possibil-ity of the break up of the United Kingdom. This can be attributed to the curious mismatch between constitutional irritation and lived expe-rience. For groups like the CEP, enormous energy is expended criticis-ing the intermittent anomaly of non-English votes on English laws and yet, because of the sheer size and predominance of England-in-Britain, life can be led as if only England existed. By extension, therefore, life could continue without Scotland, Wales and Northern Ireland since they are already only an appendage to the substantial bulk of English things. This strength is also a weakness for those campaigning for an English Parliament because it also allows most English people to ignore the anomalies of devolution, because they too appear insignificant in the wider scheme of (English) matters. Certainly survey evidence and its academic interpretation provide a rather different picture of public opinion than the one conveyed on English patriotic weblogs (for an excellent site see http://www.toque.co.uk/blog/). The impression (so far) is not one of simmering outrage but one of national equanimity.

On the figures of the 2001 British Social Attitudes Survey one scholar estimated that there were 'no signs of any English backlash against asymmetry, and no indication that devolution leads to an urgent need for structural change in England' (Sandford 2002: 791). In 2006 John Curtice's judgement, based on systematic analysis of a series of opinion poll data, was that 'England has yet to embrace with much enthusiasm any form of change to the way that it is governed'. Indeed, even putting it in that fashion appeared to overstate the case since he also felt that 'people in England still have neither a distinctive sense of national identity nor a strong sense of regional pride'. Even those who do, thought Curtice, 'are not particularly inclined to feel that this should be reflected in their country's constitutional structure' (2006a: 138). As a result it was difficult to argue that there was any English 'backlash' that would challenge the future of the United Kingdom and the only problem Curtice could envisage was that the 'rough edges' of devolution might place some strain on the business of government (2006b: 108). Some guide to the reasons for this equanimity, or even indifference, to specific English forms of governance may be found in the work of social psychologists. There is a tendency, whatever the secret pleasures that may be had in grousing about the other nations in the United Kingdom, to treat the category 'British' as a 'common ingroup'. Rather than treating Northern Ireland, Scotland and Wales as 'others' against which to define Englishness, the stance often taken is one 'of empathy, displaying recognition of the existence, and sensitivities' of these parts of the United Kingdom. Indeed, national self-identity was frequently treated in what may be called a distinctively English fashion, 'as an essentially private matter' which defined neither the boundaries of community nor the social networks within which people interacted (Condor and Abell 2006).

Furthermore, the moral panic that often attended popular expressions of nationality appear to be misplaced (see for instance Marqusee 2006). 'Were it the case that the members of the white population generally identified personally with an ethnic sense of Englishness and used this as a basis for determining the boundaries of civil society and citizenship' then there would be cause to be alarmed for traditional civilities. However, there was little evidence from social psychological research to suggest this was true for most people (Condor et al. 2006: 158). The image conveyed in all cases is a very familiar and very English one. Activists may suggest the impression of English discontent but, as Edmund Burke argued, one should not mistake political reality because a few grasshoppers under a fern make the field ring with noise, while thousands of cattle, 'reposed beneath the shadow of the British oak', are silent. This reads perhaps like a very complacent interpretation of the English public mood and perhaps there is some need for caution. One explanation for the apparent equanimity of English public opinion may also be 'that virtually no public debate has taken place on issues of the governance of England' and that perhaps such a debate is only beginning (Sandford 2002: 791). Writing in 1998, Noel Malcolm feared that 'once separate primary political consciousnesses have been developed that make people think of themselves first of all as English as opposed to Scottish, and so on, then the sort of mentality is developing in which issues like the West Lothian question can become acute'. Like the cud-chewing great cattle under that British oak, Malcolm thought that it was the genial political indolence of most English people that held the United Kingdom together (1998: 52). If that remains the case it may not always be the case – here there is indeed hope for English nationalists – and there have been counter indications to suggest that not everyone is so sanguine about challenges to English national identity (N. Lawson 2005: 9–10). However, the disposition of the major parties is to prevent that day arriving, even though the specifically English dimension of that disposition has been more openly expressed.

For example in a keynote speech to the Institute for Public Policy Research, significantly titled *An English Identity within Britain* (2005a), David Blunkett thought that the English had been reluctant in the past to champion their nationality. This was beginning to change 'suggesting an increasing sense of English self-consciousness'. Superficially, Blunkett subscribed to the Kumar thesis of a 'lack' which proposed that whereas the other nations within the United Kingdom had retained their distinctive identities, the English had found it more difficult to do so: 'This partly explains why the English have been left without their own distinct institutions, icons and civic celebrations.' The more likely explanation is that English institutions, icons and celebrations had become British, shared rather than exclusive, not lacking but so present as to have become invisible – or, to use Michael Billig's term, 'banal' (Billig 1995). That they had become British, however, in no way diminished their Englishness because only nationalists think in those categories: either that the Englishness of Britain is an imperialistic imposition or that the Britishness of England is a Celtic plot. Nor does there appear to be much political significance in that other curiosity to which Blunkett referred, what the staff of the 1969 Royal Commission on Local Government had once called the 'Marbella Test', a test which supposedly distinguished the English from the other national identities within the United Kingdom. So, when on holiday at a Spanish resort, non-English tourists from Britain will normally describe 'home' as Northern Ireland, Scotland or Wales. For the English home tends to be their locality. According to Blunkett's reading of the Marbella Test for the inhabitants of the big cities, Manchester, Birmingham or Sheffield is the answer to the question of where home is: 'For those who hail from smaller towns or villages, the answer is always twofold: this or that village in so and so county.' Unfortunately for this implied support for Labour's policy of regional devolution, this is true only up to a point, since the peculiarity of the English in the Marbella Test is apparent rather than real and the result of a very *British* contrast. Because English tourists are statistically more likely to meet other English tourists, to respond to the question 'Where are you from?' with 'England' would be self-evident since the question is already an invitation to specify which part of England. It is an assumption of the British who are not English that to reply to the same question with, for example, 'Jordanstown, County Antrim' would not really enlighten the questioner (who is, statistically, most likely to be English). Again, it is the size of England within the United Kingdom that generates the exception. Blunkett's intention was to be doubly positive, to assert that there is 'a case for a renewed sense of English identity' but 'within an overarching Britishness'. Though the substantive illustration of what England meant to him was couched in the patriotic terms of the Whig interpretation of history, the political conclusion was defined in exemplary civic fashion. 'The disintegration theorists – who believe that England can only renew itself by breaking the Union – fail to appreciate that celebrating Englishness does not deny our Britishness or vice versa, or any other identities we hold. Here in Britain,' concluded Blunkett like a sort of streetwise Sir Ernest Barker, 'we know how to do plural identities' (Blunkett 2005a). And it was to 'do' plural identities in a British way that he had originally commissioned Crick to plan the introduction of tuition and tests for those seeking citizenship, as well as affirmation ceremonies for those becoming citizens. This would be part of the 'glue' that the Government believed necessary to hold the plurality of Britain together (Blunkett 2005b).

Conservatives agreed with the sentiments but had the opportunity to have fun at their opponent's expense. For Boris Johnson, New Labour had come to power to do away with old Britain but had only 'rediscovered the vitality of old symbols in a way that is hilarious and rather moving' and in the citizenship procedures introduced in 2004 'Norman Tebbit's cricket test has been given ceremonial form by David Blunkett'. What had been discovered was something conservatism had professed all along: that institutions and traditions are valuable. Having been wrong on economic arguments, the left had now conceded that it was also wrong on the cultural arguments (Johnson 2004b: 14). There were those who remained unconvinced, arguing that collective identities like Englishness were 'unravelling', becoming 'redundant', and that despite the efforts of Blunkett to apply the glue, 'citizenship can be decoupled from a sense of belonging' and was becoming inevitably global (Bunting 2005). Here is an example of a familiar contest between, in this case, the *Daily Telegraph* (patriotic) view and the *Guardian* (citizenship) view. Yet it has been persuasively argued that these are both a misreading of the character of Englishness. 'Too often,' as Philip Dodd has argued, 'it appears as if the two alternatives are to be English or to be cosmopolitan, that is, to belong to England or to belong to the world – whereas there are many ways of belonging to the world.' There are also many ways of belonging to England and being British has been one of the most significant and the most enduring (Dodd 1995: 28).

That there is an English Question is not in doubt. That it is political is not in doubt nor that it is connected with the West Lothian Question. As critics have recently complained, the Labour Government after 1997 was unwilling to discuss an answer to it. The former Lord Chancellor, Lord Irvine, thought that it was not a question that should be asked, a response which drew angry, but also some intelligent, responses from the English nationalist 'blogging' network (see for example www.thecep.org.uk/news/). Similarly, when asked by a Scottish journalist how the Chancellor, Gordon Brown, proposed to deal with the problem of Scottish votes on English laws one anonymous English Labour MP said: 'Well, he can pretend it doesn't exist. Which is exactly what he has been doing' (cited in Cusick 2005). Such calculated political recourse to avoidance or amnesia has so far matched rather than denied the public mood. In the past, survey evidence has suggested that there was no pressing public desire to see the English Question resolved, insofar as, that is, people actually *do* see it as a 'question'. More recent indications of public opinion in this regard have been mixed. On the one hand, a YouGov poll for the *Daily Telegraph* in May 2006 found that 45 per cent of respondents were 'bothered' but 49 per cent not bothered by the fact that the Scot John Reid had become responsible, as Home Secretary, for mainly English (and Welsh) matters (YouGov 2006). On the other hand, an ICM poll for the BBC's *Politics Show* found that 55 per cent of English respondents did not think that it was right for a Scot to become Prime Minister (BBC 2006a). Of course, what polls do not detect is the intensity of such views or their salience for those who express them. However, the mixed responses show that the complacent assumption that there is no political issue to think about is a misreading. Hazell thought that presently the English electorate was opting for the status quo, albeit a *new* status quo 'in which Scotland, Wales and Northern Ireland have their own political institutions, but England remains governed by the UK Government in Whitehall and the UK Parliament at Westminster'. He did admit, however, that the situation was not static but fluid. The English Question, he concluded, 'is not an exam question which the English are required to answer' and it can remain unresolved 'for as long as the English want' (2006a: 240). Today one cannot say with certainty when or for how long.

11

Put out even more flags

Academics spend a lot of their time worrying professionally about the identity of others and this book has worried at length about the English and their Englishness. It was the shock of experiencing the ubiquitous display of the Cross of St George on a visit to the North-West of England in the early summer of World Cup 2002 that provoked the interest in addressing the subject. The shock was a mix of the familiar and the unexpected. The public display of flags is familiar to anyone from Northern Ireland but it was unexpected to encounter them so prominently in England. In Northern Ireland when they are displayed *en masse*, flags are used either to demarcate territory by the proclamation of allegiance or to intimidate and deter outsiders. In the English case neither of these things seemed to apply since the flags were everywhere – a large proportion of them were flying from cars – and the spirit of their display was not designed to intimidate (and Northern Ireland experience makes one very sensitive to that sort of threat). The ubiquity of the Cross of St George, therefore, diluted any partisan political intent. Racists proclaiming: 'this is ours and not yours' were using the same symbol as those proclaiming: 'this is ours as well as yours'. The common symbol will not overcome that difference but it cannot now be used to deepen it. This may be an obvious statement to most English people but why it *is* obvious was what seemed to warrant some explanation. As World Cup 2006 got under way it still seemed a question worth addressing if only because there were those prepared to ask: 'Is it just me, or is anyone else slightly worried about the number of St George's flags flying from road vehicles right now?' (Harker 2006). From the Labour Government's perspective in 2006, the answer for once was clear. Yes, it was just him. The Prime Minister ordered the England flag to be flown in Downing Street on the days when England was playing in the tournament and his Secretary of State for Culture, Media and Sport flew the flag on her car. Even the Chancellor of the Exchequer and the

Leader of the Opposition got involved in a personal dispute about which of them was the more genuine England football supporter. In that 'serious but not serious' style that has become increasingly required in English politics, the Conservative MP and journalist Boris Johnson described the official acknowledgement of the flag in 2006 as the cultural equivalent of the storming of the Bastille or the Winter Palace: 'It is a revolution that was born among the scaffolders and the taxi drivers and the pub owners, and then spread to the bourgeoisie to the point where the Labour elite knew they could no longer contain it: they had to co-opt it' (Johnson 2006). For all the exaggeration of Johnson's remark it does contain a certain truth. Speaking on BBC Radio Four in January 2000, the then Home Secretary Jack Straw had warned of the dark and dangerous forces lurking within the English nation, a nation which had used a 'propensity to violence' to 'subjugate' the other nations in the United Kingdom and which had then exported that violence to Europe and the British Empire (BBC 2000). If some in the Labour Party still did think that, it was no longer wise to say so openly. The self-loathing tendency in English politics had not disappeared but it was no longer guaranteed such a sympathetic, possibly guilt-induced, hearing even on the left. But what did all this mean?

The most insightful comment on the 2002 experience was that of Jim White who argued that the history of English football hooliganism had indeed been shameful and what the English wanted was 'permission to go collectively mental, like they have seen other countries do on the point of sporting victory'. This was the desire, rather than the anxiety, of imitation and in the racially balanced, multi-ethnic England team, fans had a 'progressive symbol of their nation' (White 2002). Here was the 'celebratory patriotism' the origins of which some believed the English had had intimations in Euro96 and which had now become integrated into the mainstream of English popular culture (Crabbe 2004: 73). What surprised many on the left as well as on the right was that English patriotism was popular and could be carnivalesque – and have nothing to do with either 'fascism' or aggressive nationalism (see Condor 2000: 195–6). It may be no coincidence either that English flag waving has been most dramatically on show at and around those venues which have integrated most efficiently popular culture and commercial success – sporting events. International sport presents occasions of the people, for the people if not by the people (they are 'produced' by commercial organisations) though ones that have become popular carnivals (they require the mass participation of spectators). Modern sport needs its televisual spectacle and spectators are encouraged to buy into that spectacle (McGuigan 1992: 18). A generation ago, J. B. Priestley was famously concerned about the development of what he called 'Admass' and he feared that the spirit of utilitarianism made Englishness peculiarly vulnerable to the threat of superficial consumerism (Priestley 1973: 240). From that point of view, the Englishness that displays itself on these occasions may have become yet another exercise in national branding, to be consumed like Union Jack T-shirts, England football jerseys or one-day international cricket shirts and it would fit with a political *Zeitgeist* that favours such enterprises as the 're-branding' of Britain (Leonard 1997). If nationalism is marketable and is what everyone else must have, then why not buy into it? Was not English World Cup merchandise expected to be worth more than £1.2 billion to manufacturers and retailers and, according to one businessman, was this not just 'a drop in the ocean' compared to what could be expected when London hosted the Olympics in 2012 (Colville 2006)? The sociologist Anthony King repeated the familiar and now radically chic idea that the Cross of St George represented a newly inclusive, cosmopolitan English identity which had replaced the old xenophobic British one but he also added for good measure that the England team's brand was marketed to maximise its commercial attraction (cited in Morgan 2006). The latter point is now a fact of business life but the former claim, as this book has argued, is too neat to be historically persuasive even though it has been politically attractive – it links intellectuals with the (sporting) public – and politically convenient – it legitimately replaces older ideological identities like socialism. It has been suggested here that the political term which best describes the emergence of the Cross of St George as a feature of contemporary Englishness is the *autonomy of populism*. Historically, conservative politics strove to contain English populism within a culture of social deference and Labour politics strove to contain it within a culture of working class solidarity, while the English liberal conscience often disdained English popular culture, fearing that it was both racist and xenophobic. The withering of social deference, the waning of working class solidarity and the retreat of intellectual snobbery has permitted populism to escape these former restraints. Extracting the Cross of St George from the Union flag – in the *carnavalesque* of sporting emotion – has become a statement of national pride. This pride can be playful or threatening, it can be subversive or loyal, it can be overbearing or understated and it can be all these things at once. But this populism, having become autonomous in the way it has, has remained recognisably English. *The Observer* (2006) believed that the English still did 'irony better than bombast' and one *Guardian* journalist (Anthony 2004) thought that the English sense of 'irony and burlesque' would always win out over 'jingoism and seriousness'. Both these views are partially true, but they are wished-for as much as actual and perhaps they have embraced a little too readily that very valuable patriotic resource, England's own PR. But there is sufficient truth in them to identify something distinctive about even English populism, the ironic tinge in its bombast and the bombastic aspect of its irony, the serious-ness in its lack of seriousness. Nevertheless, the continuities are just as striking as the discontinuities.

Orwell, for example, once asked what did his England of 1940 have in common with the England of 1840? His answer: the same thing that an adult has with the photograph of the child of five his mother still kept on the mantelpiece. 'Orwell's English and the English of today,' as Colls interpreted him 'cannot be compared as if they are two spec-imens in a box. They can only be explained through a line connecting how they thought about themselves then with how we think about ourselves, and them, now.' Being English 'is the consistent factor' but this too was subject to change (2002: 2). While there is less deference and more display, less stiff upper lip and more self-disclosure, less class and more mass, less understatement and more overstatement there is also much that remains familiar. The one thing that does remain famil-iar – the one thing which can often lead to interpretative misunder-standing – is the everyday self-satisfaction of being English, a self-satisfaction that can safely indulge those who trade in self-loathing. Because it is still so understood and so taken-for-granted, the incautious can assume that it is actually lacking. Moreover, it is often assumed that there is something peculiarly traditional and conserva-tive about Englishness whereas the truth is more subtle. England is not 'traditional' in the way in which other nations – like the French, for example – are 'radical' (for one comparison see Flavell 1998). In England, rather, the traditional and the radical take a distinctive form in the idiom of English politics, a relationship which has been captured intelligently by David Aaronovitch. England remains, he thought, as Orwell described it 'characterised by a complacent gentleness in which fascists do not get elected to very much, and where populists are treated with suspicion'. Significantly for Aaronovitch 'tradition and modernity operate in a constant dialectic' (Aaronovitch 2003; on Orwell see Dose 1992). For all the hypocrisy, betrayals, frustrations, disappointments and petty tyrannies of English history and English public life, that is a virtue worth acknowledging today, as it was in Orwell's day. Oakeshott once argued that 'the charm of a compromise and appeals to that love of moderation' was often fatal to the power of English philosophy but 'it has been favourable to English politics' (Oakeshott 1986: 196). One of the favours it did for English politics was to manage without the logic of classic nationalism though to secure for English politics the legitimacy and authority which such nationalism delivered elsewhere. The developments since 1997 recounted in this book have promoted the idea that this too has changed, that England is about to escape with a leap and a bound from the prison-house of the nations – to use an Austro-Hungarian term – which is the United Kingdom. Unionism has been discounted by the nations it once embraced and a 'union state without unionism' can survive for some time but not forever (McLean and McMillan 2006: 256). Some anticipated this with melancholy, fearing an 'English backlash' more serious to the Union than any threat from either the Scottish or Welsh nationalism (Cochrane 2006). Some anticipated it with joy, indulging in 'Scottophobia' along the way (*The Herald* 2006), a tradition at least as old as the accession of James I to the English throne. One of the leading English Gaberlunzies described Scottish influence in the governance of England as the rule of the Scotia Nostra and called to witness, with menace rather than with promise, Chesterton's 'secret people of England' who were now 'beginning to stir' (Littlejohn 2006; see also Heffer 2006c).

Though the evidence of increased English identification appears to confirm a nationalistic 'moment'- as Kumar would define it – and so some consequent development of English separatism, there is good reason to be cautious because 'predictions derived from earlier theories of political generations have not always been notably successful' (Heath et al. 1999: 173). Despite the prevalence of the Cross of St George in English culture, another scholar observed that there had been little 'grassroots' awakening of interest in the governance of England (Sandford 2002: 789). Though recent research into British social attitudes discovered that people in England had indeed become more willing to call themselves English rather than British following devolution in the rest of the United Kingdom, it appeared that public opinion in England had simply adjusted to the new status quo. There was also reason to be cautious about accepting that the anxieties of intellectuals, which a good proportion of the electorate also shared in some measure, would have a necessary political effect. As a YouGov survey found, the old staples of fair play, tolerance, civility and political institutions still ranked highly amongst public values and it did not find a deeply disturbed introspection about what it meant to be British or English. For those who feared that English patriotism was the equivalent of a sneaking regard for the British National Party (BNP) and the sort of racism that would have no 'black' in either the Union Jack or the Cross of St George, the same YouGov survey showed that the athlete Kelly Holmes was in a dead heat with the Queen for the person in whom people had most pride (King 2005). Moreover, the 'icons of Englishness' suggested by the public to the Government-sponsored (£1 million) *Icons Online* project were a mix of the tourist board familiar – Big Ben, York Minster; the regionally evocative – the Lindisfarne Gospels, Hadrian's Wall; the culturally diverse – Morris Dancing, The Notting Hill Carnival; and the – by now inevitable – Cross of St George. There was nothing on this list to suggest a radically disaffected nation, perhaps confirming the view of Curtice and Heath that the English had retained a post-devolution equanimity, even complacency (2000: 172). Of course, one should also be cautious about making predictions derived from *their own* theory of a political generation and, as supporters of an English Parliament or even English independence would argue, the social attitudes survey evidence is now dated and has been overtaken by events. England *has* begun to stir and the Conservative Party, for one, is beginning to respond to this shift in opinion and to fly the English flag in the sense that Gladstone once flew his kite at Hawarden. 'I'm beginning to think,' Alan Duncan, Shadow Secretary of State for Trade, Industry and Energy, told the BBC's Politics Show 'it is almost impossible now to have a Scottish Prime Minister because it would be at odds with the basic construction of the British constitution' (BBC 2006b). A majority of English voters (52 per cent), according to a YouGov poll in June 2006, still thought otherwise and did not think that sitting for a Scottish constituency should debar one from being Prime Minister (*Daily Telegraph* 2006).

The politics of flags, of course, was not exhausted by the Cross of St George flying over Number 10 or on the car roof of a Government Minister. On 14 January 2006, in a widely ranging speech to the Fabian Society's conference on the 'The Future of Britishness', the Chancellor of the Exchequer, Gordon Brown (and of course that potential Prime Minister about whom Duncan had been speaking), argued that national identity was not just an academic debate but a question of avoiding a divided society. He believed that it was necessary to 'rediscover and to build from our history' the shared values 'that bind us together and give us common purpose' and Brown took his inspiration from Jonathan Freedland's *Bringing Home the Revolution* (1998). Freedland's book had argued that the spirit of radical Britishness had been instituted in the United States whereas its conservative alter ego had secured itself at home. This was a novel twist (in its pro-Americanism) on an old theme and the theme was that of liberty. 'Brown and Liberty' – or how 'modern' British liberty was required to address the challenges of globalisation – was the theme of the Chancellor's speech and it paid due homage as well to Orwell's attack on the left's hostility to patriotism. According to Brown, the left 'should feel pride in British patriotism and patriotic purpose founded on liberty for all, responsibility by all, and fairness to all'. The media interpreted Brown's speech to advocate the celebration of Britishness with a public holiday of 'British Unity' along the lines of the United States' Fourth of July or the French Bastille Day, a public holiday that would involve the flying of the Union flag in every garden (for press response see *Daily Mail* 2006; *Guardian* 2006; Helm 2006; Webster 2006). The conformity of the reporting suggests that this is how the Chancellor desired his remarks to be 'spun' but a reading of the speech itself makes his position more equivocal. The proposal, insofar as it was a proposal, was put as a rhetorical question, not as a commitment: 'What is our equivalent for a national celebration of who we are and what we stand for?' and 'What is our equivalent of the national symbolism of a flag in every garden?' (Brown 2006). Though this was interpreted by the Chancellor's critics – and not only amongst Conservatives – as a cynical ploy by a Scot both to overcome the West Lothian Question and to legitimise his claims to be Prime Minister, Brown had been engaged with this issue intermittently for over a decade (see for example Brown 1997). Unfortunately, there were those in the Labour Party who remained addicted to a corporate marketing culture of politics and thought of national identity as some sort of vacuous 'mission statement' – 'Most other countries have a national mission embodied in their constitution' (Wills 2006) – the sort of thing which makes most sensible people justifiably cringe. Such absurdities apart, the recent discussion about Britishness and Englishness revealed another example of the historic conversation between citizenship and patriotism (see Stapleton's seminal discussion 2005b).

As this book has argued, citizenship and patriotism are abstractions from a complex reality, a reality which is politically ambivalent and open to revision. All nationalities, Englishness included, are something of a hybrid incorporating both the formalities of citizenship and the sentiments of patriotism. The relationship produces the paradox noted by A. D. Smith: that the solidarity sustaining the diversity of modern political citizenship rights requires a sense of unity and attachment to a particular homeland (Smith 1996: 458). It has become one of the conventions of the conversation about national identity to assume that

'British' now means the formalities of citizenship while English (or Scottish, Welsh and Irish) means the sentiment of particular attachment. Recently, this can be traced to Linda Colley's influential work *Britons* (1992) which argued that Britain was 'an invented nation superimposed, if only for a while, onto much older alignments and loyalties' (1992: 5). For Colley, the natural loyalties of Welsh, Irish, Scottish and English were bound to wax once the artifice of British began to wane (1992: 375). The history of this has been challenged by others (see, for example, Clark 1997: 802) but it is the logical neatness of its formula that suggests a misreading. The logical confusion of nomenclature in the United Kingdom – and, by implication, the logical implausibility of the future of that state – was, famously, the starting point for Norman Davies's equally influential *The Isles: A History* (1999) but that argument too has been challenged as a misreading (Aughey 2001: 5–9). In sum, Britishness has tended to become understood as nothing more than 'a civic device to bind people together without recourse to ethnicity' (Marr 2000: 47). That makes Britishness entirely exterior and formal compared with the interior and sentimental nature of national identity. This has given rise to two radically competing views. In the first, the civic exterior becomes dispensable insofar as one can persuade people, as nationalists seek to do, that it is more authentic if the interior of Englishness has its unique expression in exterior (parliamentary) form. In the second, the patriotic interior becomes dispensable through dilution as the exterior includes all, a condition in which 'we must put out more flags – or none' (Garton Ash 2006; see also Colley 2006). However, a more accurate reading would suggest that the supposed confusion of language between British and English or between nation and state or between civic and ethnic has reflected accurately the interpenetration of these terms in the United Kingdom. The most subtle contemporary political discussions of national identity have been aware of this (see, for example, Goodhart 2006: 28) but even someone thought today to be the byword for political incorrectness, Rudyard Kipling, was aware of it too. It was their 'immensely mixed origin', he thought, that made the English feel civically 'akin to all in the universe' (a tendency amongst intellectuals today) but that it was 'by the things that we take for granted without word', that is a patriotic civility, that the English lived and thought (Kipling 1920).

A very different thinker, Sir Ernest Barker, also argued that the key to grasping English/British national distinctiveness was not a question of absolutes, civic or patriotic, but it was all *a question of degree* – and that 'degree' or measure was at the very heart of the English idiom of politics. 'There is a sense,' Barker accepted, 'in which the Scottish and the Welsh peoples are nations of the first degree, content with the social expression of their quality.' This was only the half of it because, on the other hand, 'the members of these peoples are also members of a nation – the British nation – which is a nation of the second degree; they are heirs of its past traditions and masters by their vote of its future destinies; nor would they be content with nationhood in the first degree unless, in another form, they also possessed it in the second.' In British history (*contra* Nairn and his followers) it was democracy which transformed the character of things and in stating why this was so, Barker set out in the English idiom the ideal of Britishness: 'A democratic State which is multi-national will fall asunder into as many democracies as there are nationalities, dissolved by the very fact of will which should be the basis of its life – unless, indeed, as we have somehow managed in our island, such a State can be both multi-national and a single nation, and' – here Barker echoed George III – 'teach its citizens at one and the same time to glory both in the name of Scotsmen or Welshmen or Englishmen and in the name of Britons' (1927: 17). Despite Barker's prejudice against and exclusion of the (Northern) Irish – a common liberal failing – his understanding is still valid. It has been the degree of interpenetration of the citizenship and patriotism within Britishness – and not the absolute distinction between British (civic) and English (patriotic) – that was the efficient secret of political union. This was a subtle ideal which worked in a fit of absence of mind, so absentmindedly that most people still have difficulty in describing it properly, what Davies was writing about in *The Isles*, and it has often worked so that many people, particularly the English, have failed to understand what they helped to bring into existence. Even a scholar as intelligent as Kumar misread the true measure of English national identity in the degree to which it was both distinct and indistinct. Today one would have to admit that the 'common national substance' of Britishness has become weaker and that the 'separate national funds' have become stronger but acknowledging this change does not entail the necessary acceptance of the prospect that Nairn outlined for the United Kingdom – 'transition from the management of decline into the management of disintegration, leading eventually to a suitable testament and funeral arrangements' (2000a: 58). His wish is father to the prediction; he may be right in the long term but the case is not proven. For Pocock, by contrast, neither the English nor any of the other nationalities of the United Kingdom needed the simplicity of clear-cut identities; rather, they needed 'a complex history and a complex politics, if they are free to argue with themselves as well as with each other'. The English, above all, should avoid at all costs revelling in their griev-ances, real or imaginary, and commit themselves to 'a politics in which multiple identities are both intermixed and respected' (Pocock 2000: 41–52). England/Britain, albeit a modified England/Britain, would appear still to be the framework that respects that complexity and though there may be an 'incredible vagueness' to Englishness, as a consequence that may be its value (Cohen 2000: 35; Kearney 2000). That judgement may also be a misreading, a wished-for rather than a logical conclusion, yet as Vernon Bogdanor observed, for the moment at least the 'brute facts of electoral behaviour' oblige one to believe that Britain is not 'so artificial a construct or so imagined a commu-nity as many historians have suggested' (Bogdanor, 2002).

For England, the consequence of its being an 'absorptive patria' has meant a real, and not imaginary or imposed, interpenetration of things British and things English. The English are, as Defoe claimed, likely to be British mongrels and while things may be done differently in Wales or Scotland or Northern Ireland they are not done *that* differently for English people to feel strangers there. Despite the stories of despicable anti-English prejudice in the so-called 'Celtic Fringe' (see MacDonell 2006), English people can and do feel at home in other parts of the United Kingdom just as those from other parts of the United Kingdom feel at home in England. Moreover, it would be very peculiar if the official political culture in all parts of the United Kingdom, which today equates righteousness with inclusiveness, diversity and the cele-bration of difference, was incapable of sustaining the real and historic multiculture of Britishness. It would be (at least from this author's point of view) a tragic case of a politics of national separatism based on the narcissism of small differences. A 'cosmopolitan Englishness' (Bryant 2003) – or a cosmopolitan Scottishness for that matter – that was unable to cope with national diversity at home would be a curious cosmopolitanism indeed. If the English are British by virtue of the history of England's political, economic and cultural weight within these islands and by virtue of its 'absorptive capacity', then the British are also (partly) English as a consequence. Billy Bragg captured succinctly the interconnected parts of this relationship when he sang: 'Cos my neighbours are half English and I'm half English too'. He is 'half English' because of the British (and imperial) encounters which has made England what it is today while his (next-door) neighbours may well be 'half English' in the sense of being Asian or black. England's geographical, British neighbours are half English too, because everyone in the United Kingdom, by fate or by choice, is half

English since the fate of England is everyone's fate. Whether they like it or not (some don't but most do), what touches England touches everyone. In short, the English are half British and the British are half English. The 2006 World Cup was the occasion for an English grievance against those Scots (in particular) who refused to support England during the competition. But for all the reproach of a Scottish First Minister who preferred Trinidad and Tobago to England, what is to be made of the fact that a Glasgow Rangers fan would support any other (foreign) team against Celtic and vice versa or, for that matter, what is to be made of the fact that Liverpool and Everton fans would behave in exactly the same way? Does it mean that this rules out any commonality between Glaswegians and Scousers? We would think not. However, cricket provides a different example and as Simon Jenkins correctly noted, England's victory against the Australians in the 2005 Ashes series was truly an event in which, despite the singing of 'Jerusalem', the game belonged 'to the nation as a whole', that is Britain (Jenkins 2005b). It was perhaps in both these senses of rivalry and commonality that the artistic director of the Royal Shakespeare Company, Michael Boyd – born in Belfast, brought up in London and educated in Edinburgh – could appreciate 'the unfinishedness of the idea of Britishness' in all its contrariness, for that is what has shaped it and made it an attractive 'messy, pluralistic place' to live, where local and national competition does not mean an absence of community (Boyd 2005). Unless or until, that is, politicians choose to make it impossible for such messiness to continue or choose no longer to conduct political relations in that idiom which Mannheim had thought distinctive – working out in practice principles which seemed to be logically opposed. Not only politicians but people must want it as well. Sustaining 'equality in diversity' is a difficult and frequently inconsistent political objective but it is not an impossible one (see Adams and Schmueker 2006: 5–6).

In Chapter 1 it was argued that to define Englishness is not so much a preface as a postscript, and it was proposed that to be English was to participate in a conversation, an imaginative rather than a purely functional engagement, about the country's history, culture and society, and this is what Orwell, and after him Colls, believed to constitute a national identity. When it comes to defining English idenntity one useful rule of thumb has been: what you see is what you don't get. A trite phrase perhaps but it does go a long way towards explaining those social and cultural characteristics that many have thought definitive of the nation: English hypocrisy, which is a way of not saying what you mean; English witticism, which is a way of avoiding serious argument; English gentility, which is a way of concealing more vulgar passions; English civility, which is a way of moderating self-interest; English tolerance, which is a way of ignoring others; English self-criticism, which is another measure of self-esteem. English literature, one can say, has been an imaginative conversation between what is seen and what is got. If the impression conveyed is often negative this is not universally so for in truth these are virtues as well as vices. The patriot should acknowledge the vices and the citizen should be protective of the virtues. There is also another dimension which goes a long way to explaining much about the politics of Englishness: what you don't see is what you do get. The uncodified British constitution has been more resilient than its written counterparts and its conventions often more robust than strict formalities, its monarchical gloss less significant than its democratic substance. English national identity, this book has argued, is a further example and to assume its absence is to misread historical experience. Things have changed and are changing (and populism and nationalism loathe anything but authenticity) yet there is much that remains familiar, in particular the diversity of English sentiment.

For Ernest Barker, a nation was defined by a diversity of 'races' but one which possessed a stock of references that could be made into a common history and out of the variety of its population could also be made 'the house of thought' in which people's 'minds may dwell there together' (Barker 1927: 18). That may be too Idealist for today's sensibility but it has the value, as Oakeshott's notion of conversation does too, of stating a truth that is easy to forget: that there is no England but thinking makes it so. *How* England has thought about itself and how others have thought about England has changed and will continue to change. The idiom of English politics and the legends of Englishness have been modified and will continue to be modified. *What* England has thought of itself has induced not only complacency but also anxiety and these complacencies and anxieties have informed the tone in which the national conversation has been conducted and will continue to be conducted. *Where* England thinks itself to be – insular, European, imperial, global – is also subject to change and the location of Englishness has an effect upon how England has thought and will continue to think of itself. This book has tried to trace those thoughts in their recent and current expression. If there is always to be an England, Englishness must mean something to those who now speak of it. And it does.

References

Aaronovitch, D. (2003) 'English actually', *Observer*, 23 November.

Ackroyd, P. (2002) *Albion – the Origins of the English Imagination*, London: Chatto and Windus.

Adair, G. (1986) *Myths and Memories*, London: Fontana.

Adams, J., Lee, S. and Tomaney, J. (2002) 'Prospects for regionalism', in J. Tomaney and J. Mawson (eds) *England: State of the Regions*, Bristol: Policy Press.

Adams, J. and Schmueker, K. (2006) *Devolution in Practice 2006: Public Policy Differences within the UK*, London: IPPR.

Alexander, D. (2005) *Europe in a Global Age*, London: Foreign Policy Centre.

Alibhai-Brown, Y. (2002) 'The excluded majority: what about the English?', in P. Griffith and M. Leonard (eds) *Reclaiming Britishness*, London: Foreign Policy Centre.

Anderson, B. (1991) *Imagined Communities: Reflections on the Origins and Spread of Nationalism*, London: Verso.

Anderson, P. (1980) *Arguments Within English Marxism*, London: NLB.

Anderson, P. (1992) *English Questions*, London: Verso.

Anderson, P. (2002) 'Internationalism: a breviary', *New Left Review* (second series) 14 (March/April), 5–25.

Anthony, A. (2004) 'I'm English – but what does that mean?', *Guardian*, 2 July.

Ascherson, N. (2000) 'On with the polling and merging', *London Review of Books*, 22:4, 17 February.

Aslett, C. (1997) *Anyone for England? A Search for British Identity*, London: Little, Brown and Company.

Aughey, A. (2001) *Nationalism, Devolution and the Challenge to the British State*, London: Pluto Press.

Aughey A. (2006a) 'The challenges to English identity', in R. Hazell (ed.) *The English Question*, Manchester: Manchester University Press.

Aughey, A. (2006b) 'Traditional Toryism', in K. Hickson (ed.) *The Political Thought of the Conservative Party since 1945*, London: Palgrave.

Ayres, S. and Pearce, G. (2004) 'Central government responses to governance change in the English regions', *Regional and Federal Studies*, 14:2, 255–80.

Bailey, D. (2001) 'The new political map of England', *Parliamentary Brief*, July, 10–12.

Baker, D., Seawright, D. and Gamble, A. (2002) 'Sovereign nations and global markets: modern British conservatism and hyperglobalism', *British Journal of Politics and International Relations*, 4:3, 399–428.

Baker, K. (1998) 'Speaking for England', *The Spectator*, 1 August.

Baker, K. (Lord Baker of Dorking) (2006) 'Blair's twilight is haunted by devolution' (letter), *Daily Telegraph*, 8 May.

Barder, B. (2001) 'Britain: still looking for that role?', *The Political Quarterly*, 72:3, 366–74.

Barker, E. (1919) 'Nationality', *History*, 4, 135–45.

Barker, E. (1927) *National Character and the Factors in its Formation*, London: Methuen.

Barker, E. (1945) *Essays on Government*, Oxford: Clarendon Press.

Barker, E. (1947) 'An attempt at perspective', in E. Barker (ed.) *The Character of England*, Oxford: Clarendon Press.

Barker E. (1950) 'The English character and attitude towards life', *England*, September, 6–9.

Barker, R. (1995) 'Whose legitimacy? Elites, nationalism and ethnicity in the United Kingdom', *new community*, 21:2, 58–66.

Barker, R. (1996) 'Political ideas since 1945, or how long was the twentieth century?', *Contemporary British History*, 10:1, 2–19.

Barnard, A. J. (2001) 'Anthropology, race and Englishness: changing notions of complexion and character', *Eighteenth Century Life*, 25 (Fall), 94–102.

Barnard, C., Deakin, S. and Hobbs, R. (2003) '"Fog in the Channel, continent isolated": Britain as a model for EU social and economic policy?', *Industrial Relations Journal*, 34:5, 461–76.

Barnes, John (1998) *Federal Britain: No Longer Unthinkable?*, London: Centre for Policy Studies.

Barnes, Julian (1999) *England, England*, London: Cape.

Barnett, A. (1999) *This Time*, London: Vintage.

Barnett, C. (1972) *The Collapse of British Power*, London: Eyre Methuen Ltd.

Barry, B. (2001) 'Muddles of multiculturalism', *New Left Review* (second series), (March/April), 49–71.

Baucom, I. (1999) *Out of Place: Englishness, Empire and the Locations of Identity*, New Jersey: Princeton University Press.

Baxendale, J. (2001) 'I had seen a lot of Englands: JB Priestley, Englishness and the People', *History Workshop Journal*, 51 Spring, 87–111.

BBC (2000) 'Are the English violent?' 16 January: http://news.bbc.co.uk/1/hi/talking_point/596717.stm.

BBC (2002) 'Blunkett names "Britishness" chief', 10 September: http://news.bbc.co.uk/1/hi/uk_politics/2248319.stm.

BBC (2006a) 'English voters "oppose Scots PM"' 15 May: http://news.bbc.co.uk/go/pr/fr/-/hi/scotland/4770685.stm.

BBC (2006b) 'John Sopel interview with Alan Duncan MP for the Politics Show', 2 July: http://news.bbc.co.uk/1/hi/programmes/politics_show/5124232.stm.

Begbie, H. (A Gentleman with a Duster) (1924) *The Conservative Mind*, London: Mills and Boon.

Bell, D. (1991) 'The "Hegelian Secret": Civil Society and American Exceptionalism', in B. E. Shafer (ed.) *Is America Different? A New Look at American Exceptionalism*, Oxford: Clarendon Press.

Bell, D. A. (2000) 'A Long Silence', *London Review of Books*, 22:24, 14 December.

Bell, D. A. (2003) 'Ruling the Roast', *London Review of Books*, 25: 18, 25 September.

Betjeman, J. (1943) 'Oh, to be in England', *The Listener*, 29:739, 295–6.

Biggs-Davison, J. (1952) *Tory Lives*, London: Putnam and Company.

Billig, M. (1995) *Banal Nationalism*, London: Sage.

Birch, A. H. (1977) *Political Integration and Disintegration in the British Isles*, London: George Allen and Unwin.

Biscoe, B. (2002) 'Centralisation is the enemy of progress', *Western Morning News*, 8 May.

Black, J. (1994) *Convergence or Divergence? Britain and the Continent*, London: Macmillan.

Black, J. (1998) 'An English identity?', *History Today*, 48, 5–7.

Blackwell, N. (2003a) *The European Constitution and the Future of Europe*, London: Centre for Policy Studies.

Blackwell, N. (2003b) *A Defining Moment? A Review of the Issues and Options for Britain Arising from the Convention on the Future of Europe*, London: Centre for Policy Studies.

Blair, T. (2000) *Superpower – not Superstate*, London: Federal Trust.

Blake, R. (1970) *The Conservative Party from Peel to Churchill*,

London: Eyre and Spottiswoode.

Blunkett D. (2005a) 'An English identity within Britain', speech to the Institute for Public Policy Research, 14 March.

Blunkett, D. (2005b) 'For far too long, we have left patriotism to the extremists', *Guardian*, 21 March.

Body, R. (2001) *England for the English*, London: New European Publications.

Bogdanor, V. (1977) 'Regionalism: the constitutional aspects', *The Political Quarterly*, 48:1, 164–7.

Bogdanor, V. (1979) 'The English Constitution and devolution', *The Political Quarterly*, 50:1, 36–49.

Bogdanor, V. (1999) *Devolution in the United Kingdom*, Oxford: Oxford University Press.

Bogdanor, V. (2002) 'Lions, Unicorns and Ostriches ...', *The Times Higher Education Supplement*, November 8.

Bond, R. and McCrone, D. (2004) 'The growth of English regionalism? Institutions and identity', *Regional and Federal Studies*, 14:1, 1–25.

Borges, J. L. (1978) *The Book of Sand* (trans. N. T. di Giovanni), New York: Dutton.

Boyd, D. (2005) 'What does it mean to be British?' (interview with D. Smith and V. Thorpe), *Guardian*, 2 August.

Boyfield, K. and Ambler, T. (2006) *EUtopia. What EU Would be best and How do we Achieve it?*, London: Adam Smith Institute.

Boyle, N. (2004) 'The hiddenness of the spirit: the disappearance of God from the English cultural framework', *The New Blackfriars Magazine*, 85:996, 195–211.

Brace, C. (1999) 'Looking back: the Cotswolds and English national identity, c.1890–1950', *Journal of Historical Geography*, 25:4, 502–16.

Bradbury, J. (2003) 'The political dynamics of sub-state regionalisation: a neo-functionalist perspective and the case of devolution in the UK', *British Journal of Politics and International Relations*, 5:4, 543–75.

Bradbury, J. and McGarvey, N. (2003) 'Devolution: problems, politics and prospects', *Parliamentary Affairs*, 56:2, 219–36.

Bragg, B. (1995) 'Looking for a new England', *New Statesman*, 17 March.

Bragg, B. (1996) 'I am looking for a *new* England', *New Statesman*, 26 July.

Bragg, B. (1999) 'Forum day', *Looking Into England*, London: The British Council.

Bragg, B. (2002a) 'Reclaim our flag', *Daily Mirror*, 3 June.

Bragg, B. (2002b) Interview, *Tasty*, 16: www.tastyfanzine.org.uk /ints16.htm.

Bragg, B. (2004) 'George on our mind' (exchange of letters with Martin Linton MP) *Guardian*, 24 April.

Bragg, M. (1976) *Speak for England*, London: Secker and Warburg.

Brockbank, R. (1948) *Round the Bend with Russell Brockbank*, London: Temple Press.

Brown, G. (1997) 'Outward bound', *The Spectator*, 8 November.

Brown, G. (2004) *Britishness*, London: The British Council.

Brown, G. (2005) 'Gordon Brown on liberty and the role of the state: the Hugo Young memorial lecture', *Guardian*, 13 December.

Brown, G. (2006) 'The future of Britishness', speech to the Fabian Society 'Future of Britishness' conference, 14 January: www.fabian-society.org.uk/press_office/display.asp?id=520&type=news&cat=43.

Browne, A. (2005a) 'The Left's war on Britishness', *The Spectator*, 23 July.

Browne, A. (2005b) 'Now for the British revolution', *The Spectator*, 4 June.

Bruter, M. (2004) 'On what citizens mean by feeling "European": perceptions of news, symbols and borderless-ness', *Journal of Ethnic and Migration Studies*, 30:1, 21–39.

Bryant, A. (1969) *The Lion and the Unicorn: A Historian's Testament*, London: Collins.

Bryant, A. (2001) *The Spirit of England*, London: The House of Stratus.

Bryant, C. G. A. (2003) 'These Englands, or where does devolution leave the English?', *Nations and Nationalism*, 9(3), 393–412.

Bulmer, S., Burch, M., Hogwood, P. and Scott, A. (2006) 'UK devolution and the European Union: a tale of cooperative asymmetry?', *Publius*, 36:1, 75–93.

Bulpitt, J. (1983) *Territory and Power in the United Kingdom: An Interpretation*, Manchester: Manchester University Press.

Bulpitt, J. (1991) 'The Conservative Party in Britain: a preliminary paradoxical portrait', paper presented to the Political Studies Association annual conference, Lancaster.

Bunting, M. (2005) 'Beyond Englishness', *Guardian*, 14 March.

Bunting, M. (2006) 'If it's English votes for English law, the UK's end is nigh', *Guardian*, 12 June.

Burrow, J. B. (1988) *Whigs and Liberals: Continuity and Change in English Political Thought*, Oxford: Clarendon Press.

Buruma, I. (1999) *Voltaire's Coconuts or Anglomania in Europe*,

London: Weidenfeld and Nicolson.

Butterfield, H. (1944) *The Englishman and his History*, Cambridge: Cambridge University Press.

Bywater, M. (2000) 'Englishness: who cares?', *New Statesman*, 3 April.

Cabinet Office/DTLR (2002) *Your Region, Your Choice: Revitalising the English Regions*, Cm 5511, London: Stationery Office.

Cameron, D. (2005) 'Re-asserting faith in our shared British values', speech to the Foreign Policy Centre, 24 August.

Campaign for an English Parliament (1998a) 'Why an English Parliament?': www.thecep.org.uk/introduction.shtml.

Campaign for an English Parliament (1998b) 'The constitutional case for an English Parliament': www.thecep.org.uk/constitutional_case.shtml.

Campaign for an English Parliament (2003) 'Response to Eric Pickles': http://www.thecep.org.uk/pressreleases/press081003.html.

Campbell, D. and Asthana, A. (2006) 'On cars, in shops and on the houses: every day's a flag day', *Observer*, 26 May.

Cannadine, D. (1995) 'British History as a "new subject": politics, perspectives and prospects', in A. Grant and K. J. Stringer (eds) *Uniting the Kingdom? The Making of British History*, London: Routledge.

Cannadine, D. (1998) *History in Our Time*, New Haven: Yale University Press.

Canovan, M. (1981) *Populism*, New York: Harcourt.

Canovan, M. (1999) 'Trust the people! Populism and the two faces of democracy', *Political Studies*, 47:1, 2–16.

Canovan, M. (1996) *Nationhood and Political Theory*, Cheltenham: Edward Elgar.

Canovan, M. (2001) 'Sleeping dogs, prowling cats and soaring doves: three paradoxes in the political theory of nationhood', *Political Studies*, 49:2, 203–15.

Carsaniga, G. (1977) *Giacomo Leopardi: The Unheeded Voice*, Edinburgh: Edinburgh University Press.

Casey, T. (2002) 'Devolution and social capital in the British regions', *Regional and Federal Studies*, 12:3, 55–78.

Cave, M. (2001) 'Paradise Regained?', *The Salisbury Review*, Winter, 49–50.

Chadwick, H. M. (1945) *The Nationalism of Europe and the Growth of National Ideology*, Cambridge: Cambridge University Press.

Clark, J. C. D. (1990a) 'National identity, state formation and patriotism: the role of history in the public mind', *History Workshop*

Journal, 29, Spring, 95–133.

Clark, J. C. D. (1990b) 'The history of Britain: a composite state in a *Europe des patries?*', in J. C. D. Clark (ed.) *Ideas and Politics in Modern Britain*, Basingstoke: Macmillan.

Clark, J. C. D. (1997) 'The strange death of British history? Reflections on Anglo-American scholarship', *Historical Journal*, 40, 787–809.

Clark, J. C. D. (2000) *English Society, 1660–1832: Religion, Ideology and Politics During the Ancien Regime*, Cambridge: Cambridge University Press.

Clark, J. C. D. (2003) *Our Shadowed Present: Modernism, Postmodernism and History*, London: Atlantic Books.

Cochrane, A. (2006) 'Once we Scots were welcome. Now the English are ready to man Hadrian's Wall', *Daily Telegraph*, 21 May.

Cohen R. (1995) 'Fuzzy frontiers of identity: the British case', *Social Identities*, 1:1, 35–62.

Cohen, R. (2000) 'The incredible vagueness of being British/English', *International Affairs*, 76:3, 575–82.

Coleraine, Lord (1970) *For Conservatives Only*, London: Tom Stacey.

Colley, L. (1992) *Britons: Forging the Nation 1707–1837*, New Haven: Yale University Press.

Colley, L. (2001) 'Multiple Kingdoms', *London Review of Books*, 23, 4, 19 July.

Colley, L. (2006) 'British values, whatever they are, won't hold us together', *Guardian*, 18 May.

Collini, S. (1985) 'The Idea of "Character" in Victorian Political Thought', *Transactions of the Royal Historical Society* (fifth series) 35, 29–50.

Collini, S. (1993) *Public Moralists: Political Thought and Intellectual Life in Britain*, London: Clarendon Press.

Collini, S. (2001) 'Hegel in green wellies', *London Review of Books*, 23:5, 8 March.

Collini, S. (2003) '"No Bulshit" bullshit', *London Review of Books*, 25:2, 23 January.

Collins, J. (2005) 'Britain destroying itself from within', *Daily Mail*, 4 August.

Collins, M. (2002) 'The fall of the English gentleman: the national character in decline, c.1918–1970', *Historical Research*, 75, 187, 90–111.

Collinson, P. (1986) 'A Chosen People? The English church and the Reformation', *History Today*, March, 14–20.

Colls, R. (1998) 'The Constitution of the English', *History Workshop Journal*, 46, 97–128.

Colls, R. (2000) 'Our friends in the South: bad day in Newcastle', *The Political Quarterly*, 71:3, 463–8.

Colls, R. (2002) *Identity of England*, Oxford: Oxford University Press.

Colls, R. (2005) review of 'The Making of English National Identity', *The Sociological Review*, 53:3, 581–3.

Colville, R. (2006) 'England flags will cover the country', *Daily Telegraph*, 29 April.

Condor, S. (1997) '"Having History": a social psychological exploration of Anglo-British autostereotypes', in C. C. Barfoot (ed.) *Beyond Pug's Tour: National and Ethnic Stereotyping in Theory and Literary Practice*, Amsterdam: Rodopi.

Condor, S. (2000) 'Pride and Prejudice: identity management in English people's talk about this country', *Discourse and Society*, 11:2, 175–205.

Condor, S. (2001) 'Nations and nationalisms: particular cases and impossible myths', *British Journal of Social Psychology*, 40, 177–81.

Condor, S. and Abell, J. (2006) 'Vernacular constructions of "national identity" in post-devolution Scotland and England', in J. Wilson and K. Stapleton (eds) *Devolution and Identity*, Aldershot: Ashgate.

Condor, S., Gibson, S. and Abell, J. (2006) 'English identity and ethnic diversity in the context of UK constitutional change', *Ethnicities*, 6:2, 123–58.

Condren, C. (1999) 'English historiography and the invention of Britain in Europe', in J. Milfull (ed.) *Britain in Europe: Prospects for Change*, Aldershot: Ashgate.

Connolly, B. (2004) speech to Bruges Group: www.brugesgroup .com/mediacentre/speeches.live?article=245.

Conservative Party (2000) *Strengthening Parliament: Report of the Commission to Strengthen Parliament*, London: Conservative Party.

Constable, C. (2006) 'Will there always be an England?': http: //susvalleypolicy.org/policynews.asp?aid=1184.

Conway, D. (2004) 'The Government's new community cohesion and race equality strategy', *Civitas Review*, 1:3, 1–3.

Conway, D. (2005) 'Why history remains the best form of citizenship education', *Civitas Review*, 2:2, 1–10.

Cooke, M. (2000) 'Five arguments for deliberative democracy', *Political Studies*, 48, 947–69.

Cooper, R. (2000) *The Post-modern State and the World Order*, London: Demos.

Cooper, R. (2005) 'All together now: Europe', *Sunday Times*, 27 February.

Cowley, J. (1999) 'A search for identity in the shock of the new', *New Statesman*, 24 May.

Cowling, M. (1980) *Religion and Public Doctrine in Modern England*, Cambridge: Cambridge University Press.

Cox, D. (2002) 'At last, the silent people speak', *New Statesman*, 22 April.

Crabbe, T. (2004) 'Englandfans – a new club for a new England? Social inclusion, authenticity and the performance of Englishness at "home" and "away"', *Leisure Studies*, 23:1, 63–78.

Crick, B. (1989) 'An Englishman considers his passport', in N. Evans (ed.) *National Identity in the British Isles*, Coleg Harlech: Coleg Harlech Occasional Papers in Welsh Studies No 3.

Crick, B. (1991) 'The English and the British', in B. Crick (ed.) *National Identities: The Constitution of the United Kingdom*, Oxford: Blackwell.

Crick, B. (1995) 'The sense of identity of the indigenous British', in B. Parekh (ed.) 'British national identity in a European context', *new community* special issue, 21:2, 167–82.

Crick, B. (1999) book review, *The Political Quarterly*, 70:4, 475–7.

Crick, B. (2002) review of 'The Red Flag and the Union Jack', *The Political Quarterly*, 368–70.

Crick, B. (2003) 'How to be British', *Spectator*, 8 March.

Cunningham, H. (1981) 'The language of patriotism, 1750–1914', *History Workshop Journal* 12, 8–33.

Curtice, J. (2006a) 'What the people say – if anything', in R. Hazell (ed.) *The English Question*, Manchester: Manchester University Press.

Curtice, J. (2006b) 'A stronger or weaker Union? Public reactions to asymmetric devolution in the United Kingdom', *Publius*, 36:1, 95–113.

Curtice, J. and Heath, A. (2000) 'Is the English lion about to roar? National identity after devolution', in R. Jowell *et al.* (eds) *British Social Attitudes, 17th Report: Focusing on Diversity*, London: Sage.

Cusick, J. (2005) 'No Prime Minister', *Sunday Herald*, 20 March.

Daily Mail (leader) (2006) 'Brown backed over "Britishness Day"', *Daily Mail*, 15 January.

Daily Telegraph (leader) (2004) 'England United', *Daily Telegraph*, 6 November.

Daily Telegraph (2006) 'YouGov poll: Brown, Scotland and the UK', *Daily Telegraph*, 24 June.

Daley, J. (2005) 'For British "tolerance" read "indifference"', *Daily Telegraph*, 7 August.

Dalyell, T. (1977) *Devolution: The End of Britain*, London: Cape.

D'Ancona, M. (2002) 'Why the right must embrace multiculturalism', in P. Griffith and M. Leonard (eds) *Reclaiming Britishness*, London: The Foreign Policy Centre.

D'Ancona, M. (2005) 'This horror began with a literary row', *Daily Telegraph*, 17 July.

D'Ancona, M. (2006) 'For Labour, the gentleman in the town hall is always right', *Daily Telegraph*, 22 February.

Daniels, S. (1993) *Fields of Vision: Landscape Imagery and National Identity in England and the United States*, London: Polity Press.

Darian-Smith, E. (1999) *Bridging Divides: The Channel Tunnel and English Legal Identity in the New Europe*, Berkeley: University of California Press.

Darwin, J. G. (1986) 'The fear of falling: British politics and imperial decline since 1900', *Transactions of the Royal Historical Society* (fifth series) 36, 27–43.

Davey, K. (1998) *English Imaginaries: Six Studies in Anglo-British Modernity*, London: Lawrence and Wishart.

Davies, N. (1999) *The Isles: A History*, London: Macmillan.

Deas, I. and Ward, K. G. (2000) 'From the "new localism" to the "new regionalism"? The implications of regional development agencies for city-regional relations', *Political Geography*, 19, 273–92.

Deedes, B. (2001) 'The real trouble with Enoch', *The Spectator*, 18 August.

Defoe, D. (1997) *The True-Born Englishman and Other Writings*, Harmondsworth: Penguin.

Delanty, G. (1996) 'Beyond the nation-state: national identity and citizenship in a multicultural society – a response to Rex', *Sociological Research Online*, 1:3: www.socresonline.org.uk/socresonline/1/3/1.html.

Devolution and Constitutional Change (2005a) 'Before the referendum: public views on elected regional assemblies in the North of England', *Briefing No 17*, February.

Devolution and Constitutional Change (2005b) 'Why the North East said "No": the 2004 referendum on an elected regional assembly', *Briefing No 19*, February.

Dicey, A. V. (1905) *Lectures on the Relationship between Law and Public Opinion in England*, London: Macmillan.

Direct Democracy (2005a) 'Parish politics may be key to success', *Daily Telegraph*, 5 June.

Direct Democracy (2005b) 'Reviving local democracy in Britain will restore pride to our communities', *Daily Telegraph*, 9 June.

Dodd, P. (1995) *The Battle Over Britain*, London: Demos.

Dose, G. (1992) '"England Your England": George Orwell on socialism, gentleness, and the English mission', *anglistik & englischunterricht*, 46/47, 241–61.

Dyson, K. H. F. (1980) *The State Tradition in Western Europe: The Study of an Idea and Institution*, Oxford: Martin Robertson.

Eagleton, T. (2002) 'In the company of confreres', *London Review of Books*, 24:24, 12 December.

Easthope, A. (1999) *Englishness and National Culture*, London: Routledge.

Eastwood, D., Brockliss, L. and John, M. (1997) 'From dynastic union to unitary state: the European experience', in L. Brockliss and D. Eastwood (eds) *A Union of Multiple Identities: The British Isles, c.1750–c.1850*, Manchester: Manchester University Press.

Edgerton, D. (2005) 'Science and the nation: towards new histories of twentieth-century Britain', *Institute of Historical Research*, 78:199, 96–112.

Edmunds, J. and Turner, B. S. (2001) 'The re-invention of England? Women and "cosmopolitan" Englishness', *Ethnicities*, 1:1, 83–108.

Elton, G. R. (1991) *Return to Essentials: Some Reflections on the Present State of Historical Study*, Cambridge: Cambridge University Press.

Elton, G. (1992) *The English*, London: Blackwell.

English, R. and Kenny, P. (eds) (2000) *Rethinking British Decline*, Basingstoke: Palgrave.

Esty, J. (2004) *A Shrinking Island: Modernism and National Culture in England*, Princeton: Princeton University Press.

Evans, E. (1994) 'National consciousness? The ambivalences of English identity in the eighteenth century', in C. Bjorn, A. Grant and K. J. Stringer (eds) *Nations, Nationalism and Patriotism in the European Past*, Copenhagen: Academic Press.

Evans, R. and Harding, A. (1997) 'Regionalisation, regional institutions and economic devolopment', *Party and Politics*, 25:1, 19–30.

Farndale, N. (2001) 'The history man', *Daily Telegraph*, 16 February.

Favell, A. (1998) *Philosophies of Integration: Immigration and the Idea of Citizenship in France and Britain*, London: Palgrave.

Fforde, M. (1990) *Conservatism and Collectivism 1886–1914*, Edinburgh: Edinburgh University Press.

Fine, R. (1994) 'The new nationalism and democracy: a critique of pro patria', *Democratization*, 1:3, 423–43.

Foster, M. B. (1935) *The Political Philosophies of Plato and Hegel*, Oxford: Clarendon Press.

Fowles, J. (1998) *Wormholes: Essays and Occasional Writings*, London: Jonathan Cape.

Freeden, M. (1998) 'Is nationalism a distinct ideology?', *Political Studies*, 46:4, 748–65.

Freedland J. (1998) *Bringing Home the Revolution: How Britain Can Live the American Dream*, London: Fourth Estate.

Freedland, J. (2005) 'The identity vacuum', *Guardian*, 3 August.

Fromkin, D. (1999) 'The importance of being English', *Foreign Affairs*, 78:5, 144–9.

Fulford, F. (2005) 'Why England's f*****!', *Daily Mail*, 26 November.

Gamble, A. (1974) *The Conservative Nation*, London: Routledge & Kegan Paul.

Gamble, A. (2006) 'The constitutional revolution in the United Kingdom', *Publius* 36:1, 19–35.

Garland, J. (2004) 'The same old story? Englishness, the tabloid press and the 2002 football World Cup', *Leisure Studies*, 23:1, 79–92.

Garside, P. and Hebbert, M. (1989) 'Introduction', in P. L. Garside and M. Hebbert (eds) *British Regionalism*, London: Mansell.

Garton Ash, T. (2001) 'Is Britain European?', *International Affairs*, 77:1, 1–13.

Garton Ash, T. (2005) 'The birth of Europe', *Guardian*, 17 March.

Garton Ash, T. (2006) 'In our search for Britishness we should put out more flags – or none', *Guardian*, 19 January.

Gelfert, H.-D. (1992) 'Picturesque England, or, the part and the whole', *anglistik & englischunterricht*, 46/47, 31–48.

Geoghegan, V. (2003) 'Edward Carpenter's England revisited', *History of Political Thought*, 24:3, 509–27.

George, S. (1998) *An Awkward Partner: Britain and the European Community*, Oxford: Oxford University Press.

Gervais, D. (1993) *Literary Englands: Versions of Englishness in Modern Writing*, Cambridge: Cambridge University Press.

Gervais, D. (2001) 'Englands of the Mind', *The Cambridge Quarterly*, 30:2, 151–68.

Gilmour, I. (2001) 'Little Mercians', *London Review of Books*, 23:13, 5 July.

Gilroy, P. (1999) 'A London sumpting dis ...', *Critical Quarterly* 41:3, 57–69.

Gilroy, P. (2005) 'Why Harry's disoriented about empire', *Guardian*, 20 January.

Giordano, B. and Roller, E. (2004) '"Te para todos"? A comparison of the process of devolution in Spain and the UK', *Environment and Planning A*, 36, 2163–81.

Goodhart, D. (2004) 'Discomfort of strangers', *Guardian*, 24 February.

Goodhart, D. (2006) *Progressive Nationalism: Citizenship and the Left*, London: Demos.

Goulbourne, H. (1991) *Ethnicity and Nationalism in Post-imperial Britain*, Cambridge: Cambridge University Press.

Grainger, J. H. (1969) *Character and Style in English Politics*, Cambridge: Cambridge University Press.

Grainger, J. H. (1986) *Patriotisms: Britain 1900–1939*, London: Routledge & Kegan Paul.

Grant, R. (1998) 'The English tradition in literature', *The Salisbury Review*, Autumn, 29–31.

Green, D. (2005) 'Patriotism is back in fashion', *Daily Telegraph*, 27 December.

Green, M. (1976) *Children of the Sun: A Narrative of 'Decadence' in England after 1918*, New York: Basic Books.

Green, S. J. D. and Whiting, R. C. (1996) 'Conclusion: on the past development and future prospects of the state in modern Britain', in S. J. D. Green and R. C. Whiting (eds) *The Boundaries of the State in Modern Britain*, Cambridge: Cambridge University Press.

Greenfeld, L. (1992) *Nationalism: Five Roads to Modernity*, Cambridge, Mass: Harvard University Press.

Greer, G. (2005) 'Shakespeare's the daddy of all Englishmen', *Sunday Times*, 24 April.

Guardian (leader) (2004) 'Island of the mind', *Guardian*, 10 June.

Guardian (leader) (2006) 'Birth of a nation builder', *Guardian*, 16 January.

Hague, W. (1998) 'Change and tradition: thinking creatively about the constitution', speech to the Centre for Policy Studies, 24 February.

Hague, W. (2006) 'Speech to Policy Exchange' full text in *Guardian*, 21 February.

Hailsham, Lord (1959) *The Conservative Case*, Harmondsworth: Penguin.

Hain, P. (2003) 'Socialist values, local solutions', *Progress*, March/April: www.progressives.org.uk/magazine/Default.asp?action=magazine &articleid=408.

Hale, A. (2001) 'Representing the Cornish: contesting heritage interpretation in Cornwall', *tourist studies*, 1:2, 185–96.

Hall, S., Massey, D. and Rustin, E. (2005) 'After identity', *Soundings* 29, 1–2.

Hampsher-Monk, I. (1995) 'Is there an English form of toleration?', *new community*, 21:2, 227–40.

Hannan, D. (2006) 'So you thought the European constitution was dead, did you?', *Daily Telegraph*, 20 March.

Harker, J. (2006) 'Flutters of anxiety', *Guardian*, 18 May.

Harris, R. (1998) 'The rise of English nationalism and the Balkanization of Britain', *National Interest*, 54:Winter, 40–51.

Harvie, C. (1991) 'English regionalism: the dog that never barked', in B. Crick (ed.), *National Identities: The Constitution of the United Kingdom*, Oxford: Blackwell.

Haseler, S. (1990) 'Britain's ancient regime', *Parliamentary Affairs*, 43:4, 415–26.

Haseler, S. (1996) *The English Tribe: Identity, Nation and Europe*, London: Macmillan.

Haseler, S. (2004) *Super-State: The New Europe and its Challenge to America*, London: I. B. Taurus.

Hastings, A. (1999) 'Special peoples', *Nations and Nationalism*, 5:3, 381–96.

Hastings, M. (2003) 'Why I am no longer a European', *Guardian*, 15 December.

Hastings, C. (2004) 'England is the country that "dare not speak its name"', *Daily Telegraph*, 17 October.

Hattersley, R. (2004) 'A European superstate is inevitable', *Guardian*, 27 September.

Hattersley, R. (2006) 'It's all about the epitaph', *Guardian*, 8 May.

Hazell, R. (2000a) 'Regional government in England: three policies in search of a strategy', in S. Chen and T. Wright (eds) *The English Question*, London: The Fabian Society.

Hazell, R. (2000b) 'Loose Ends', *Prospect* 56, 20 October, 16–17.

Hazell, R. (2006a) 'Introduction: what is the English Question?', in R Hazell (ed.) *The English Question*, Manchester: Manchester University Press.

Hazell, R. (2006b) 'Conclusion: what are the answers to the English Question?', in R. Hazell (ed.) *The English Question*, Manchester: Manchester University Press.

Hazell, R. (2006c) 'The English Question', *Publius: The Journal of Federalism*, 36, 37–56.

Hazell, R., Russell, M., Seyd, B., Sinclair, D. (2000) 'The British constitution in 1998–99: the continuing revolution', *Parliamentary Affairs* 53:2, 219–41.

Healey, J. (2000) 'Conclusion', in E. Balls and J. Healey (eds) *Towards a New Regional Policy: Delivering Growth and Full Employment*, London: The Smith Institute.

Heath, A., Taylor, B., Brook, L. and Park, A. (1999) 'British National

Sentiment', *British Journal of Political Science*, 29-1, 155–75

Heathorn, S. (1996) '(Re) Discovering the national character: some recent work on the history of English nationalism and its influence on the construction of British national identity', *Canadian Review of Studies in Nationalism*, 23:1–2, 9–18.

Heffer, S. (1998) *Like the Roman: The Life of Enoch Powell*, London: Pheonix.

Heffer, S. (1999) *Nor Shall My Sword: The Reinvention of England*, London: Weidenfeld and Nicolson.

Heffer, S. (2002a) 'Now, more than ever, she is the Queen of England', *Daily Telegraph*, 2 June.

Heffer, S. (2002b) 'The case for anarchy', *The Spectator*, 18 May.

Heffer, S. (2002c) 'The next great exodus' *The Spectator*, 30 March.

Heffer, S. (2004) 'It's not devolution, it's divorce', *The Spectator*, 17 July.

Heffer, S. (2005) 'Labour has left a scar on the soul of Britain', *Daily Telegraph*, 26 October.

Heffer, S. (2006a) 'The soft approach to militant Muslims is a gift to the far Right', *Daily Telegraph*, 7 February.

Heffer, S. (2006b) 'The English will be heard, by George', *Daily Telegraph*, 22 April.

Heffer S. (2006c) 'Being ruled by Scots is no joke for the English majority', *Daily Telegraph*, 17 May.

Helm, T. (2006) 'Fly the flag in every garden', *Daily Telegraph*, 14 January.

Helmer, R. (2001) 'Democracy and the European Union': www.congressfordemocracy.org.uk/Helmer%20speech.html.

Henderson, R. (2003) 'English national identity', *Steadfast Magazine* issue 7: www.hsite.co.uk/steadf/articles/i7-henderson.html.

Henderson, R. (2004) 'Institutionalised Anglophobia', *Steadfast Magazine*, issue 12: www.hsite.co.uk/steadf/articles/i12-henderson.html.

Henderson, R. (2005) 'Institutionalised Anglophobia', *Steadfast Magazine* issue 12: www.hsite.co.uk/steadf/articles/i12-henderson.html.

Henry, J. (2005) 'Cambridge dons to halt decline of history lessons', *Daily Telegraph*, 24 July.

Hensher, P. (2002) 'What makes us who we are', *The Spectator*, 11 May.

Herald (leader) (2006) 'Scottophobia lives on today', *Herald*, 15 May.

Hetherington, P. (2003) 'Talking about devolution', *Guardian*, 5 November.

Hewison, R. (2003) 'Britannia rules no more', *New Statesman*, 6 October.

Hickman, M. J., Morgan, S., Walter, B. and Bradley, J. (2005) 'The limitations of whiteness and the boundaries of Englishness', *Ethnicities*, 5:2, 160–82.

Hill, A. (2004) 'The English identity crisis: who do you think you are?', *Observer*, 13 June.

Hitchens, P. (2005) 'Conservatives do not have a party', *The Spectator*, 18 June.

Hoggart, R. (1998) 'The way we were', *The Political Quarterly*, 69:4, 464–7.

House of Lords (2006) speech by Lord Baker of Dorking moving the second reading of the Parliament (Participation of Members of the House of Commons) Bill, *House of Lords Hansard*, 10 February.

Howe, D. (2002) 'An ex-colony can celebrate Independence Day, but England should drop St George's', *New Statesman*, 29 April.

Howe, S. (1989) 'Labour patriotism, 1939–83', in R. Samuel (ed.) *Patriotism: The Making and Unmaking of British National Identity, Volume 1: History and Politics*, London: Routledge.

Howe, S. (2003) 'Internal colonization? British politics since Thatcher as post-colonial trauma', *Twentieth Century British History*, 14, 3, 286–304.

Howell, D. (2006) *The Commonwealth and the UK: a New Foreign Policy Appropriate to the 21st Century*, London: Centre for Policy Studies.

Howse, C. (2002) 'Ackroyd's England', *Daily Telegraph*, 21 September.

Huizinga, J. H. (1958) *Confessions of a European in England*, London: Heinemann.

Hutton, W. (2002) 'Great television, but is it great history?', *Observer*, 16 June.

Hutton, W. (2005) 'What Eurosceptics won't say', *Observer*, 13 February.

Ichijo, A. (2003) 'The uses of history: Anglo-British and Scottish views of Europe', *Regional and Federal Studies*, 13:3, 23–43.

Ingelbien, R. (2002) *Misreading England: Poetry and Nationhood since the Second World War*, Amsterdam: Rodopi.

Ingelbien, R. (2004) 'Imagined communities/imagined solitudes: versions of Englishness in postwar literature', *European Journal of English Studies*, 8:2, 159–71.

Ionescu, G. and Gellner, E. (eds) (1969) *Populism: Its Meanings and National Characteristics*, London: Weidenfeld and Nicolson.

Jacques, M. (2004) 'Our problem with abroad', *Guardian*, 23 August.

Jeffery, C. (2006) 'Devolution and local government', *Publius: The Journal of Federalism*, 36:1, 57–73.

Jenkins, S. (2004) *Big Bang Localism: A Rescue Plan for British Democracy*, London: Policy Exchange.

Jenkins, S. (2005a) 'A French yes lets Britain go to plan C – tearing this EU down', *The Times*, 22 May.

Jenkins, S. (2005b) 'Forget the bling and egotists, this is the beautiful game', *Guardian*, 14 September.

Jessop, B. (1974) *Traditionalism, Conservatism and British Political Culture*, London: George Allen and Unwin.

Jewell, H. M. (1994) *The North-South Divide. The Origins of Northern Consciousness in England*, Manchester: Manchester University Press.

John, P., Musson, S. and Tickell, A. (2002) 'England's problem region: regionalism in the south east', *Regional Studies*, 36:7, 733–41.

John, P. and Whitehead, A. (1997) 'The renaissance of English region-alism in the 1990s', *Policy and Politics*, 25:1, 7–17.

Johnson, B. (2004a) 'England expects ... a fairer deal', *Daily Telegraph*, 10 June.

Johnson, B. (2004b) *Being British: The 2004 Keith Joseph Memorial Lecture*, London: Centre for Policy Studies.

Johnson, B. (2006) 'C'mon Gordon, join the rest of us and fly the flag for England', *Daily Telegraph*, 8 June.

Johnson, D. (2001) 'Who can transcend illusion?', *Daily Telegraph*, 22 December.

Johnson, N. (1977) *In Search of the Constitution: Reflections on State and Society in Britain*, Oxford: Pergamon.

Johnson, N. (2000a) 'Then and now: the British constitution', *Political Studies*, 48:1, 118–31.

Johnson, N. (2000b) *Can Self-government Survive? Britain and the European Union*, London: Centre for Policy Studies.

Johnson, N. (2004) *Reshaping the British Constitution: Essays in Political Interpretation*, London: Palgrave.

Johnson, R. W. (1985) *Politics of Recession*, London: Macmillan.

Johnston, P. (2004) 'North-east delivers huge rebuff to Prescott's regional assembly', *Daily Telegraph*, 6 November.

Johnston, P. (2005) 'Home front', *Daily Telegraph*, 21 November.

Johnston, R. J. and Pattie, C. J. (1989) 'A nation dividing?: Economic well-being, voter response and the changing electoral geography of Great Britain', *Parliamentary Affairs*, 42:1, 37–51.

Johnstone, R. (1987) 'Images of Belfast', in F. Ormsby (ed.) *Northern*

Windows, Belfast: Blackstaff Press.

Jones, E. (1998) *The English Nation: The Great Myth*, Stroud: Sutton Publishing.

Jones, G. (2006) 'Tories challenge Brown to solve Scottish paradox', *Daily Telegraph*, 22 February.

Jones, M. and MacLeod G. (1999) 'Towards a regional renaissance? Reconfiguring and rescaling England's economic governance', *Transactions of the Institute of British Geographers*, 24, 295–313.

Jones, M. and MacLeod, G. (2004) 'Regional spaces, spaces of regionalism: territory, insurgent politics and the English question', *Transactions of the Institute of British Geographers* 29, 433–52.

Kagan, R. (2003) *Paradise and Power: America and Europe in the New World Order*, London: Atlantic Books.

Kaiser, W. (2002) 'A never-ending story: Britain in Europe', *British Journal of Politics and International Relations*, 4:1, 152–65.

Kaplan, A. (2004) 'The tenacious grasp of American exceptionalism', *Comparative American Studies*, 2:2, 153–9.

Kavanagh, D. (1985) 'Whatever happened to consensus politics?', *Political Studies*, 33:4, 529–46.

Kearney, H. (1995) *The British Isles: A History of Four Nations*, Cambridge: Cambridge University Press.

Kearney, H. (2000) 'The importance of being British', *Political Quarterly* 71:1, 15–26.

Kearney, H. (2003) 'Myths of Englishness', *History Workshop Journal* 56, 251–7.

Keating, M. (1989) 'Regionalism, devolution and the state, 1969–1989', in P. L. Garside and M. Hebbert (eds) *British Regionalism*, London: Mansell.

Keating, M. (2006) 'From functional to political regionalism: England in comparative perspective', in R. Hazell (ed.) *The English Question*, Manchester: Manchester University Press.

Kenner, H. (1988) *A Sinking Island: The Modern English Writers*, New York: Random House.

Kenny, M. (1995) *The First New Left: British Intellectuals after Stalin*, London: Lawrence and Wishart.

Kent, J. (1998) 'William Temple, the Church of England and British national identity', in R. Weight and A. Beach (eds) *The Right to Belong: Citizenship and National Identity in Britain, 1930–1960*, London: I. B. Taurus.

Kettell, S. (2004) 'Why New Labour wants the Euro', *The Political Quarterly*, 75:1, 52–9.

Kidd, C. (2001) 'Highway to modernity', *London Review of Books*, 23:5, 8 March.

King, A. (2005) 'What does it mean to be British?', *Daily Telegraph*, 27 July.

Kingsnorth, P. (2004) 'Reclaim our Englishness and throw out the burgers', *New Statesman*, 15 November.

Kipling, R. (1898) 'The Bridge Builders', *The Day's Work*, 6, 41–2, in E. Stokes '"The voice of the hooligan": Kipling and the Commonwealth experience', in N. McKendrick (ed.) *Historical Perspectives: Studies in English Thought and Society in Honour of J. H. Plumb* (1974), London: Europa Publications.

Kipling, R. (1920) 'England and the English', speech to the Royal Society of St George: http://theenglandproject.net/documents /englandandtheenglish.html.

Kitson Clark, G. (1950) *The English Inheritance: An Historical Essay*, London: S. C. M. Press.

Knowles, M. (2005) 'Only an English Parliament can put things right for England', *Yorkshire Post*, 30 August.

Kohn, H. (1940) 'The genesis and character of English nationalism', *Journal of the History of Ideas*, 1:1, 69–94.

Kruger, D. (2005) 'Orwell can tell us what Englishness is', *Daily Telegraph*, 28 July.

Kruger, D. (2006) 'Cameron must see Brown for the Scottish bourgeois he is', *Daily Telegraph*, 15 February.

Kumar, K. (2003a) *The Making of English National Identity*, Cambridge: Cambridge University Press.

Kumar, K. (2003b) 'Britain, England and Europe. Cultures in contraflow', *European Journal of Social Theory*, 6:1, 5–23.

Kumar, K. (2006) 'Empire and English nationalism', *Nations and Nationalism*, 12:1, 1–13.

Kundnani, A. (2000) 'Stumbling on: race, class and England', *Race and Class*, 41:4, 1–18.

Kundnani, A. (2001) 'In a foreign land: the new popular racism', *Race and Class*, 43:2, 41–60.

Laborde, C. (2000) 'The concept of the state in British and French political thought', *Political Studies*, 48:2, 540–57.

Laity, P. (2001) 'Short cuts', *London Review of Books*, 23:10, 24 May.

Laity, P. (2002) 'Dazed and confused', *London Review of Books*, 24:23, 28 November.

Lampedusa, G. di (1972) *The Leopard*, London: Fontana.

Langford, P. (2000) *English Identified: Manners and Character 1650–1850*, Oxford: Oxford University Press.

Langlands, R. (1999) 'Britishness or Englishness? The historical problem of national identity in Britain', *Nations and Nationalism* 5:1, 53–69.

Larkin, P. (2003) *Collected Poems*, London: Faber and Faber.

La Rochefoucauld, F. Duc de (1981) *Maxims* (trans. L. Tancock), Harmondsworth: Penguin Books.

Lawrence, J. (1998) *Speaking for the People: Party, Language and Popular Politics in England, 1867–1914*, Cambridge: Cambridge University Press.

Lawson, M. (2005) 'Renaissance for the nationality that dared not speak its name', *Guardian*, 15 October.

Lawson, N. (2005) *Dare More Democracy*, London: Compass.

Lea, R. (2006) 'Why the Commonwealth is set to bowl over the world', *Daily Telegraph*, 13 March.

Le Carré, J. (1968) *A Small Town in Germany*, London: Heinemann.

Leonard, M. (1997) *Britain TM: Renewing our Identity*, London: Demos.

Leonard, M. (1998a) *Rediscovering Europe*, London: Demos.

Leonard, M. (1998b) 'Europe's legitimacy gap', in I. Christie (ed.) *Euro Visions: New Dimensions of European Integration*, London: Demos.

Leonard, M. (2005a) *Why Europe Will Run the 21st Century*, London: Fourth Estate.

Leonard, M. (2005b) 'Ascent of Europe', *Prospect*, March.

Leonard, M. (2005c) 'The project for a new European century': www.theglobalist.com/DBWeb/StoryId.aspx?StoryId-4464.

Linklater, M. (2006) 'The anti-Scottish worm has turned', *The Times*, 11 January.

Linsell, T. (2003) 'Dreams, nightmares and the great upheaval', *Steadfast Magazine*, issue 7, Spring: www.hsite.co.uk/steadf /articles/i7–linsell.html.

Littlejohn, R. (2006) 'Why should England put up with either of these tartan terrors?', *Daily Mail*, 16 May.

Lloyd, J. (2002) 'The end of multiculturalism', *New Statesman*, 27 May.

Loades, D. (1982) 'The origins of English Protestant nationalism', *Studies in Church History*, 18, 297–307.

Loveland, I. (1996) 'Parliamentary sovereignty and the European Community: the unfinished revolution', *Parliamentary Affairs*, 49:4, 517–35.

Lowenthal, D. (1989) 'Nostalgia tells it like it wasn't', in C. Shaw and M. Chase (eds) *The Imagined Past: History and Nostalgia*,

Manchester: Manchester University Press.

Lucas, J. (1990) *England and Englishness*, London: The Hogarth Press.

Lunn, K. (1996) 'Reconsidering Britishness: the construction and significance of national identity in twentieth-century Britain', in B. Jenkins and S. A. Sofos (eds) *Nation and Identity in Contemporary Europe*, London: Routledge.

Lynch (1999) *The Politics of Nationhood: Sovereignty, Britishness and Conservative Politics*, London: Macmillan.

MacColl, A. (2004) 'The construction of England as a Protestant "British" nation in the sixteenth century', *Renaissance Studies*, 18:4, 582–608.

MacDonell, H. (2006) 'Anti-English feeling "at its strongest in nationalists"', *Scotsman*, 4 July.

MacRae, D. (1969) 'Populism in England', in G. Ionescu, and E. Gellner (eds) *Populism: Its Meanings and National Characteristics*, London: Weidenfeld and Nicolson.

MacShane, D. (2004) 'The left must say yes to Europe', *Le Monde*, 1 September.

Malcolm, N. (1995) 'The case against "Europe"', *Foreign Affairs*, 74:1, 52–68.

Malcolm, N. (1998) 'A reply', in J. Barnes, *Federal Britain: No Longer Unthinkable?*, London: Centre for Policy Studies.

Malik, K. (2005) 'Born in Bradford', *Prospect*, October, 54–6.

Mandelson, P. (2001) 'Bridging the gap', *Progress: Policy Forum*: www.progressives.org.uk/magazine/Default.asp?action=magazine &articleid=99.

Mandler, P. (2000) '"Race" and "nation" in mid-Victorian thought', in S. Collini, R. Whatmore and B. Young (eds) *History, Religion, and Culture: British Intellectual History 1750–1950*, Cambridge: Cambridge University Press.

Mandler, P. (2004) 'The problem with cultural history', *Cultural and Social History*, 1, 94–117.

Marin, M. (1999) 'The Englishness that dare not speak its name', *Daily Telegraph*, 19 November.

Marin, M. (2001) 'It's not just foreigners who find Britain a foreign land', *Daily Telegraph*, 10 March.

Marin, M. (2006) 'England is waking up to the patriot game', *Sunday Times*, 15 January.

Marquand, D. (1993) 'The twilight of the British state? Henry Dubb versus sceptred awe', *Political Quarterly*, 64:2, 210–21.

Marquand, D. (1995) 'After Whig imperialism: can there be a new

British identity?', in B. Parekh (ed.) 'British National Identity in a European Context', *new community* special issue, 21:2, 183–93.

Marquand, D. and Tomaney, J. (2000) 'Democratising England', paper prepared for the Regional Policy Forum, November.

Marqusee, M. (2006) 'Rebranding a team: English nationalism in the World Cup', *Counterpunch*, 12 June: www.counterpunch.org /marqusee06122006.html.

Marr, A. (1998) 'Stuff the hope and glory', *New Statesman*, 27 November.

Marr, A. (2000) *The Day Britain Died*, London: Profile Books.

Marshall, P. J. (1994) 'Imperial Britain', *The Journal of Imperial and Commonwealth History* 23:3, 379–94.

Maslen, E. (2004) 'The miasma of Englishness at home and abroad in the 1950s', in D. Rogers and J. McLeod (eds) *The Revision of Englishness*, Manchester: Manchester University Press.

Massie, A. (2002) 'Maddest of tribunals', *Times Literary Supplement* 9 August, 12–13.

Masterman, C. F. G. (1910) *The Condition of England*, London: Methuen.

Mather, J. (2000) 'Labour and the English regions: centralised devolution?', *Contemporary British History*, 14:3, 10–38.

Matless, D. (1990) 'Definitions of England, 1928–89. Preservation, modernism and the nature of the nation', *Built Environment*, 16:3, 179–91.

Matless, D. (2001) *Landscape and Englishness*, London: Reaktion Books.

Mawson, J. (1998) 'English regionalism and New Labour', *Regional and Federal Studies*, 8:1, 158–75.

McCrone, D. (2002) 'Who do you say you are? Making sense of national identities in modern Britain', *Ethnicities*, 2:3, 301–20.

McCrone, D. (2006) 'A nation that dare not speak its name?' *Ethnicities* 6:2, 267–78.

McGuigan, J. (1992) *Cultural Populism*, London: Routledge.

McLaughlin, E. (2005) 'From reel to ideal: The Blue Lamp and the popular cultural reconstruction of the English "bobby"', *Crime and Culture*, 1:1, 11–30.

McLean, I. and McMillan, A. (2006) *State of the Union*, Oxford: Oxford University Press.

Mebyon Kernow (2004) 'Cornish nationalism or English regionalism?': www.mebyonkernow.org/?action=Print&SID=142.

Meny, Y. (2002) '*De la democratie en Europe*: old concepts and new challenges', *Journal of Common Market Studies*, 41:1, 1–13.

Miller, D. (1995a) *On Nationality*, Oxford: Clarendon Press.

Miller, D. (1995b) 'Reflections on British national identity', *new community* 21:2, 153–66.

Milward, A. S. (1999) *The European Rescue of the Nation-State*, London: Routledge.

Minogue, K. (1992) 'Transcending the European State', in P. Robertson (ed.) *Reshaping Europe in the Twenty-First Century*, Basingstoke: Macmillan, in association with the Bruges Group.

Minogue, K. (1996) 'Introduction: on Conservative realism', in K. Minogue (ed.) *Conservative Realism: New Essays on Conservatism*, London: HarperCollins.

Minogue, K. (2004a) 'Is Britain a moral exemplar to the nations?': www.brugesgroup.com/mediacentre/speeches.live?article=200.

Minogue, K. (2004b) 'The fate of Britain's national interest': www.brugesgroup.com/mediacentre/index.live?article=2o6.

Minogue, K. (2005) 'Introduction', in P. West, *The Poverty of Multiculturalism*, London: Civitas.

Mitchell, A. (1992) 'Nationhood: the end of the affair?', *Political Quarterly*, 63:2, 122–42.

Monbiot, G. (2005) 'The new chauvinism', *Guardian*, 9 August.

Moore, C. (2004) 'There's no point in voting Labour now, but can the Tories cash in?', *Daily Telegraph*, 2 October.

Moore, C. and Heffer, S. (eds) (1989) *A Tory Seer: The Selected Journalism of T. E. Utley*, London: Hamish Hamilton.

Morgan, I. (2006) 'England flag points to "a new national identity"', *24dash.com*, 8 June: www.24dash.com/content/news/viewNews .php?navID=7&newsID=6642.

Morgan, K. (2001) 'The new territorial politics: rivalry and justice in post-devolution Britain', *Regional Studies*, 35:4, 343–8.

Morgan, K. (2002) 'The English Question: regional perspectives on a fractured nation', *Regional Studies*, 36:7, 797–810.

Morrison, B. (2002) 'Placism, not racism', *Guardian*, 5 October.

Morton, H. V. (1927) *In Search of England*, London: Methuen.

Mount, F. (1993) *The British Constitution Now*, London: Macmillan.

Mudde, C. (2004) 'The populist zeitgeist', *Government and Opposition*, 35:4, 541–63.

Nairn, T. (1977) *The Break-up of Britain: Crisis and Neo-Nationalism*, London: NLB.

Nairn, T. (1988) *The Enchanted Glass: Britain and its Monarchy*, London: Radius.

Nairn, T. (1989) 'Britain's royal romance', in R. Samuel (ed.) *Patriotism: The Making and Unmaking of the British National*

Identity, vol. 3, London: Routledge.

Nairn, T. (1996) 'The incredibly shrinking state', *Demos Quarterly*, 9, 29–34.

Nairn, T. (1997) *Faces of Nationalism: Janus Revisited*, London: Verso.

Nairn, T. (2000a) *After Britain*, London: Granta.

Nairn, T. (2000b) 'Ukania under Blair', *New Left Review* (second series) 1:1, 69–104.

Nairn, T. (2002) *Pariah*, London: Verso.

Neil, A. (2005) 'The fall of the Scottish Raj', *Daily Telegraph*, 20 August.

New Statesman (editorial) (1999) 'Vote for the British melting pot', *New Statesman*, 3 May.

New Statesman (editorial) (2000) 'They don't live here any more' *New Statesman*, 16 October.

Nunning, V. (2001) 'The invention of cultural traditions: the construction and deconstruction of Englishness and authenticity in Julian Barnes's *England, England*', *Anglia*, 119: 58–76.

Nunning, V. (2004) 'The importance of being English: European perspectives on Englishness', *European Journal of English Studies*, 8:2, 145–58.

Oakeshott, M. (1948) 'Contemporary British politics', *The Cambridge Journal* 1, 474–90.

Oakesshott, M. (1975) *On Human Conduct*, Oxford: Clarendon Press.

Oakeshott, M. (1986) *Experience and its Modes*, Cambridge: Cambridge University Press.

Oakeshott, M. (1989) *The Voice of Liberal Learning*, New Haven: Yale University Press.

Oakeshott, M. (1991) *Rationalism in Politics and Other Essays*, Indianapolis: The Liberty Press.

Observer (leader) (2006) 'All this Britishness is just a trifle un-British', *Observer*, 15 January.

O'Neill, M. (2000) 'Great Britain: from Dicey to devolution', *Parliamentary Affairs*, 53:1, 69–95.

Orwell, G. (1941) *The Lion and the Unicorn: Socialism and the English Genius*, London: Secker and Warburg.

Orwell, G. (2001) *Orwell's England* (ed. P. Davison) Harmondsworth: Penguin.

O'Sullivan, N. (2004) *European Political Thought Since 1945*, Basingstoke: Palgrave.

Ousby, I. (1990) *The Englishman's England: Taste, Travel and the Rise of Tourism*, Cambridge: Cambridge University Press.

Painter, J. (2000) 'A Third Way for Europe? Discourse, regulation and the European question in Britain', *Tijdschrift voor Economische en Sociale Geografie*, 91:3, 227–36.

Palmer, A. (2000) review of 'England: an Elegy', *Sunday Telegraph*, 12 November.

Palmer, C. (2002) 'Christianity, Englishness and the southern English countryside: a study of the work of H. J. Massingham', *Social and Cultural Geography*, 3:1, 25–38.

Parekh, B. (1994) 'Discourses on national identity', *Political Studies*, 42, 492–504.

Parekh, B. (1995) 'Introduction', *new community*, 21:2, 147–51.

Parekh, B. (2000) 'Defining British national identity', *The Political Quarterly*, 71:1, 4–14.

Parker, S. (2003) 'Regional government: the issue explained', *Guardian*, 23 May.

Parris, M. (2006) 'If you want local choice, you'll have to play the hated postcode lottery', *The Times*, 18 February.

Parry, R. (1991) 'State and nation in the United Kingdom', in U. Ra'anan, M. Mesner, K. Armes and K. Martin (eds) *State and Nation in Multi-ethnic Societies: The Breakup of Multinational states*, Manchester: Manchester University Press.

Patten, C. (2002) 'Let's get emotional', *The Spectator*, 18 May.

Paxman, J. (1998) *The English: A Portrait of a People*, London: Michael Joseph.

Pearce, G. and Ayres, S. (2006) 'Regional mobilisation in England: the role of the government's Regional Offices', paper presented to Political Studies Association/Economic and Social Research Council Devolution and Constitutional Change Programme Conference, Queen's University Belfast, 11–13 January.

Perkins, M. A. (2004) *Christendom and European Identity: The Legacy of a Grand Narrative Since 1789*, Berlin and New York: Walter de Gruyter.

Peterkin, T. (2005) 'Britain run by Scottish Raj, claims Paxman', *Daily Telegraph*, 14 March.

Plumb, J. H. (1969) 'The historian', in A. J. P. Taylor *et al.*, *Churchill: Four Faces and the Man*, Harmondsworth: Penguin Books.

Pocock, J. G. A. (1995) 'Conclusion: contingency, identity, sovereignty', in A. Grant and K. J. Stringer (eds) *Uniting the Kingdom? The Making of British History*, London: Routledge.

Pocock, J. G. A. (2000) 'Gaberlunzie's Return', *New Left Review* (second series) 5, 41–52.

Political Quarterly (editorial) (1998) 'And so to England', *The*

Political Quarterly, 69:1, 1–3.

Porter, R. (1992) 'Introduction', in R. Porter (ed.) *Myths of the English*, London: Polity Press.

Powell E. (1968) 'Like the Roman, I see the River Tiber foaming with much blood': www.sterlingtimes.org/powell_speech.doc.

Power (2006) *Power to the People: The Report of Power: An Independent Inquiry Into Britain's Democracy*, London: Power Inquiry.

Preston, P. W. (1994) *Europe, Democracy and the Dissolution of Britain*, Aldershot: Dartmouth Press.

Preston, P. W. (2004) *Relocating England*, Manchester: Manchester University Press.

Priestley, J. B. (1934) *English Journey: Being a Rambling but Truthful Account of What One Man Saw*, London: Heinemann.

Priestley, J. B. (1973) *The English*, London: Heinemann.

Read, H. (1933) *The English Vision: An Anthology*, London: Eyre & Spottiswoode.

Rees-Mogg, W. (2005) 'The battle for England', *The Times*, 9 May.

Rees-Mogg, W. (2006) 'For goodness' sake don't mention Europe: it doesn't fit our new image', *The Times*, 10 April.

Reicher, S., Hopkins N. and Condor S. (1997) 'The lost nation of psychology', in C. C. Barfoot (ed.) *Beyond Pug's Tour: National and Ethnic Stereotyping in Theory and Literary Practice*, Amsterdam: Rodopi.

Reichl, S. (2004) 'Flying the flag: the intricate semiotics of national identity', *European Journal of English Studies*, 8:2, 205–17.

Reyes, O. (2002) 'Skinhead Conservatism: the failure of contemporary British populism', *Essex Papers in Politics and Government* 20, Colchester: Department of Government, Essex University.

Rezzori, G. von (1984) *Memoirs of an Anti-Semite*, London: Picador.

Risse, T., Engelmann-Martin, D., Knopf, H.-J. and Roscher, K. (1999) 'To Euro or not to Euro? The EMU and identity politics in the European Union', *European Journal of International Relations*, 5:2, 147–87.

Robbins, K. (1982) 'Religion and identity in modern British history', *Studies in Church History*, 18, 465–87.

Robbins, K. (2003) 'Nationhood and identity' (book review), *Nations and Nationalism*, 9:3, 451.

Roberts, A. (2002) 'A history of the English speaking peoples', *History Today*, May, 53–5.

Rose, R. (1982a) 'Is the UK a state? Northern Ireland as a test case', in P. Madgwick and R. Rose (eds) *The Territorial Dimension in*

United Kingdom Politics, London: Macmillan.

Rose, R. (1982b) *Understanding the United Kingdom*, London: Longman.

Rose, R. (1985) *Politics in England: Persistence and Change*, London, Faber and Faber.

Rowse, A. L. (1945) *The English Spirit*, London: Macmillan.

Runnymede Trust (2000) *The Future of Multi-Ethnic Britain: The Parekh Report*, London: Profile.

Russell, M. and Lodge, G. (2006) 'The government of England by Westminster', in R. Hazell (ed.) *The English Question*, Manchester: Manchester University Press.

Salmon, J. H. M. (1999) 'Liberty by degrees: Raynal and Diderot on the British constitution', *History of Political Thought*, 20:1, 87–107.

Samuel, R. (ed.) (1989) *Patriotism: The Making and Unmaking of the British National Identity*, vol. 1, London: Routledge.

Sandford, M. (2002) 'What place for England in an asymmetrically devolved UK?' *Regional Studies* 36:7, 789–96.

Sandford, M. (2006) *English Regions Devolution Monitoring Report* (January), University College London: The Constitution Unit.

Santayana, G. (1922) *Soliloquies in England and Later Soliloquies*, London: Constable and Company.

Schlaeger, J. (2004) 'Continuities', *European Journal of English Studies*, 8:2, 233–42.

Schopenhauer, A. (1892) *Essays* (selected and translated by T. Bailey Saunders), London: Swan Sonnenschein.

Schopflin, G. (2000) *Nations, Identity, Power: The New Politics of Europe*, London: Hurst.

Schwab, G. (1985) 'Introduction', in C. Schmitt, *Political Theology: Four Chapters on the Concept of Sovereignty*, (trans. G. Schwab), Boston: MIT Press.

Schwarz, B. (1999) '*Philosophes* of the Conservative nation: Burke, Macauley, Disraeli', *Journal of Historical Sociology*, 12:3 183–217.

Scotland on Sunday (leader) (2006) 'We have home rule, why not England?', *Scotland on Sunday*, 22 January.

Scott, D. (2005) 'The real crisis in Europe is about power and its allocation', *Daily Telegraph*, 11 July.

Scott, J.W. (2001) 'Fantasy echo: history and the construction of identity', *Critical Inquiry* 27, 284–304.

Scruton, R. (1986) *The Meaning of Conservatism* (2nd edn) Harmondsworth: Penguin.

Scruton, R. (1993) 'How to be a non-liberal, anti-socialist conservative', *The Intercollegiate Review*, Spring, 17–23.

Scruton, R. (1999) 'Whatever happened to reason?' *City Journal*, 9:2, Spring: www.city-journal.org.

Scruton, R. (2000) *England: An Elegy*, London: Chatto and Windus.

Scruton, R. (2001) 'Pop and corn', *Blunt Edge* 1, April: www.artspacegallery.co.uk/OtherWWW/FULLER_BE/BE_index .html.

Scruton, R. (2002) 'A question of temperament', *The Wall Street Journal*, 10 December.

Scruton, R. (2004a) *The Need for Nations*, London: Civitas.

Scruton, R. (2004b) 'Friends, Muslims, countrymen, lend us your ears', *Sunday Times*, 15 February.

Scruton, R. (2004c) 'Why shouldn't we fly the English flag?' *Daily Mail*, 11 June.

Scruton, R. (2005) 'The dangers of internationalism', *Intercollegiate Review*, Fall/Winter, 29–35.

Scruton, R. (2006) 'Values are not learnt through teaching', *Daily Telegraph*, 16 May.

Sear, C. (2003) 'The West Lothian Question': www.parliament.uk /commons/lib/research/notes/snpc-02586.pdf.

Seenan, G. (2005) 'The Scottish Raj', *Guardian*, 18 March.

Sen, A. (2000) 'Other people', fourth Annual British Academy Lecture: www.britac.ac.uk/pubs/review/_pdfs/review04–09–sen.pdf.

Seton-Watson, H. (1979) 'History', in C. Maclean (ed.) *The Crown and the Thistle*, Edinburgh, Scottish Academic Press.

Shah, I. (2000) *The Englishman's Handbook: Or How to Deal with Foreigners*, London: Octagon.

Shanahan, F. (2006) 'Let's have home rule for the English', *Sun*, 21 April.

Shils, E. (1972) *The Intellectuals and the Powers and Other Essays*, Chicago: University of Chicago Press.

Shore, C. (1998) 'The myth of a European identity', in I. Christie (ed.) *Euro Visions: New Dimensions of European Integration*, London: Demos.

Shore, C. (2000) *Building Europe: The Cultural Politics of European Integration*, London: Routledge.

Shore, C. (2001) *European Union and the Politics of Culture*, London: The Bruges Group.

Shore, C. (2004) 'Whither European citizenship? Eros and civilisation revisited', *European Journal of Social Theory*, 7:1, 27–44.

Sissons, M. (2005) 'Please allow us to get away Scot-free', *The Times*, 31 December.

Smith, A. D. (1995) *Nations and Nationalism in a Global Era*, London: Polity Press.

Smith, A. D. (1996) 'Culture, community and territory: the politics of ethnicity and nationalism', *International Affairs*, 72:3, 445–58.

Smith, A. D. (2003) 'Adrian Hastings on nations and nationalism', *Nations and Nationalism*, 9:1, 25–8.

Smith, B. (1977) 'Confusions in regionalism', *Political Quarterly* 48:1, 14–29.

Smith, S. (1986) 'Unnatural relations', *Poetry Review*, 76:1/2, 9–13.

Soffer, R. N. (1994) *Discipline and Power: The University, History, and the Making of an English Elite*, Stanford: Stanford University Press.

Soffer, R. N. (1996) 'The Conservative historical imagination in the twentieth century', *Albion*, 27:4, 1–17.

Spiering, M. (1992) *Englishness: Foreigners and Images of National Identity in Postwar Literature*, Amsterdam: Rodopi.

Spiering, M. (2004) 'British Euroscepticism', in R. Harmsen and M. Spiering (eds) *Euroscepticism: Party Politics, National Identity and European Integration*, Amsterdam: Rodopi.

Stapleton, J. (1994) *Englishness and the Study of Politics. The Social and Political Thought of Ernest Barker*, Cambridge: Cambridge University Press.

Stapleton, J. (1998) 'English political thought', in A. Dobson and J. Stanyer (eds) *Contemporary Political Studies*, London: PSA.

Stapleton, J. (1999a) 'Englishness, Britishness, and patriotism in recent political thought and historiography', *British Journal of Politics and International Relations*, 1:1, 119–30.

Stapleton, J. (1999b) 'Resisting the centre at the extremes: English liberalism in the political thought of interwar Britain', *British Journal of Politics and International Relations*, 1:3 270–92.

Stapleton, J. (2000a) 'Political thought and national identity in Britain, 1850–1950', in S. Collini, R. Whatmore and B. Young (eds) *History, Religion, and Culture: British Intellectual History 1750–1950*, Cambridge: Cambridge University Press.

Stapleton, J. (2000b) 'Cultural conservatism and the public intellectual in Britain, 1930–70', *The European Legacy*, 5:6, 795–813.

Stapleton, J. (2001) *Political Intellectuals and Public Identities in Britain since 1850*, Manchester: Manchester University Press.

Stapleton, J. (2004) 'Sir Arthur Bryant as a 20th-century Victorian', *History of European Ideas*, 30, 217–40.

Stapleton, J. (2005a) *Sir Arthur Bryant and National History in Twentieth-Century Britain*, Lanham: Lexington Books.

Stapleton, J. (2005b) 'Citizenship versus patriotism in twentieth-century England', *The Historical Journal* 48:1 151–78.

Starkey, D. (1999) 'By 2050 England will have recreated itself: vision-ary, multi-ethnic, free. Is this farewell to the bulldog breed?': www.chronicle-future.co.uk/debate2right.html.

Starkey, D. (2001) 'England striker', *Sunday Times* colour supplement, 25 March.

Starkey, D. (2004) 'What history should we be teaching in Britain in the 21st century?': www.history.ac.uk/education/conference /starkey.html.

Statham, P. and Gray, E. (2005) 'The public sphere and debates about Europe in Britain', *Innovation*, 18:1, 61–81.

Steele, J. (2006) 'The textbook whitewash of our brutish empire is a lie', *Guardian*, 22 January.

Stenhouse, D. (2003) 'Stand up and vote for England', *The Times*, 15 November.

Stephens, S. (2005) 'Britain and Europe: an unforgettable past and an unavoidable future', *The Political Quarterly*, 76:1, 12–21.

Steyn, M. (2004a) 'It's dangerous to get rid of men in tights', *Daily Telegraph*, 21 September.

Steyn, M. (2004b) 'EUtopia is over – join the real world', *Daily Telegraph*, 28 September.

Steyn, M. (2005) 'A victory for multiculti over common sense', *Daily Telegraph*, 19 July.

Stoker, G. (2000) 'Is regional government the answer to the English Question?', in S. Chen and T. Wright (eds) *The English Question*, London: The Fabian Society.

Stoker, G. (2004) 'New localism, progressive politics and democracy', *Political Quarterly*, 75:1, 117–29.

Stringer, K. (1994) 'Social and political communities in European history: some reflections on recent studies', in C. Bjorn, A. Grant and K. J. Stringer (eds) *Nations, Nationalism and Patriotism in the European Past*, Copenhagen: Academic Press.

Stuart, G. (2003) *The Making of Europe's Constitution*, London: The Fabian Society.

Sylvester, R. (2004) 'Euroscepticism encourages Britain's dark stream of racism, says minister', *Daily Telegraph*, 7 August.

Taggart, P. (2000) *Populism*, Buckingham: Open University Press.

Tannsjo, T. (1992) *Populist Democracy: A Defence*, London: Routledge.

Taylor, A. J. P. (1976) *Essays in English History*, Harmondsworth: Penguin.

Taylor, P. J. (1991) 'The English and their Englishness: "a curiously mysterious, elusive and little understood people"', *Scottish*

Geographical Magazine, 107:3, 146–61.

Taylor, P. J. (1993) 'The meaning of the North: England's "foreign country" within?', *Political Geography* 12:2, 136–55.

Taylor, P. J. (1994) *A Dream of England: Landscape, Photography and the Tourist's Imagination*, Manchester: Manchester University Press.

Taylor, P. J. (1997) 'Is the United Kingdom big enough for both London and England?', *Environment and Planning A*, 29, 766–70.

Taylor, P. J. (2001) 'Which Britain? Which England? Which North?', in D. Morley and K. Robins (eds) *British Cultural Studies: Geography, Nationality, and Identity*, Oxford: Oxford University Press.

Tebbit, Lord (2004) 'The Rt Hon. Lord Tebbit of Chingford speaks to Robert Ould': www.brugesgroup.com/mediacentre/interviews .live?aricle=141.

Thompson, E. P. (1980) *Writing by Candlelight*, London: Merlin.

Thompson, E. P. (1978) *The Poverty of Theory and Other Essays*, London: Merlin.

Thomson, A. (2005) 'After the years of being embarrassed about our past, people want to sing Land of Hope and Glory', *Daily Telegraph*, 27 July.

Tindale, S. (1996) 'Devolution on demand: options for the English regions and London', in S. Tindale (ed.) *The State and the Nations: The Politics of Devolution*, London: IPPR.

Tomaney, J. (1999) 'New Labour and the English Question', *The Political Quarterly*, 70:1, 75–82.

Tomaney, J. (2000) 'End of the empire state? New Labour devolution in the United Kingdom', *International Journal of Urban and Regional Research*, 24:3, 675–88.

Tomaney, J. (2002) 'The evolution of regionalism in England', *Regional Studies*, 36:7, 721–31.

Tomaney, J. (2006) 'The idea of English regionalism', in R. Hazell (ed.) *The English Question*, Manchester: Manchester University Press.

Tomaney, J., Hetherington, P. and Pinkney, E. (2003) 'The English Regions', *Nations and Regions: The Dynamics of Devolution*, quarterly monitoring programme, The Constitution Unit, June.

Tomaney, J. and Ward, N. (2000) 'England and the new regionalism', *Regional Studies*, 34:5, 471–8.

Travers, T. (1998) 'The freedom to be more unequal', *New Statesman* (special supplement), 26 June.

Travers, T. and Esposito, L. (2003) *The Decline and Fall of Local Democracy: A History of Local Government Finance*, London:

Policy Exchange.

Travers, T. and Kleinman, M. (2003) *The Politics of London: Governing an Ungovernable City*, London: Palgrave.

Trentmann, F. (1994) 'Civilization and its discontents: English neo-romanticism and the transformation of anti-modernism in twentieth century western culture', *Journal of Contemporary History*, 29:4, 583–625.

Turner, B. (1992) 'Ideology and Utopia in the formation of an intelligentsia: reflections on the English cultural conduit', *Theory, Culture and Society*, 9, 183–210.

Turner, D. (1996) interview with Roger Scruton *Right Now!*, 9, October.

Turner, D. (2003) interview with Andrew Roberts, *Right Now!*, 41, July.

Vander Weyer, M. (2004) 'Regional forecast', *The Spectator*, 4 September.

Wainwright, H. (2004) 'Reclaiming "the public" through the people', *Political Quarterly*, 75:1 (special supplement), 141–56.

Wakefield, M. (2001) 'Empire of the slum', *The Spectator*, 18 August.

Walden, G. (2004) 'Anthropologist, study thyself' (review), *New Statesman*, 10 May.

Walker, D. (2002) *In Praise of Centralism: A Critique of the New Localism*, London: The Catalyst Forum.

Wallwork, J. and Dixon, J. A. (2004) 'Foxes, green fields and Britishness: on the rhetorical construction of place and national identity', *British Journal of Social Psychology*, 43, 21–39.

Ward, I. (2000) 'A charmed spectacle: England and its constitutional imagination', *Liverpool Law Review* 22, 235–51.

Ward, P. (1998) *Red Flag and Union Jack: Englishness, Patriotism and the British Left, 1881–1924*, Woodbridge: The Boydell Press.

Ward, P. (2005) *Unionism in the United Kingdom, 1918–1974*, Basingstoke: Palgrave.

Watson, G. (1973) *The English Ideology: Studies in the Language of Victorian Politics*, London: Allen Lane.

Watson, G. (2000) *Not Ones for Theory: England and the War of Ideas*, Cambridge: The Lutterworth Press.

Watson, M. (2005) 'England's Scottish clan', *History Today* 55:6, June, 17–18.

Webster, P. (2006) 'British Day of unity tops Brown agenda', *The Times*, 14 January.

Webster, W. (2005) *Englishness and Empire 1939–1965*, Oxford: Oxford University Press.

Weight, R. (1999) 'Raise St George's standard high', *New Statesman*, 8 January.

Weight, R. (2002) *Patriots: National Identity in Britain 1940–2000*, Basingstoke: Macmillan.

Wellings B. (2002) 'Empire-nation: national and imperial discourses in England', *Nations and Nationalism*, 8:1, 95–109.

Westwood, S. (2000) 'Re-branding Britain: sociology, futures and futurology', *Sociology*, 34:1, 185–202.

Wheatcroft, G. (2005) *The Strange Death of Tory England*, Harmondsworth: Penguin.

Wheatcroft, G. (2006) 'Fear of West Lothian', *Guardian*, 24 January.

White, J. (2002) 'Cheerful fans of Svengland flew the flag proudly', *Scotland on Sunday*, 23 June.

White, J. (2005) 'Now that England's in decline, everyone turns out to be a Welshman', *Daily Telegraph*, March 14.

White, J. (2006) 'How our modest nation can fly the flag', *Daily Telegraph*, 16 January.

Whittle, P. (2006) 'How my neighbourhood was lost to the multiculture', *Sunday Times Review*, 22 January.

Wiener, M. (1981) *English Culture and the Decline of the Industrial Spirit, 1850–1980*, Cambridge: Cambridge University Press.

Willets, D. (1998) 'Who do we think we are?', lecture at the Centre for Policy Studies at the Conservative Party Conference, 8 October.

Wills, M. (2006) 'Being British is different now', *Sunday Times*, 15 January.

Woods, V. (2006) 'Why don't they want me to be English?', *Daily Telegraph*, 21 January.

Woodward, W. (2006) 'Cameron promises UK bill of rights to replace Human Rights Act', *Guardian*, 26 June.

Worsthorne, P. (1998) 'England don't arise!', *The Spectator*, 19 September.

Wright, P. (1985) *On Living in an Old Country*, London: Verso.

Wright, T. (2000) 'Introduction: England, whose England?', in S. Chen and T. Wright (eds) *The English Question*, London: Fabian Society.

Wright, T. (2006) 'The English Question', *Guardian*, 19 April.

Wroe, N. (2000) 'Thinking for England', *Guardian*, 28 October.

YouGov (2006) 'Cabinet reshuffle': www.Yougov.com/archives/pdf/TEL060101007_1.pdf.

Young, G. M. (1947) 'Government', in E. Barker (ed.) *The Character of England*, Oxford: Clarendon Press.

Young, H. (1998) *This Blessed Plot: Britain and Europe from Churchill to Blair*, London: Macmillan.

Young, I. M. (2002) *Inclusion and Democracy*, Oxford: Oxford University Press.

Žižek, S. (1996) *The Indivisible Remainder: Essays on Schelling and Related Matters*, London: Verso.

Žižek, S (2000) 'History against historicism', *European Journal of English Studies*, 4:2, 101–10.

Index